GERMAN SENTENCE BUILDERS

SECOND EDITION

A lexicogrammar approach
Beginner to Pre-Intermediate

 THE LANGUAGE GYM

SECOND EDITION

Imprint: Independently Published

Edited by Isabelle Porter & Martin Ringenaldus

About the authors

Gianfranco Conti taught for 25 years at schools in Italy, the UK and in Kuala Lumpur, Malaysia. He has also been a university lecturer, holds a Master's degree in Applied Linguistics and a PhD in metacognitive strategies as applied to second language writing. He is now an author, a popular independent educational consultant and professional development provider. He has written around 2,000 resources for the TES website, which awarded him the Best Resources Contributor in 2015. He has co-authored the best-selling and influential book for world languages teachers, "The Language Teacher Toolkit" and "Breaking the sound barrier: Teaching learners how to listen", in which he puts forth his Listening As Modelling methodology. Gianfranco writes an influential blog on second language acquisition called The Language Gym, co-founded the interactive website language-gym.com and the Facebook professional group Global Innovative Language Teachers (GILT). Last but not least, Gianfranco has created the instructional approach known as E.P.I. (Extensive Processing Instruction).

Dylan Viñales has taught for 15 years, in schools in Bath, Beijing and Kuala Lumpur in state, independent and international settings. He lives in Kuala Lumpur. He is fluent in five languages, and gets by in several more. Dylan is, besides a teacher, a professional development provider, specialising in E.P.I., metacognition, teaching languages through music (especially ukulele) and cognitive science. In the last five years, together with Dr Conti, he has driven the implementation of E.P.I. in one of the top international schools in the world: Garden International School. This has allowed him to test, on a daily basis, the sequences and activities included in this book with excellent results (his students have won language competitions both locally and internationally). He has designed an original Spanish curriculum, bespoke instructional materials, based on Reading and Listening as Modelling (RAM and LAM). Dylan co-founded the fastest growing professional development group for modern languages teachers on Facebook, Global Innovative Languages Teachers, which includes over 12,000 teachers from all corners of the globe. He authors an influential blog on modern language pedagogy in which he supports the teaching of languages through E.P.I. Dylan is the lead author of Spanish content on the Language Gym website and oversees the technological development of the site. He is currently undertaking the NPQML qualification, after which he plans to pursue a Masters in second language acquisition.

Thomas Weidner has been teaching languages since 2011, starting out as a language assistant in a large secondary school in London and completing his PGCE qualification at Bristol University in 2013. He now teaches at Sidcot School, a Quaker school in the Southwest of England, where he works with students at both primary and secondary levels, teaching German and Spanish up to the GCSE, A-level and IB qualifications. Thomas is a native German, who holds a Master's degree in Sports Sciences and worked in the international development sector for seven years before turning to languages as his profession. Now fluent in 5 languages, he believes in language skills as a tool for personal opportunity, a key driver for bringing people together and enabling an international dialogue towards peace and a sustainable future for all. Thomas has been experimenting and working with the E.P.I. in the classroom approach since 2017. He has found it an excellent way to engage and empower language learners to feel confident about their language skills and to make progress. Since 2020, Thomas is the lead-author for German content on the Language Gym.

 **THE LANGUAGE GYM**

Acknowledgements

Translating and adapting this book from its Spanish original into German has been a time-consuming, yet hugely rewarding endeavour. Thomas would like to thank his wife Chrissy for her support and above all for being a wonderful partner. He would also like to thank his children, Carys (7) and Theo (3), for being super-patient with him and (almost) never complaining when he wasn't there to play this summer, but perhaps should have been.

Secondly, huge thanks to our editor for this edition, Isabelle Porter, from Stuttgart, Germany and now teaching German, French and Spanish at Queen Elizabeth's Hospital in Bristol. Her contributions have gone *far* beyond proofreading for accuracy, to advising on best selection of language content and offering inter-cultural insights along the way. With her fabulous dedication, sense of humour and eagle-eye, she has been a tremendous asset to our team. In a similar vein, a massive thank you to Magdalena Weidner, experienced German as a Second Language and English as a Foreign Language teacher in Hesse, Germany (and Thomas' mum), for her invaluable input and eye for detail.

Thirdly, we'd like to thank the many colleagues from the German teaching community who have given their moral support and professional feedback to this book, both online (GILT, Conti Deutsch group on Facebook) and face to face. Here, a special thanks to Katrin Sredzki-Seamer from the National Modern Languages SCITT in Sheffield for her critical eye and suggestions in the content selection process, and to Thomas' colleagues at Sidcot School, North Somerset, for their fabulous comradeship and support.

Lastly, a heartfelt thanks to Tom Ball, Damian Graizevsky and David James, at Garden International School, for being fantastic colleagues, inspiring leaders, and for helping to create a world class working environment, where it was possible to lay the foundations for E.P.I. and produce the bank of Sentence Builders that are the foundation for this booklet.

In addition, a shout-out to the talented Ross Padgett, former Head of Art at Garden International School for his superb work designing the book cover.

Vielen Dank.

Introduction

Hello and welcome to the first 'text' book designed to be an accompaniment to a German, Extensive Processing Instruction course. The book has come about out of necessity, because such a resource did not previously exist.

How to use this book if you have bought into our E.P.I. approach

This book was originally designed as a resource to use in conjunction with our E.P.I. approach and teaching strategies. Our course favours flooding comprehensible input, organising content by communicative functions and related constructions, and a big focus on reading and listening as modelling. The aim of this book is to empower the beginner-to-pre-intermediate learner with linguistic tools - high-frequency structures and vocabulary - useful for real-life communication. Since, in a typical E.P.I. unit of work, aural and oral work play a huge role, this book should not be viewed as the ultimate E.P.I. coursebook, but rather as a **useful resource** to **complement** your Listening-As-Modelling and Speaking activities.

Sentence Builders – Online Versions

Please note that all these sentence builders will be available in bilingual and German only versions on the Language Gym website, available to download, editable and optimised for displaying in the classroom, via the Locker Room section (available via subscription).

How to use this book if you don't know or have NOT bought into our approach

Alternatively, you may use this book to dip in and out of as a source of printable material for your lessons. Whilst our curriculum is driven by communicative functions rather than topics, we have deliberately embedded the target constructions in topics which are popular with teachers and commonly found in published coursebooks.

If you would like to learn about E.P.I. you could read one of the authors' blogs. The definitive guide is Dr Conti's "Patterns First – How I Teach Lexicogrammar" which can be found on his blog (www.gianfrancoconti.com). There are also blogs on Dylan's wordpress site (mrvinalesmfl.wordpress.com) such as "Using sentence builders to reduce (everyone's) workload and create more fluent linguists" which can be read to get teaching ideas and to learn how to structure a course, through all the stages of E.P.I.

The book "Breaking the Sound Barrier: Teaching Learners how to Listen" by Gianfranco Conti and Steve Smith, provides a detailed description of the approach and of the listening and speaking activities you can use in synergy with the present book.

The basic structure of the book

The book contains 19 macro-units which concern themselves with a specific communicative function, such as 'Describing people's appearance and personality', 'Comparing and contrasting people', 'Saying what you like and dislike' or 'Saying what you and others do in your free time'. You can find a note of each communicative function in the Table of Contents. Each unit includes:

- a sentence builder modelling the target constructions;
- a set of vocabulary building activities which reinforce the material in the sentence builder;
- a set of narrow reading texts exploited through a range of tasks focusing on both the meaning and structural levels of the text;
- a set of translation tasks aimed at consolidation through retrieval practice;
- a set of writing tasks targeting essential writing micro-skills such as spelling, functional and positional processing, editing and communication of meaning.

Each sentence builder at the beginning of a unit contains one or more constuctions which have been selected with real-life communication in mind. Each unit is built around that construction but not solely on it. Based on the principle that each E.P.I instructional sequence must move from modelling to production in a seamless and organic way, each unit expands on the material in each sentence builder by embedding it in texts and graded tasks which contain both familiar and unfamiliar (but comprehensible and learnable) vocabulary and structures. Through lots of careful recycling and thorough and extensive processing of the input, by the end of each unit the student has many opportunities to encounter and process the new vocabulary and patterns with material from the previous units.

Alongside the macro-units you will find:

- grammar units: one or two pages of activities at regular intervals. They explicitly focus on key grammar structures which enhance the generative power of the constructions in the sentence builders. At this level, they mainly concern themselves with the present tense conjugations of key verbs, give learners an introduction to the use of cases and provide opportunities to build confidence with the German word order.
- question-skills units: one or two pages on understanding and creating questions. These micro-units too occur at regular intervals in the book, so as to recycle the same question patterns in different linguistic contexts;
- revision quickies: these are retrieval practice tasks aimed at keeping the previously learnt vocabulary alive. These too occur at regular intervals;
- self-tests: these occur at the end of the book. They are divided into two sections, one for less confident and one for more confident learners.

The point of all the above micro-units is to implement lots of systematic recycling and interleaving, two techniques that allow for stronger retention and transfer of learning.

 **THE LANGUAGE GYM**

Other important *caveats*

1) This is a '**no frills**' book. This means that there are a limited number of illustrations (only on unit title pages). This is because we want every single little thing in this book to be useful. Consequently, we have packed a substantive amount of content at the detriment of its look. In particular, we have given serious thought to both **recycling** and **interleaving**, in order to allow for key constructions, words and grammar items to be revisited regularly so as to enhance exponentially their retention.

2) **Listening** as modelling is an essential part of E.P.I. There will be an accompanying listening booklet released shortly which will contain narrow listening exercises for all 19 units, following the same content as this book.

3) **All content** in this booklet matches the content on the **Language Gym** website. For best results, we recommend a mixture of communicative, retrieval practice games, combined with Language Gym games and workouts, and then this booklet as the follow-up, either in class or for homework.

4) An **answer booklet** is also available, for those that would like it. We have produced it separately to stop this booklet from being excessively long.

5) This booklet is suitable for **beginner** to **pre-intermediate** learners. This equates to a **CEFR A1-A2** level, or a beginner **Y6-Y8** class. You do not need to start at the beginning, although you may want to dip in to certain units for revision/recycling. You do not need to follow the booklet in order, although many of you will, and if you do, you will benefit from the specific recycling/interleaving strategies. Either way, all topics are repeated frequently throughout the book.

We hope that you and your students will find this book useful and enjoyable.

Gianfranco, Dylan and Thomas

TABLE OF CONTENTS

	Unit Title	Communicative function	Page
1	Talking about my age	Describing yourself and other people	**1**
2	Saying when my birthday is	Describing yourself and other people	**7**
3	Describing hair and eyes	Describing yourself and other people	**13**
4	Saying where I live and am from Unit 4a: Talking about the weather	Indicating location	**19**
5	Talking about my family members, saying their age and how well I get along with them. Counting to 100.	Describing people and relationships	**31**
	Revision Quickie 1: Numbers 1-100 / Dates / Birthdays		**36**
6	Part 1: Describing myself and another family member	Describing yourself and other people	**37**
	Grammar Time 1: SEIN (Part 1)		**40**
	Grammar Time 2: HABEN (Part 1)		**43**
	Part 2: Describing my family and saying why I like/dislike them Unit 6a: Talking about skills	Describing people, relationships and expressing opinions	**45**
7	Talking about pets (I have and would like to have); asking key questions	Describing people/animals and asking questions	**54**
	Grammar Time 3: HABEN (Part 2) - Pets and description		**60**
	Grammar Time 4: A, THE, and MY in the nominative and accusative cases		**61**
	Question Skills 1: Age / descriptions / pets		**63**
8	Saying what jobs people do, why they like/dislike them and where they work	Describing people, expressing opinions and indicating location	**65**
	Grammar Time 5: WOHNEN & ARBEITEN and other regular verbs in the present tense		**70**
	Unit 8a: Using FINDEN + accusative to express an opinion	Expressing opinions	
	Grammar Time 6: SEIN (Part 2) - Jobs		**74**
9	Comparing people's appearance and personality	Comparing and contrasting	**76**
	Revision Quickie 2: Family / Pets / Jobs		**81**
10	Saying what's in my school bag / classroom / describing colour	Stating what you have and describing objects	**82**
	Grammar Time 7: HABEN + indefinite article + noun		**88**
	Grammar Time 8: HABEN + indefinite article + adjective + noun		**91**
11	Talking about food (Part 1): Likes / dislikes / reasons	Describing food and expressing opinions	**94**

 **THE LANGUAGE GYM**

	Grammar Time 9: ESSEN & TRINKEN + gern/lieber/am liebsten		100
12	Talking about food (Part 2): Likes / dislikes / mealtimes	Describing routine behaviour in the present, indicating time and expressing opinions	103
	Grammar Time 10: Word order in main clauses		108
	Question Skills 2: Jobs / School bag / Food		111
13	Talking about clothes and accessories I wear, how often and when	Describing people, routine behaviour in the present and indicating time	112
	Grammar Time 11: TRAGEN + indefinite article + adjective + noun		117
	Grammar Time 12: Word Order in subordinate clauses		119
	Revision Quickie 3: Jobs, food, clothes and numbers 20-100		121
14	Saying what I and others do in our free time	Describing routine behaviour in the present and indicating time	122
	Grammar Time 13: SPIELEN, MACHEN, GEHEN + Use of adverbials to add interest		128
	Grammar Time 14: 3 types of linking words		131
15	Talking about the weather and free time	Describing events and routine behaviour in the present and indicating location	133
	Grammar Time 15: SPIELEN, MACHEN, GEHEN (Part 2) & SEIN, HABEN (Part 3)		139
	Revision Quickie 4: Weather / Free time / Clothes		141
	Question Skills 3: Weather / Free time / Clothes		142
16	Talking about my daily routine	Describing routine behaviour in the present, indicating time and sequencing actions	143
	Revision Quickie 5: Clothes / Food / Free Time / Describing people		150
17	Describing my house, indicating where it is located & saying what I like/dislike about it	Indicating location, describing things and expressing likes/dislikes	152
	Grammar Time 16: WOHNEN + locations in the dative case		158
	Grammar Time 17: REFLEXIVES (Part 1)		160
	Grammar Time 18: ES GIBT + indefinite article + adjective + noun		162
18	Saying what I do at home, how often, when and where	Indicating routine behaviour in the present, time, frequency and location	165
	Grammar Time 19: Destinations vs Locations		171
	Grammar Time 20: SPIELEN, MACHEN, GEHEN (Part 3)		173
19	Talking about future plans for holidays	Making plans for the future, indicating time, location and expressing opinions	175
	Revision Quickie 6: Daily routine / House / Home life / Holidays		181
	Question Skills 4: Daily routine / House / Home life / Holidays		183
20	Vocabulary Tests		184

THE LANGUAGE GYM

UNIT 1
Talking about my age

In this unit you will learn:

- How to say your name and age
- How to say someone else's name and age
- How to count from 1 to 15
- A range of common German names
- The words for brother and sister

Ich bin fünfzehn Jahre alt.

Sie ist zehn Jahre alt.

Ich bin sechs Jahre alt.

Er ist dreißig Jahre alt.

UNIT 1
Talking about my age

Ich	heiße	Alex	und	ich bin	ein	1	Jahr alt _year old_
_I_	_am called_	Ben	_and_	_I am_	zwei	2	Jahre alt _years old_
		Clara			drei	3	
		Dennis			vier	4	
		Finn			fünf	5	
		Hannah			sechs	6	
		Jonas			sieben	7	
		Julia			acht	8	
Mein Bruder	**heißt**	Leonie		**er ist**	neun	9	
	is called	Luzi		_he is_	zehn	10	
My brother		Max			elf	11	
		Michi			zwölf	12	
Meine Schwester		Nina		**sie ist**	dreizehn	13	
		Paul		_she is_	vierzehn	14	
My sister		Sarah			fünfzehn	15	
		Simon			sechzehn	16	
		Stefan			siebzehn	17	
		Tim			achtzehn	18	
		Toni			neunzehn	19	
		Yildiz			zwanzig	20	
					einundzwanzig	21	
					...		

Author's note:

When you are counting, the word for number 1 in German is "eins".

E.g. 1, 2, 3... = „eins, zwei, drei"

Unit 1. Talking about my age: VOCABULARY BUILDING

1. Match up

ein Jahr	seven years
zwei Jahre	four years
drei Jahre	five years
vier Jahre	six years
fünf Jahre	eleven years
sechs Jahre	ten years
sieben Jahre	twelve years
acht Jahre	nine years
neun Jahre	two years
zehn Jahre	eight years
elf Jahre	one year
zwölf Jahre	three years

2. Complete with the missing word

a. Ich bin _____ Jahre alt.   *I am fourteen years old.*

b. Mein Bruder _____ Max.   *My brother is called Max.*

c. Ich _____ Stefan.   *I am called Stefan.*

d. Mein Bruder _____ zwei.   *My brother is two.*

e. Meine Schwester ist _____.   *My sister is four.*

f. _____ heiße Anna.   *My name is Anna.*

vier	ist	heißt
ich	vierzehn	heiße

3. Translate into English

a. Ich heiße …

b. Ich bin sechs Jahre alt.

c. Ich bin zwölf Jahre alt.

d. Er ist vierzehn Jahre alt.

e. Sie ist acht Jahre alt.

f. Er heißt …

g. Mein Bruder ist …

h. Meine Schwester ist …

i. Sie heißt …

4. Broken words

a. ich b_____   *I am*

b. ich hei_____   *I'm called*

c. meine Schwe_____   *my sister*

d. zw_____   *twelve*

e. fünfz_____   *fifteen*

f. e_____   *eleven*

g. ne_____   *nine*

h. vier_____   *fourteen*

i. a_____   *eight*

5. Rank the people below from oldest to youngest as shown in the example

Nina ist fünfzehn Jahre alt.	1
Finn ist dreizehn Jahre alt.	
Julia ist fünf Jahre alt.	
Toni ist ein Jahr alt.	
Max ist zwölf Jahre alt.	
Selim ist drei Jahre alt.	
Lena ist acht Jahre alt.	
Luzi ist elf Jahre alt.	

6. For each pair of people write who is the oldest, as shown in the example

A	B	older
Ich bin elf Jahre alt.	Ich bin drei Jahre alt.	A
Ich bin acht Jahre alt.	Ich bin sieben Jahre alt.	
Ich bin vierzehn Jahre alt.	Ich bin neun Jahre alt.	
Ich bin ein Jahr alt.	Ich bin sechs Jahre alt.	
Ich bin zwölf Jahre alt.	Ich bin vier Jahre alt.	
Ich bin dreizehn Jahre alt.	Ich bin fünfzehn Jahre alt.	
Ich bin zehn Jahre alt.	Ich bin zwei Jahre alt.	

Unit 1. Talking about my age: READING

Ich heiße Alex. Ich bin zwölf Jahre alt und ich wohne in Berlin. Das ist die Hauptstadt von Deutschland! Ich habe einen Bruder. Er heißt Max und er ist vierzehn Jahre alt.

Ich heiße Tim. Ich bin zehn Jahre alt und ich wohne in Bern. Das ist die Hauptstadt der Schweiz. Ich habe eine Schwester. Sie heißt Barbara und sie ist fünf Jahre alt. Ich habe auch einen Bruder. Er heißt Finn und er ist neun Jahre alt.

Ich heiße Laura. Ich bin dreizehn Jahre alt und ich wohne in Wien. Das ist die Hauptstadt von Österreich. Ich habe einen Bruder. Er heißt Roberto und er ist fünfzehn Jahre alt.

Ich heiße Luise. Ich bin neun Jahre alt und ich wohne in Brüssel. Das ist die Hauptstadt von Belgien. Ich habe eine Schwester. Sie heißt Luzi und sie ist elf Jahre alt. Ich habe auch einen Bruder. Er heißt Pierre und er ist vierzehn Jahre alt.

1. Find the German for the following items in Alex' text

a. I live in

b. that is the capital

c. I have a brother

d. I am twelve years old

e. he is called

f. of Germany

g. he is fourteen years old

2. Answer these questions about Tim

a. Where does Tim live?

b. How old is he?

c. How many siblings does he have?

d. What are their names and ages?

Ich heiße Marcel. Ich bin vierzehn Jahre alt und ich wohne in Vaduz. Das ist die Hauptstadt von Liechtenstein. Ich habe keine Geschwister, aber ich habe einen Cousin. Er heißt Linus und er ist zwölf Jahre alt. Ich habe auch eine Cousine. Sie heißt Maja und sie ist sieben Jahre alt.

3. Complete the table below

	Age	Home country	How many siblings	Ages of siblings
Laura				
Tim				
Alex				

Ich heiße Anna. Ich bin elf Jahre alt und ich wohne in Bozen. Das ist in Südtirol. Ich habe keine Schwester, aber ich habe zwei Brüder. Sie heißen Martin und Johannes. Martin ist mein großer Bruder, er ist dreizehn Jahre alt. Johannes ist mein kleiner Bruder, er ist sieben Jahre alt.

4. Luise, Marcel or Anna?

a. Who lives in northern Italy?

b. Who has an 11-year-old sister?

c. Who has no siblings, but 2 cousins?

d. Who has an older brother aged 13?

e. Who has a 14-year-old brother?

 THE LANGUAGE GYM

Unit 1. Talking about my age: TRANSLATION

1. Bad translation: spot and correct (in the English) any translation mistakes you find below

a. Ich heiße Olivia.	*Her name is Olivia.*
b. Ich habe zwei Schwestern.	*I have two brothers.*
c. Meine Schwester heißt Petra.	*My mother is called Petra.*
d. Mein Bruder ist fünf Jahre alt.	*My sister is 5.*
e. Ich bin fünfzehn Jahre alt.	*I am fourteen.*
f. Mein Bruder ist acht.	*My brother is seven.*
g. Ich habe keine Geschwister.	*I have no sisters.*
h. aber ich habe einen Onkel	*but I have an aunt*
i. Ich bin elf Jahre alt.	*I am 13 years old.*
j. Er heißt Jens.	*She is called Jens.*

2. Translate from German into English

a. Mein Bruder heißt Jonas.	f. Ich wohne in Berlin.
b. Ich bin fünfzehn Jahre alt.	g. Meine Schwester ist dreizehn Jahre alt.
c. Mein Bruder ist sechs Jahre alt.	h. Ich habe einen Bruder und eine Schwester.
d. Meine Schwester heißt Annika.	i. Ich habe keine Schwester.
e. Ich bin sieben Jahre alt.	j. Franzi ist neun Jahre alt.

3. Translate from English to German

a. I am called Max. I am seven years old.

b. My brother is fourteen.

c. I am twelve years old.

d. My sister is called Julia.

e. I am fifteen.

f. I have a brother and a sister.

g. My name is Miriam and I am thirteen.

h. I have no sister, but I have a brother.

i. I am called Sebastian. I am ten. I have a brother and a sister.

Unit 1. Talking about my age: WRITING

1. Complete the words

a. I___ h_____ Max.

b. I___ b___ vierz_____ J_____ a____.

c. I___ h_____ ein___ Br_____r.

d. Me___e Schw_____ he_____ Lisa.

e. I___ h_____e Kathrin.

f. Me___ Br_____ h_____t Niko.

g. ___h b____ d___i J_____ ____t.

h. M_____e Sch_____ h_____ Miriam.

2. Write out the number in German

nine	n_____
ten	z_____
twelve	z_____
fifteen	f_____
fourteen	v_____
eight	a_____
thirteen	d_____
eleven	e_____

3. Spot and correct the spelling mistakes

a. Ich heißen Mark.

b. Ich bin driezehn Jahr alt.

c. Mein Bruder is funf Jahre alt.

d. Meine Swester heiße Birte.

e. Ich hieße Patrick.

f. Meine Bruder heiße Matthias.

4. Complete with a suitable word

a. Meine Schwester _____ Laura.

b. _____ Bruder ist fünfzehn Jahre alt.

c. Ich _____ Timo.

d. Ich habe einen _____.

e. Ich habe eine _____.

f. Sie _____ Andrea.

g. Mein Bruder ist neunzehn _____ alt.

5. Guided writing – write 4 short paragraphs in the first person singular ['I'] each describing the people below

Name	Age	Lives in	Country	Brother's name and age	Sister's name and age
Yildiz	14	Berlin	Germany	Ahmed 9	Ellen 8
Simon	15	Zürich	Switzerland	Alex 13	Valentina 10
Michael	11	Innsbruck	Austria	Thomas 7	Gerda 12
Eva	10	Bozen	South Tyrol	Antonio 6	Chiara 1

6. Describe this person in the third person:

Name: Lars

Age: 12

Lives in: Hamburg

Brother: Tim, 10 years old

Sister: Sarah, 14 years old

UNIT 2
Saying when my birthday is

In this unit you will learn to say:

- Where you and another person (e.g. a friend) come from
- When your birthday is
- Numbers from 15 to 31
- Months
- Names of German-speaking locations
- Where you live

UNIT 2
Saying when my birthday is

Ich heiße Max *My name is Max*	**ich komme aus Berlin** *I come from Berlin* **ich bin X Jahre alt** *I am X years old*	**und** *and* **mein Geburtstag ist am** *my birthday is on the*	1. – **ersten*** 2. - **zweiten** 3. - **dritten** 4. - **vierten** 5. - **fünften** 6. - **sechsten** 7. - **siebten** 8. - **achten** 9. - **neunten** 10. - **zehnten** 11. - **elften** 12. - **zwölften** 13. - **dreizehnten** 14. - **vierzehnten** 15. - **fünfzehnten** 16. - **sechzehnten** 17. - **siebzehnten** 18. - **achtzehnten** 19. - **neunzehnten** 20. - **zwanzigsten** 21. - **einundzwanzigsten** 22. - **zweiundzwanzigsten** 23. - **dreiundzwanzigsten** 24. - **vierundzwanzigsten** 25. - **fünfundzwanzigsten** 26. - **sechsundzwanzigsten** 27. - **siebenundzwanzigsten** 28. - **achtundzwanzigsten** 29. - **neunundzwanzigsten** 30. - **dreißigsten** 31. - **einunddreißigsten**	**Januar** *January* **Februar** **März** **April** **Mai** **Juni** **Juli** **August** **September** **Oktober** **November** **Dezember**
Meine Freundin heißt Lena *My friend is called Lena* **Mein Freund heißt Toni** *My friend is called Toni*	**er/sie kommt aus München** *he/she comes from Munich* **er/sie ist X Jahre alt** *he/she is X years old*	**und** *and* **sein/ihr Geburtstag ist am** *his/her birthday is on the*		

Author's notes:

(1) To say when your birthday is, you can also use: 'Ich habe (am ersten Juni) Geburtstag'. This literally translates as 'I have (on the first of June) birthday.' You will see examples of this in the activities of this unit.

(2) In the table above, the ordinal numbers 1-31 are given, as you need them to give a date in German. You can find the cardinal numbers (i.e. the ones you need for counting) for the numbers 1-21 in the sentence builder of Unit 1. Discuss with your teacher any pattern that you notice!

Unit 2. Saying when my birthday is: VOCABULARY BUILDING

1. Complete with the missing word

a. Ich _____ Mia.   *My name is Mia.*

b. Meine _____ heißt Anna.   *My friend is called Anna.*

c. _____ Freund heißt Paul.   *My friend is called Paul.*

d. mein _____ ist   *my birthday is*

e. am _____ Juni   *on the fifth of June*

f. am _____ März   *on the 18th of March*

g. am neunten _____   *on the 9th of July*

h. _____/_____ Geburtstag ist am   *his/her birthday is on the*

2. Match up

April	May
Juli	my birthday
Dezember	my friend (f)
Mai	April
Januar	July
Februar	he/she is called
mein Geburtstag	December
mein Freund	I am called
meine Freundin	February
ich heiße	January
er/sie heißt	my friend (m)

3. Translate into English

a. am zwölften Oktober

b. am achten Februar

c. am neunzehnten Juni

d. am fünfundzwanzigsten März

e. am elften August

f. am siebzehnten Dezember

g. am dreißigsten Mai

h. am vierzehnten April

4. Add the missing letter

a. Geburt_tag   c. Ma_   e. A_ril   g. J_nuar   i. Jul_   k. De_ember

b. M_rz   d. Febr_ar f. Jun_   h. A_gust   j. No_ember l. Sept_mber

5. Broken words

a. a___ d_____ S_____   *on the 30ᵗʰ of Sept*

b. a___ f_____ J_____   *on the 5ᵗʰ of July*

c. a___ n_____ A_____   *on the 9ᵗʰ of Aug*

d. a___ d_____ J_____   *on the 3ʳᵈ of Jan*

e. a___ z_____ O_____   *on the 20ᵗʰ of Oct*

f. a___ n_____ D_____   *on the 19ᵗʰ of Dec*

g. a___ s_____ A_____   *on the 16ᵗʰ of April*

h. a___ v_____ M_____   *on the 24ᵗʰ of May*

i. a___ z_____ M_____   *on the 12ᵗʰ of March*

6. Complete with a suitable word

a. Ich _____ Hansi.

b. Mein _____ ist am zweiten Mai.

c. Ich bin neun _____ alt.

d. Meine _____ heißt Laura.

e. Laura _____ zehn Jahre alt.

f. Ihr _____ ist am dritten Juni.

g. Mein _____ ist am ersten Juli.

h. Mein _____ heißt Max.

i. _____ Geburtstag ist am vierten März.

j. Sein Geburtstag ist _____ ersten April.

k. _____ heiße Gerd Müller.

Unit 2. Saying when my birthday is: READING

Hallo, ich heiße Ben. Ich bin zwölf Jahre alt und ich komme aus Hamburg. Mein Geburtstag ist am zwölften Januar. Mein Freund heißt Luis und er ist dreizehn Jahre alt. Sein Geburtstag ist am achtundzwanzigsten Mai. In meiner Freizeit spiele ich gern Gitarre. Luis auch, wie cool!

Meine Tante heißt Charlotte. Sie ist dreißig Jahre alt und sie ist Lehrerin. Sie hat am einundzwanzigsten September Geburtstag. Charlotte hat einen großen Bruder. Sein Geburtstag ist am siebten Januar.

Hi, wie geht's! Ich heiße Julian. Ich bin einundzwanzig Jahre alt und ich komme aus Graz. Das ist im Süden von Österreich. Ich habe am zehnten September Geburtstag. Meine Freundin heißt Annika und sie ist neunzehn Jahre alt. Sie hat am fünfzehnten April Geburtstag. In meiner Freizeit spiele ich gern Trompete.

Hallo Leute, ich heiße Lena. Ich bin sieben Jahre alt und ich wohne in Leipzig, im Osten von Deutschland. Mein Geburtstag ist am fünften November. Ich habe zwei Brüder, Jens und Maik. Jens ist elf Jahre alt und er ist total nett. Sein Geburtstag ist am dreißigsten März. Maik ist total gemein. Er ist dreizehn Jahre alt und er hat am fünften Januar Geburtstag.

Hallo, na? Ich heiße Anton. Ich bin achtzehn Jahre alt und ich komme aus Aachen. Das ist im Westen von Deutschland. Mein Geburtstag ist am neunten August. Meine kleine Schwester ist vier Jahre alt. Sie ist sehr nett. Sie hat am neunten August Geburtstag. So wie ich!

Mein Freund heißt Luis und er ist siebzehn Jahre alt. Sein Geburtstag ist am fünfundzwanzigsten Oktober.

1. Find the German for the following items in Ben's text

a. I am called

b. I am 12 years old

c. I come from Hamburg

d. My birthday is

e. on the twelfth

f. his birthday is

g. in my free time

h. my aunt

i. is called

j. she is 30

k. on the 21st

l. she has a big brother

m. on the seventh of January

2. Answer the following questions about Lena's text

a. How old is she?

b. Where does she live?

c. When is her birthday?

d. How many brothers does she have?

e. Which brother is totally mean?

f. How old is Maik?

g. When is his birthday?

3. Complete with the missing words

Ich heiße Max. Ich _____ dreizehn _____ alt und ich _____ aus Köln. Mein _____ ist am achtundzwanzigsten Mai. Mein Bruder _____ zehn _____ alt und sein Geburtstag ist _____ dritten April.

4. Find someone who ...

a. ... has a birthday in November

b. ... is from the South of Austria

c. ... has a birthday in late March

d. ... has an aunt who is 30 years old

e. ... has one totally kind and one totally mean sibling

f. ... shares a birthday with a sibling

g. ... is 21 years old

h. ... has a little sister

i. ... likes playing the guitar, like their friend

Unit 2. Saying when my birthday is: TRANSLATION

1. Bad translation: spot and correct (in the English) any translation mistakes you find below

a. Mein Geburtstag ist am sechsundzwanzigsten Mai.
His birthday is on the 27th of May.

b. Ich heiße Laura und ich komme aus der Schweiz.
Your name is Laura and you are from Germany.

c. Ich bin vierundzwanzig Jahre alt.
I am 25 years old.

d. Mein Freund heißt Stefan und er kommt aus Köln.
I am called Stefan and I come from Cologne.

e. Ich bin fünfunddreißig Jahre alt.
I am 34 years old.

f. Ihr Geburtstag ist am vierten April.
My birthday is on the 14th of April.

g. Meine Freundin Ute kommt aus Österreich.
My sister Ute comes from Australia.

2. From German to English

a. mein Geburtstag ist

b. am fünften Mai

c. meine Freundin heißt

d. ihr Geburtstag ist

e. am ersten Juni

f. am vierzehnten Februar

g. am fünfundzwanzigsten Dezember

h. sein Geburtstag ist

i. am elften März

3. Phrase-level translation

a. my name is

b. I am eleven years old

c. my birthday is

d. on the seventh of March

e. my friend is called Maria

f. she is twelve years old

g. her birthday is

h. on the 23rd of June

i. on the 19th of May

Author's note: go back to 3.e. Did you make Maria a girl - "Freundin"? Well done if you did! ☺

4. Sentence-level translation

a. My name is Julia. I am 20 years old. I live in Germany. My birthday is the 5th of July.

b. My brother is called Peter. He is 17 years old. His birthday is the 1st of April.

c. My friend is called Luis. He is 21 years old and his birthday is on the 12th of December.

d. My friend is called Angela. She is 19 years old and her birthday is on the 22nd of June.

e. My friend is called Xaver. He is 18 years old. His birthday is on the 3rd of January.

Unit 2. Saying when my birthday is: WRITING

1. Complete with the missing letters

a. Ich hei_ _ Luis.

b. Ich kom_ _ a_ _ Frankfurt.

c. Mei_ Geburtst_ _ ist am zweit_ _ M_ _.

d. E_ i_ _ dreize_ _ Jah_ _ al_.

e. Mein_ _ Freund_ _ he_ _ _ Johanna.

f. Johanna kom_ _ au_ Frankfurt.

g. Mei_ Freu_ _ Nico kom_ _ a_ _ Köln.

h. Nico is_ el_ Ja_ _ _ _ a_ _.

2. Spot and correct the spelling mistakes

a. Mein Geburtstag is am vierten Januar.

b. Ich hieße Luis.

c. Ich komme ous Frankfurt.

d. Meine Freundin heiße Johanna.

e. Johanna ist funfzehn Jahre alt.

f. Ich bin vierzehn jahre alt.

g. Ich habe am ersten Marz Geburtstag.

h. Ich bin zwansig Jahre alt.

3. Answer the questions in German

a. Wie heißt du?

b. Wie alt bist du?

c. Wann ist dein Geburtstag?

d. Wie alt ist dein Bruder/deine Schwester?

e. Wann ist sein/ihr Geburtstag?

4. Write out the dates below in words as shown in the example

a. on 15.05   am fünfzehnten Mai

b. on 11.07

c. on 20.04

d. on 07.02

e. on 24.12

f. on 01.06

g. on 04.01

h. on 14.03

5. Guided writing – write 4 short paragraphs in the 1st person singular ['I'] describing the people below

Name	Town/City	Age	Birthday	Name of brother	Brother's birthday
Jana	Wien	15	21.07	Lukas	03.02
Maik	München	11	25.12	Philipp	20.08
Clara	Kiel	12	02.11	Martin	04.06
Samuel	Bern	17	01.01	Leo	13.10

6. Describe this person in the third person:

Name: Toni

Age: 12

Lives in: Salzburg

Birthday: 14.02

Brother: Roman, 15 years old

Birthday: 06.12

UNIT 3
Describing hair and eyes

In this unit you will learn:
- To describe what a person's hair and eyes are like
- To describe details about their faces (e.g. beard and glasses)
- Colours
- I wear & he/she wears

You will also revisit:
- Common German names
- The verbs "haben" and "sein" in the first and third person singular
- Numbers from 1 to 15

UNIT 3
Describing hair and eyes

Ich heiße *I am called / My name is* **Er/Sie heißt** *He/She is called*	Amelie Christian Daniela Eike Franzi Miriam Nils Julia Susi		**und** *and*	**ich bin** *I am* **er/sie ist** *he/she is*	sechs 6 sieben 7 acht 8 neun 9 zehn 10 elf 11 zwölf 12 dreizehn 13 vierzehn 14 fünfzehn 15	**Jahre alt** *years old*
Ich habe *I have* **Er/Sie hat** *He/She has*	**kurze** *short* **lange** *long* **mittellange** *medium-length* **glatte** *straight* **lockige** *curly* **wellige** *wavy* **blonde** *blonde* **braune** *brown* **graue** *grey* **schwarze** *black* **rote** *red* **weiße** *white*	**Haare** *hair*	**und** *and*	**blaue** *blue* **braune** *brown* **graue** *grey* **grüne** *green*	**Augen** *eyes*	
Ich trage *I wear* **Er/Sie trägt** *He/she wears*	**eine Brille** *glasses* **keine Brille** *no glasses* **einen Bart** *a beard* **keinen Bart** *no beard*		**und** *and* **aber** *but*	**Kontaktlinsen** *contact lenses* **Ohrringe** *earrings* **keine Ohrringe** *no earrings*		

Unit 3. Describing hair and eyes: VOCABULARY BUILDING

1. Complete with the missing word

a. Ich habe br_____ Haare.   *I have brown hair.*

b. Ich habe bl_____ Haare.   *I have blonde hair.*

c. Ich trage einen B_____.   *I wear a beard.*

d. Ich habe blaue A_____.   *I have blue eyes.*

e. Ich trage keine Br_____.   *I don't wear glasses.*

f. Ich habe mitt_____ Haare.   *I have mid-length hair.*

g. Ich habe dunkelbr_____ Augen.   *I have dark-brown eyes.*

h. Ich habe rote H_____.   *I have red hair.*

2. Match up

ich habe	I wear
schwarze Haare	no hair
blonde Haare	a beard
keine Haare	green eyes
eine Brille	black hair
einen Bart	short hair
blaue Augen	I have
grüne Augen	red hair
kurze Haare	blonde hair
ich trage	glasses
rote Haare	blue eyes

3. Translate into English

a. lockige Haare

b. blaue Augen

c. ich trage eine Brille

d. ich trage einen Bart

e. grüne Augen

f. rote Haare

g. dunkelbraune Augen

h. keine Haare

4. Add the missing letter

a. lan_e   c. _aare   e. bla_e   g. loc_ige   i. br_une   k. Au_en

b. Bri_le   d. B_rt   f. gr_ne   h. g_atte   j. mit_ellange   l. ich tr_ge

5. Broken words

a. I____ h_____ l_____ H_____.   *I have curly hair.*

b. I____ t_____ e_____ B_____.   *I wear glasses.*

c. I____ h_____ k_____ H_____.   *I have short hair.*

d. I____ h_____ k_____ B_____.   *I don't have a beard.*

e. I____ h_____ b_____ A_____.   *I have brown eyes.*

f. E____ h____ e_____ B_____.   *He has a beard.*

g. I____ b___ a_____ J_____ a____.   *I am eight years old.*

h. I____ h_____ L_____.   *My name is Lena.*

i. I___ t____ k_____ B_____.   *I don't wear glasses.*

6. Complete with a suitable word

a. Ich bin zehn _____ alt.

b. Ich _____ einen Bart.

c. Ich _____ Sascha.

d. Ich trage eine _____.

e. Ich habe lange rote _____.

f. Ich habe keinen _____.

g. Ich _____ braune Augen.

h. Ich habe _____ Haare.

i. Ich trage keine _____.

j. Ich trage _____.

k. Ich habe _____ Augen.

l. Ich _____ elf Jahre alt.

THE LANGUAGE GYM

Unit 3. Describing hair and eyes: READING

Ich heiße Lisa. Ich bin zwölf Jahre alt und ich wohne in Berlin. Das ist die Hauptstadt von Deutschland. Ich habe lange, glatte schwarze Haare und blaue Augen. Ich trage eine Brille. Mein Geburtstag ist am neunten September. Meine Schwester hat glatte Haare. Sie ist zehn Jahre alt.

Ich heiße Manuel. Ich bin fünfzehn Jahre alt und ich wohne in Vaduz. Das ist die Hauptstadt von Liechtenstein.

Ich habe kurze, lockige rote Haare und blaue Augen. Ich trage keine Brille. Mein Geburtstag ist am vierzehnten Dezember.

Ich heiße Alex. Ich bin neun Jahre alt und ich wohne in München. Das ist die Hauptstadt von Bayern. Ich habe mittellange, wellige braune Haare und braune Augen. Ich trage keine Brille, aber ich trage Kontaktlinsen. Mein Geburtstag ist am fünften Dezember.

Mein Bruder heißt Timo. Er ist fünfzehn Jahre alt. Er hat lange, glatte rote Haare und blaue Augen. Er trägt eine Brille. Sein Geburtstag ist am dreizehnten November. Er hat Sommersprossen und er ist sehr muskulös.

Ich heiße Aline. Ich bin elf Jahre alt und ich wohne in Hannover. Das ist die Hauptstadt von Niedersachsen. Ich habe lange, lockige dunkelbraune Haare und grüne Augen. Ich trage eine Brille. Mein Geburtstag ist am neunten Mai. Ich habe drei Haustiere, ein Pferd, einen Hund und eine Katze.

Meine Schwester heißt Sabina. Sie ist vierzehn Jahre alt. Sie hat lange, glatte blonde Haare und grüne Augen, so wie ich. Sie trägt auch eine Brille, so wie mein Vater. Ihr Geburtstag ist am zweiten Juni. Sie ist sehr intelligent.

Ich heiße Paul. Ich bin zehn Jahre alt und ich wohne in Wien. Das ist die Hauptstadt von Österreich. Ich habe kurze, glatte blonde Haare und grüne Augen. Ich trage eine Brille. Mein Geburtstag ist am achten April.

1. Find the German for the following items in Lisa's text

a. I am called

b. I live in

c. I wear glasses

d. my birthday is

e. on the ninth of

f. I have

g. long hair

h. blue eyes

i. she is

2. Answer the following questions about Manuel's text

a. How old is he?

b. Where is Vaduz?

c. What colour is his hair?

d. Is his hair wavy, straight or curly?

e. What length is his hair?

f. What colour are his eyes?

g. When is his birthday?

3. Complete with the missing words

Ich heiße Nils. Ich _____ zehn Jahre alt und ich _____ in Bern. Das ist die _____ der Schweiz. Ich habe kurze, glatte blonde _____ und grüne _____. Ich trage eine _____. Mein _____ ist am achten April.

4. Find someone who: answer the questions below about all 5 texts

a. Who has a sister called Sabina?

b. Who is eleven years old?

c. Who celebrates their birthday on the 9th of May?

d. How many people wear glasses?

e. Who has short red hair and blue eyes?

f. Who has a very intelligent sister?

g. Whose birthday is in April?

h. Who is muscular and has freckles?

THE LANGUAGE GYM

Unit 3. Describing hair and eyes: TRANSLATION

1. Bad translation: spot and correct (in the English) any translation mistakes you find below

a. Ich habe schwarze Haare.   *I have blonde hair.*

b. Er hat grüne Augen.   *He has brown eyes.*

c. Ich habe einen Bart.   *He has a beard.*

d. Sie heißt Maria.   *I am called Maria.*

e. Er hat kurze Haare.   *I have short hair.*

f. Ich habe braune Augen.   *I have green eyes.*

g. Ich wohne in München.   *He comes from Munich.*

3. Phrase-level translation

a. blonde hair

b. I am called

c. I have

d. blue eyes

e. straight hair

f. he has

g. ten years old

h. I have green eyes

i. long curly hair

j. she has brown eyes

k. black hair

2. From German to English

a. Ich habe braune Haare.

b. Ich habe grüne Augen.

c. Er hat kurze Haare.

d. Sie trägt eine Brille.

e. Er hat Sommersprossen.

f. Ich trage eine Brille.

g. Aber ich habe keinen Bart.

h. Ich habe lange blonde Haare.

i. Sie trägt Ohrringe.

4. Sentence-level translation

a. My name is Ben. I am nine years old. I have long, brown hair and blue eyes.

b. I am twelve years old. I have green eyes and short, straight blonde hair.

c. I am called Lena. I live in Munich. I have long, blonde hair and brown eyes.

d. My name is Johannes. I live in Hamburg. I have short, wavy black hair.

e. I am thirteen years old. I have medium-length red hair and blue eyes.

f. I am fifteen years old. I have long, curly black hair and brown eyes.

Unit 3. Describing hair and eyes: WRITING

1. Split sentences

Ich habe kurze	Augen.
Ich trage eine	Brille.
Ich habe blaue	in Köln.
Ich bin zehn	am ersten Mai.
Ich wohne	blonde Haare.
Ich heiße	Jahre alt.
Mein Geburtstag ist	Jonas.

2. Rewrite the sentences in the correct order

a. schwarze ich Haare habe

b. keinen Bart habe ich

c. heiße ich Max

d. rote ich habe Haare

e. Bruder mein Augen braune hat

f. hat Haare blonde Schwester meine

3. Spot and correct the grammar and spelling errors

a. Ich habe schwarz Haare.

b. Mein Bruder heiße Max.

c. Er habe braune Haare.

d. Sei heißt Maria.

e. Ich habe fierzehn Jahre alt.

f. Ich habe glatte Hare.

g. Ich habe grune Augen.

h. Ich tragen keine Brille.

i. Er tragt eine Brille.

j. Ich habe keine Bart.

4. Anagrams

a. raHae   Haare

b. traB

c. gueAn

d. hrJae

e. wzarsche

f. genla

g. treo

h. llreBi

5. Guided writing – write 3 short paragraphs in the first person singular ['I'] describing the people below

Name	Age	Lives in	Hair	Eyes	Glasses	Beard
Alex	12	Berlin, Germany	long curly brown	green	wears	does not have
Tina	11	Vienna, Austria	short straight red	blue	doesn't wear	does not have
Chris	15	Bern, Switzer-land	medium-length wavy brown	brown	wears	has

6. Describe this person in the third person:

Name: Martin

Age: 15

Hair: short, wavy, brown

Eyes: blue

Glasses: no

Beard: yes

THE LANGUAGE GYM

UNIT 4
Saying where I live and am from

Unit 4a - Talking about the weather

In this unit you will learn to talk about:

- Where you live and are from
- If you live in a flat or a house
- What your accommodation looks like
- Where it is located
- The names of renowned cities in German-speaking countries
- What the weather is like where you live

You will also revisit:
- Introducing yourself
- Telling age and birthday

UNIT 4
Saying where I live and am from

Ich heiße Leonie und ... *My name is Leonie and ...*	ich wohne *I live*	in einem kleinen Haus	*in a small house*	im Stadtzentrum *in the town centre*
		in einem großen Haus	*in a big house*	am Stadtrand *in the suburbs*
		in einem schönen Haus	*in a pretty hous*	auf dem Land *in the countryside*
		in einem hässlichen Haus	*in an ugly house*	
		in einer Wohnung *in a flat*	in einem alten Gebäude *in an old building*	in den Bergen *in the mountains*
			in einem modernen Gebäude *in a modern building*	an der Küste *on the coast*

	ich komme aus *I come from*	Berlin Hamburg München Köln *Cologne* Frankfurt Stuttgart	Das ist ... *That is ...*	die Hauptstadt *the capital* im Norden *in the north* im Osten *in the east*	von Deutschland *of Germany*
		Wien *Vienna* Graz Linz Salzburg Innsbruck		im Süden *in the south* im Südwesten *in the southwest*	von Österreich *of Austria*
		Zürich Basel Bern Winterthur Luzern *Lucerne*		im Westen *in the west* im Zentrum *in the centre of*	der Schweiz *of Switzerland*

Author's notes: *(1) The table above shows you the largest cities in Germany, Austria and in the German-speaking parts of Switzerland. Use a map to find out where exactly these cities are located! (2) German is the language with the second most native speakers in Europe with (approx. 100 million), behind Russian (approx. 120 million). In seven countries in Europe, German is either the official language (Germany, Austria, Liechtenstein) or a co-official language (Switzerland, Belgium, Luxembourg, and South Tyrol in Italy).*

Unit 4. Saying where I live and am from: VOCABULARY BUILDING

1. Complete with the missing word

a. Ich komme _____ Berlin.   *I come from Berlin.*

b. Ich wohne in einem _____ Haus.   *I live in a pretty house.*

c. Ich mag meine _____.   *I like my flat.*

d. Ich _____ in einer kleinen Wohnung.   *I live in a small flat.*

e. Ich wohne in einem alten _____, ...   *I live in an old house, ...*

f. ... im _____ von Österreich.   *... in the south of Austria.*

g. Ich wohne in einem _____ Haus.   *I live in an ugly building.*

h. Ich wohne am _____.   *I live in the suburbs.*

2. Match up

im Stadtzentrum	big
Wohnung	small
groß	old
Gebäude	flat
alt	in the centre
am Stadtrand	on the coast
an der Küste	I come from
ich komme aus	in the suburbs
hässlich	ugly
klein	I live in
ich wohne in	building

3. Translate into English

a. ich komme aus der Schweiz

b. ich wohne in einem Haus

c. meine Wohnung ist klein

d. in einer kleinen Wohnung

e. in einem alten Gebäude

f. ich komme aus München

g. ich wohne im Stadtzentrum

h. das ist im Norden von Deutschland

4. Add the missing letter
a. Ham_urg   c. In_sbruck   e. Zü__ich   g. Ber_in   i. Öster_eich

b. Vad_z   d. Lu_ern   f. Wi_n   h. M_nchen   j. Leip_ig

5. Broken words

a. I___ w_____ i__ N_____ v____ D_____.
I live in the north Germany.

b. I__ w_____ i_ e_____ a_____ H_____.
I live in an old house.

c. D___ i_ d____ H_____ d____ S_____.
That is the capital of Switzerland.

d. I__ w_____ i_ e_____ W_____ a___ S_____.
I live in a flat in the suburbs.

e. I__ w_____ i_ e____ k_____, aber s_____ W_____.
I live in a small but pretty flat.

f. D___ i____ i_ W_____ v____ D_____.
That is in the west of Germany.

g. I___ k_____ a___ Z_____.
I am from Zurich.

6. Complete with a suitable word

a. Ich komme _____ Frankfurt.

b. Ich _____ in einer schönen Wohnung.

c. Ich wohne in _____ alten Haus.

d. Ich wohne im _____ von Köln.

e. Das ist im _____ von Deutschland.

f. Ich wohne in einer kleinen _____.

g. Ich komme aus _____.

h. Ich wohne auf dem _____.

i. Linz ist im Nordosten von _____.

j. Zürich ist im Norden der _____.

k. Ich wohne in einem Haus am _____.

Unit 4. "Geography test": Using your own knowledge (and a bit of help from Google/your teacher) match the numbers to the cities

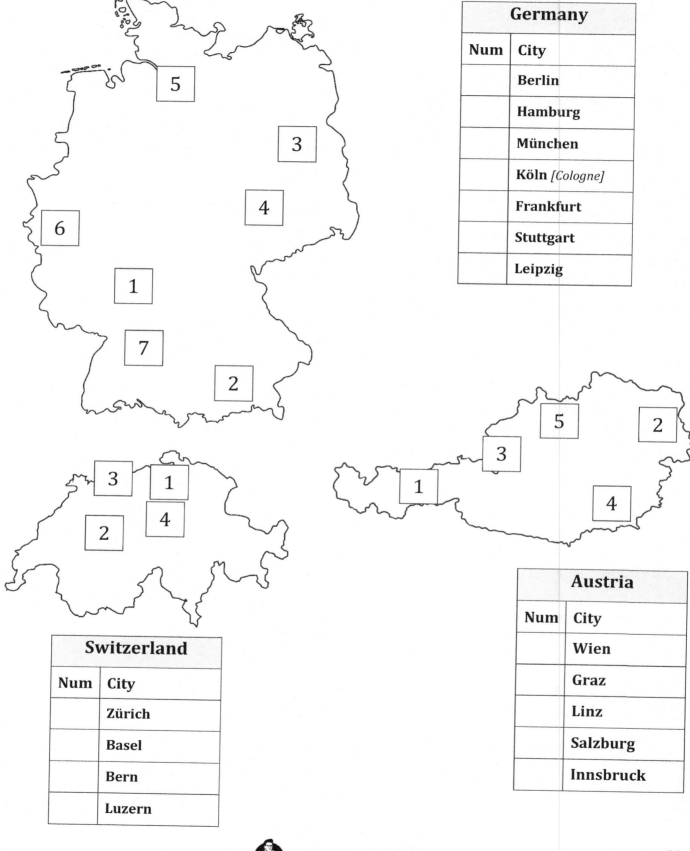

Germany	
Num	**City**
	Berlin
	Hamburg
	München
	Köln [Cologne]
	Frankfurt
	Stuttgart
	Leipzig

Switzerland	
Num	**City**
	Zürich
	Basel
	Bern
	Luzern

Austria	
Num	**City**
	Wien
	Graz
	Linz
	Salzburg
	Innsbruck

Unit 4. Saying where I live and am from: READING

Ich heiße Christian. Ich bin einundzwanzig Jahre alt und mein Geburtstag ist am achten August. Ich komme aus Wien – das ist die Hauptstadt von Österreich! Ich wohne in einem schönen Haus im Stadtzentrum.

Ich habe zwei Brüder: Lars und Michael. Ich mag Lars nicht, aber Michael ist total nett.

Mein Freund Max wohnt in Graz. Das ist im Südosten von Österreich. Er wohnt in einer Wohnung in einem alten Gebäude, auch im Stadtzentrum.

Ich heiße Daniel. Ich bin fünfzehn Jahre alt und ich wohne in Bern. Das ist die Hauptstadt der Schweiz. In meiner Familie gibt es vier Personen: meine Eltern, meinen Bruder Anton und mich. Ich habe am zehnten September Geburtstag, genau wie Anton. Wir sind Zwillinge!

Ich heiße Stefanie. Ich bin neun Jahre alt und ich wohne in Hamburg, im Norden von Deutschland. In meiner Familie gibt es vier Personen: meine Eltern, meine Schwester Amelie und mich. Mein Geburtstag ist am sechsten Mai und Amelies Geburtstag ist am dreißigsten März. Sie ist elf Jahre alt. Mein Haus ist groß und schön! Es ist am Stadtrand und ich mag es sehr.

Ich heiße Kathi. Ich bin zweiundzwanzig Jahre alt und ich wohne in Berlin, das ist die Hauptstadt von Deutschland. Ich wohne mit meiner Freundin Marina in einer großen und modernen Wohnung am Stadtrand. Mein Geburtstag ist am dritten Juni und Marinas Geburtstag ist am zwölften Juli.

Ich habe einen Hund in meiner Wohnung. Er heißt „Litti" und er kommt aus Köln. Er ist sehr groß! Sein Geburtstag ist am ersten April und er ist drei Jahre alt. Ich habe auch eine Spinne. Sie heißt Luisa und sie ist sehr klein, aber gefährlich! Ihr Geburtstag ist auch am ersten April. Also mache ich eine Party für beide Haustiere zusammen. Das ist sehr praktisch.

1. Find the German for the following in Kathi's text

a. I'm called

b. I am 22 years old

c. I live

d. in a big flat

e. in the suburbs

f. on the 3rd of June

g. I have a dog

h. he is very big

i. he is 3 years old

j. I also have a spider

k. small, but dangerous

2. Complete the statements below based on Christian's text

a. I am _____ years old.

b. My birthday is on the ____ of _____ .

c. I live in a _____ house.

d. My house is in the _____ of town.

e. I don't like Lars, but Michael is really _____.

f. My friend Max _____ in Graz.

g. He lives in an old _____.

3. Answer the questions on the four texts above

a. How old is Daniel?

b. Why do Daniel and Anton have the same birthday? *(what do you think a 'Zwilling' is?)*

c. Whose birthday is on the twelfth of July?

d. Who only likes one of his siblings?

e. Who does not live in the capital of their country?

f. Who has a friend that lives in a different city?

g. Who has two pets that share a birthday?

h. Why is it convenient that they share a birthday?

i. Whose dog comes from Cologne?

4. Correct any of the statements below [about Stefanie's text] which are incorrect

a. Stefanie wohnt in Hamburg, in der Mitte von Deutschland.

b. In ihrer Familie gibt es *(=In her family, there are)* fünf Personen.

c. Ihr Geburtstag ist im Mai.

d. Amelies Geburtstag ist am vierten März.

e. Stefanie wohnt in einem großen, aber hässlichen Haus am Stadtrand.

f. Sie mag das Haus nicht.

Unit 4. Saying where I live and am from: TRANSLATION/WRITING

1. Translate into English

a. ich wohne

b. in einem Haus

c. in einer kleinen Wohnung

d. ich komme aus

e. groß

f. in einem alten Gebäude

g. alt

h. mein Freund Max wohnt

i. im Stadtzentrum

j. am Stadtrand

k. an der Küste

l. er kommt aus

m. in Köln

n. im Norden von

2. Gapped sentences

a. Ich wohne in einer großen _____ ...
I live in a large flat ...

b. ... in einem neuen _____.
... in a new building

c. Ich wohne in einem kleinen _____ ...
I live in a small house ...

d. ... im _____ von München.
... in the north of Munich.

e. Ich _____ ____ Berlin, das ist die Hauptstadt von Deutschland.
I come from Berlin, that is the capital of Germany.

3. Complete the sentences with a suitable word

a. Ich wohne in _____, das ist die Hauptstadt von Österreich.

b. Ich komme aus München, im _____ von Deutschland.

c. Ich wohne in einem schönen _____ an der _____.

d. Mein Freund wohnt in einer _____ Wohnung.

e. Er kommt aus _____, das ist im _____ der Schweiz.

f. Ich wohne in einem modernen _____ im Stadtzentrum.

4. Phrase-level translation [En to Ger]

a. I live

b. I come from

c. in a house

d. in a pretty flat

e. in an ugly house

f. in an old house

g. in a modern building

h. in the town centre

i. in the suburbs

j. on the coast

k. in Switzerland

5. Sentence-level translation [En to Ger]

a. I come from Cologne. That is in the west of Germany. I live in a pretty and big house in the suburbs.

b. I come from Bern. That is the capital of Switzerland. I live in a small and ugly flat in the town centre.

c. I come from Innsbruck. That is in the west of Austria. I live in a flat in a new building in the town centre. My flat is big but ugly.

d. I come from Munich. That is in the south of Germany. I live in a big and modern house in the suburbs. I like it a lot.

Unit 4. Saying where I live and am from: WRITING

1. Complete with the missing letters

a. Ich hei_ _ Manuel.

b. Ich woh_ _ in ein_ _ klein_ _ Wohnu_ _.

c. I_ _ wo_ _ _ _ i_ ein_ _ groß_ _ Ha_ _.

d. I_ _ kom_ _ au_ Deutschl_ _ _.

e. Da_ is_ i_ Nordost_ _ v_ _ Österre_ _ _.

f. E_ komm_ au_ Züri_ _ i_ d_ _ Schw_ _ _ _.

g. I_ _ wo_ _ _ _ i_ e_ _ _ _ _ alt_ _ Gebä_ _ _.

h. D_ _ ist d_ _ Haupts_ _ _ _ _ d_ _ Sc_ _ _ _ _ _.

2. Spot and correct the spelling mistakes

a. Ich komme aus Koln.

b. Ich wohne in einer klienen Wohnung.

c. Ich wohne in einem häslichen Haus.

d. Ich wohne in einem modern Gebäude.

e. Ich wohne am Stattrand.

f. Ich wohne im Norden von Deutshland.

g. Ich komme aus der Schweitz.

h. Sie kommt aus Munchen.

3. Answer the questions in German

a. Wie heißt du?

b. Wie alt bist du?

c. Wann hast du Geburtstag?

d. Woher kommst du?

e. Wo wohnst du?

f. Wohnst du in einem Haus oder in einer Wohnung?

4. Anagrams (cities in German-speaking countries)

a. lnKö   *Köln*

b. chenMün

c. zGar

d. zerLun

e. rgubmHa

f. rnBe

g. eWni

h. ttgSrautt

i. nnIkcursb

j. chriZü

5. Guided writing – write 5 short paragraphs in the 1st person singular ['I'] describing the people below

Name	Age	Birthday	City	Country
Tina	14	18.06	Bern	Switzerland
Jonas	11	20.10	Stuttgart	Germany
Paul	15	07.02	Innsbruck	Austria
Luzi	12	15.01	Leipzig	Germany
Stefanie	13	30.11	Vienna	Austria

6. Describe this person in the third person:

Name: Florian

Age: 16

Birthday: 4 November

City/Country of origin: Hamburg Germany

Country of: residence: Lucerne, Switzerland

Unit 4a – Talking about the weather

Wie ist das Wetter? - *How is the weather?*

Subject-Verb	Frequency adverbs	Weather Adjectives		Adverbial
Das Wetter ist *The weather is*	**normalerweise** *normally* **immer** *always*	**schön** **gut** **okay** **schlecht** **furchtbar**	*nice* *good* *alright* *bad* *terrible*	**im Frühling** *in the spring* **im Sommer** *in the summer* **im Herbst** *in the autumn*
Es ist *It is*	**oft** *often* **manchmal** *sometimes* **selten** *rarely* **nie** *never*	**bedeckt** **bewölkt** **heiter** **heiß** **kalt** **neblig** **schön** **sonnig** **stürmisch** **warm** **windig**	*overcast* *cloudy* *clear skies* *hot* *cold* *foggy* *nice* *sunny* *stormy* *warm* *windy*	**im Winter** *in the winter* **im Januar, Februar, ...** *in January, February, ...* **wo ich wohne** *where I live* **in Berlin, Wien, ...** *in Berlin, Vienna, ...* **im Norden, Süden, ...** *in the north, south, ...*

Die Sonne scheint <u>oft</u>.	*The sun <u>often</u> shines.*
Es gibt <u>oft</u> Gewitter.	*There are <u>often</u> thunderstorms.*
Es regnet <u>oft</u>.	*It <u>often</u> rains.*
Es schneit <u>oft</u>.	*It <u>often</u> snows.*

Author's notes:

(1) When building your sentences, just like in English, you can move any adverb or adverbial to the front of the sentence. If you do this, make sure that you swap the subject and the verb around. Example:

       V - S

Im Frühling <u>ist es</u> oft sonnig. *[In spring, it is often sunny]*

(2) The four sentences at the bottom show that in a German main clause a frequency adverb like 'oft' [=often] cannot be placed between the subject and the verb – which is exactly what happens in English (except when the verb is 'to be')! Use the sentence builders in this booklet to compare German and English word order from time to time, and you will get really good at noticing the differences and similarities between the two languages and get comfortable with them.

 **THE LANGUAGE GYM**

Unit 4a. Talking about the weather: VOCABULARY BUILDING

1. Match up

bedeckt	cold
warm	clear skies
furchtbar	terrible
die Sonne	it is
stürmisch	thunderstorm
kalt	overcast
heiter	the sun
es ist	foggy
neblig	warm
windig	stormy
Gewitter	windy

2. Complete with the missing word

a. Im Sommer ist es oft sehr _____ in Berlin, ...
In the summer, it is often very hot in Berlin, ...

b. ... aber es ist meistens _____ im Winter.
... but it is usually cold in the winter.

c. Im Norden von Deutschland ist es oft _____.
In the north of Germany, it is often windy.

d. Im Sommer gibt es manchmal ein starkes _____.
In the summer, there ist sometimes a strong thunderstorm.

e. Ich liebe es, wenn das Wetter _____ ist.*
I love it when the weather is nice.

3. Translate into English

a. Im Norden ist es schön.

b. Im Osten ist es windig.

c. Im Südwesten regnet es.

d. Im Westen scheint die Sonne.

e. In Berlin ist es heiter und warm.

f. In Basel ist es bedeckt, aber warm.

g. In Wien ist es sehr heiß.

h. Wo ich wohne, schneit es oft.

4. Add the missing letter

a. sch_n   c. im Nor_en   e. he_ter   g. st_rmisch   i. im Frü_ling

b. ka_t   d. im S_den   f. wo ich wo_ne   h. im S_mmer   j. im Her_st

5. Broken words

a. I___ S_____ i__ e_____ n_____ w_____.
In the summer, it is normally warm.

b. M_____ s_____ d___ S_____.
Sometimes, the sun shines.

c. I___ H_____ i__ e___ o___ b_____.
In the autumn, it is often overcast.

d. W___ i___ w_____, s_____ e__ n____.
Where I live, it never snows.

e. D___ W_____ i___ o_____ sehr s_____.
The weather is often very nice.

f. Heute i__ d____ W_____ o_____.
Today, the weather is ok.

g. W___ i__ d___ W_____ n_____ i_ Zürich?
What is the weather normally like in Zurich?

6. Complete with a suitable word

a. Es ist oft _____ in Berlin.

b. Im Sommer ist es normalerweise _____.

c. Das Wetter ist _____ schön.

d. Es ist oft _____ im Herbst.

e. Im Winter _____ es oft.

f. Wo ich wohne, gibt es nie _____.

g. Ich liebe es, wenn es _____ ist*.

h. Wo ich wohne, schneit es _____.

i. In Innsbruck ist es warm im _____.

j. Ich finde es super, wenn es _____*.

* "wenn" [=when/whenever] introduces a subordinate clause in German, just like in English. In German, in a subordinate clause the verb stands at the end.

Ich heiße Eduardo. Ich bin dreizehn Jahre alt und ich komme aus Madrid. Das ist die Hauptstadt von Spanien! Ich wohne in einer Wohnung im Stadtzentrum. Ich finde das Wetter hier okay. Es ist oft sonnig und warm und im Winter ist es nicht zu kalt. Aber im Sommer ist es manchmal zu heiß! Dann fahre ich in den Norden an die Küste.

Hi Leute, ich heiße Dylan. Ich bin fünfzehn Jahre alt und ich wohne in einem schönen Haus in Kuala Lumpur, in der Hauptstadt von Malaysia. Ich finde das Wetter hier super! Es ist immer warm und es gibt oft Regen. Dann sitze ich auf dem Balkon. Manchmal gibt es Gewitter, das ist das Beste! Ich liebe die Blitze und den Donner!

Ich heiße Mo. Ich bin achtundzwanzig Jahre alt und ich wohne in Liverpool im Nordwesten von England. Ich wohne in einem alten Haus am Stadtrand. Ich liebe meine Stadt, aber das Wetter finde ich nicht so schön. Es ist oft sehr kalt und es regnet viel. Ich komme aus Ägypten, da ist es immer sonnig und heiß!

1. Find the German for the following in Eduardo's text

a. I come from

b. the capital

c. I live

d. in the town centre

e. I find

f. the weather here

g. it is often

h. and in the winter

i. too cold

j. sometimes

k. too hot

l. then I drive to the north

2. Complete the statements below based on Dylan's text

a. I am _____ years old.

b. I live in a _____ house in the _____ of Malaysia.

c. I find the weather here _____.

d. It is always _____ and there is often _____.

e. Then, I sit on the _____.

f. Sometimes, there is a _____.

g. I love the lightning and the _____,

h. that is the _____.

Ich heiße Annika. Ich bin zwölf Jahre alt und ich wohne auf Sylt. Das ist eine Insel im Norden von Deutschland. Ich wohne in einem großen Haus direkt am Strand. Das Wetter hier ist ganz okay. Manchmal scheint die Sonne und manchmal regnet es. Ich liebe es, wenn es windig ist. Dann kann ich surfen gehen!

Ich heiße Robert und ich bin sechzehn Jahre alt. Ich wohne in Zürich in der Schweiz, in einer großen Wohnung in der Stadtmitte. Ich liebe das Wetter hier. Im Sommer ist es oft sonnig und ich kann in einem Café in der Sonne sitzen. Im Winter schneit es oft. Dann fahre ich in die Berge und ich fahre Ski.

Meine große Schwester heißt Veronika. Sie ist Biologin und sie ist auf einer Expedition in der Antarktis! Sie sagt, das Wetter da ist unglaublich. Es ist immer eiskalt, aber jetzt im Sommer scheint die Sonne vierundzwanzig Stunden am Tag. Krass, oder?

3. Eduardo, Dylan, Annika or Mo?

a. Who is the oldest?

b. Who doesn't like the weather where they live?

c. Who loves thunderstorms?

d. Who lives right by the beach?

e. Who loves it when it is windy?

f. Who lives in a flat?

g. Who comes from a place that is always sunny and hot?

h. Who loves their town?

i. Who leaves their city when it gets too hot?

4. Correct any of the statements below [about Robert's text] which are incorrect

a. Robert wohnt in einem Haus.

b. Robert liebt das Wetter, wo er wohnt.

c. Er sitzt in einem Café, wenn es kalt ist.

d. Im Winter schneit es nie.

e. Robert hat eine große Schwester.

f. Sie ist auf einer Expedition in der Arktis.

g. Da (=there) ist es sehr heiß.

 **THE LANGUAGE GYM**

Unit 4a. Talking about the weather: TRANSLATION & WRITING

1. Translate into English

a. Es ist immer kalt.

b. Es ist oft warm.

c. Im Sommer ist es heiß.

d. Im Winter schneit es.

e. Es regnet oft in Berlin.

f. Ich wohne ...

g. in einem schönen Haus.

h. in einer alten Wohnung.

i. Es ist zu kalt.

j. Ich liebe es, ...

k. ... wenn es regnet.

2. Bad translation: spot and correct any translation mistakes (in the English) you find below

a. Wo ich wohne, regnet es oft.
Where I live, it often snows.

b. Das Wetter ist normalerweise sehr gut.
The weather is normally very bad.

c. Im Sommer ist das Wetter oft schön.
In the summer, the weather is sometimes nice.

d. Ich wohne in einer modernen Wohnung am Stadtrand.
I live in a modern house in the suburbs.

e. Ich liebe es, wenn es schneit.
I love it when it rains.

f. Es ist immer heiß und es regnet nie.
It is always hot and it never rains.

g. Manchmal scheint die Sonne.
Sometimes, the sun shines.

h. Im Januar ist es oft bewölkt.
In January, it is often clear skies.

3. Spot and correct the grammar and spelling errors

a. Die Wetter ist immer schön in Berlin.

b. Im Sommer es ist oft warm in Wien.

c. Es oft schneit im Winter.

d. Ich leibe es, wenn es heiß ist.

e. Ich finde das wetter nicht schön im winter.

f. Ich wohnen in einer modernen Wohnung.

g. Hier ist es manchmal su kalt.

4. Complete with the missing letters

a. Im S_mmer i_t es man_hmal _u hei_.

b. Im Fr_hling gi_t e_ o_t Ge_itter.

c. I_h wo_ne in eine_ Hau_ am Sta_trand.

d. H_er is_ e_ im_er bede_kt und ka_t.

e. Ich l_ebe _s, we_n das Wette_ sch_n is_.

f. W_ ic_ w_hne, re_net e_ jeden Tag*.

g. I_ d_r Sch_eiz s_hneit _s o_t im _inter.

*jeden Tag = *every day*

5. Guided writing – write 3 short paragraphs in the 1st person singular ['I'] describing the people below

Name	Age	City	Lives in	Weather in summer	Weather in the winter
Anna	13	Hamburg	modern flat	often overcast	cold and it often rains
Andrea	14	Buenos Aires	big house	sunny and hot	too cold
Olaf	12	Reykjavík	old house	nice but not so warm	it often snows

6. Describe this person in the 3rd person

Name & Age:
Akari, 16

Lives in:
a nice flat in Tokyo*

Weather in the summer:
often warm and sunny

In the winter:
rarely snows, not too cold

in German, it is "Tokio"

UNIT 5
Talking about my family members, saying their age and how well I get on with them. Counting to 100.

Revision quickie 1: Numbers 1-100 / Dates / Birthdays

In this unit you will learn to talk about:
- How many people there are in your family and who they are
- If you get on with them
- Words for family members
- What their age is
- Numbers from 31 to 100

You will also revisit
- Numbers from 1 to 31
- Hair and eyes description

UNIT 5
Talking about my family members, saying their age and how well I get on with them. Counting to 100.

Es gibt vier Personen in meiner Familie.			
There are four people in my family.			

			ein	1	Jahr alt
			zwei		
	meine Oma Adele		drei		
	my granny Adele		vier		
			fünf		
Es gibt...	**meine Mutter Lisa**	**Sie ist**	sechs		
There is/are...	*my mother Lisa*	*She is*	sieben		
	meine Tante Mareike		acht		
	my aunt Mareike	**Meine Tante**	neun		
		ist	zehn		
	meine große/kleine Schwester Anna	*My aunt is*	elf	11	
	my big/little sister Anna		zwölf	12	
...und es gibt...	**meine Cousine Klara**		dreizehn	13	
...and there is...	*my girl cousin Klara*		vierzehn	14	
			fünfzehn	15	
			sechzehn	16	
			siebzehn	17	Jahre alt
			achtzehn	18	
Außerdem gibt es...	**meinen Opa Martin**		neunzehn	19	
Furthermore there is...	*my grandad Martin*		zwanzig	20	
	meinen Vater Stefan		einundzwanzig	21	
	my father Stefan		zweiundzwanzig	22	
		Er ist	dreißig	30	
	meinen Onkel Tim	*He is*	einunddreißig	31	
	my uncle Tim		zweiunddreißig	32	
...und mich!	**meinen großen/kleinen Bruder Max**	**Mein Onkel ist**	vierzig	40	
...and me!	*my big/little brother Max*	*My uncle is*	fünfzig	50	
			sechzig	60	
			siebzig	70	
	meinen Cousin Jonas		achtzig	80	
	my cousin Jonas		neunzig	90	
			hundert	100	

Ich verstehe mich (nicht) gut	**mit meinem Onkel**	*with my uncle*
I (don't) get on well	**mit meiner Tante**	*with my aunt*
	mit meinen Eltern	*with my parents*

Author's note:
Can you see the different ways that the word "my" can look like in German? What patterns can you see? Take a note and show your teacher!

Unit 5. Talking about my family + Counting to 100: VOCAB BUILDING

1. Complete with the missing word

a. In meiner F_____ gibt es ...   *In my family there are ...*

b. Es gibt _____ Personen, ...   *There are five people, ...*

c. meinen _____ Peter   *my grandad Peter*

d. _____ Opa ist achtzig Jahre alt.   *My grandad is 80 years old.*

e. Es gibt auch meine _____.   *There is also my mother.*

f. Sie ist _____ alt.   *She is fourty years old.*

g. Ich verstehe mich _____ ...   *I get on well ...*

h. ... mit meinem _____.   *... with my brother.*

2. Match up

sechzehn	21
zwölf	12
einundzwanzig	13
zehn	79
dreiunddreißig	52
dreizehn	16
achtundvierzig	10
zweiundfünfzig	48
fünf	15
fünfzehn	33
neunundsiebzig	5

3. Translate into English

a. ich verstehe mich gut

b. es gibt meine Oma Lisa

c. es gibt auch meinen Onkel

d. ich habe auch eine Schwester

e. in meiner Familie gibt es

f. ich verstehe mich nicht gut

g. mit meinem Vater

h. mein Vater ist vierzig Jahre alt

4. Add the missing letter

a. Fam_lie   c. P__rsonen   e.Br__der   g. Mut_er   i. ich verste_e mich gut   k. drei_ig

b. es g_bt   d. au__h   f. gr__ß   h. Co__sine   j. au__erdem gibt es   l. ze_n

5. Broken words

a. E_ g_____ s_____ P_____ i_ m_____ F_____.
There are 6 people in my family.

b. M_____ S_____ i___ d_____ J_____ a___.
My sister is 13 years old.

c. i_ m_____ F_____ g_____ e__
in my family there are

d. m_____ O_____ h_____
my uncle is called

e. M_____ V_____ i___ n_____ J_____ a_____.
My father is 39 years old.

f. I__ v_____ m___ n___ g___ m___ m_____ B_____.
I don't get on well with my brother.

g. I__ v_____ m____ g__ m__ m_____ S_____.
I get on well with my sister.

6. Complete with a suitable word

a. In meiner Familie _____ es ...

b. Es _____ sechs Personen.

c. Ich habe auch einen _____.

d. Er ist _____ Jahre alt.

e. Meine _____ Luise ist vierzig Jahre alt.

f. Ich verstehe mich _____ mit meinem Vater.

g. Es gibt auch meinen _____ Max.

h. Ich _____ mich gut mit meiner Oma.

i. Ich verstehe _____ nicht gut mit meiner Tante.

j. Ich habe keine _____, leider!

Unit 5. Talking about my family + Counting to 100: VOCABULARY DRILLS

1. Match up

es gibt	people
in meiner Familie	there are
mit meinem Bruder	with my brother
sieben	I get on well
ich verstehe mich gut	in my family
Personen	seven

2. Complete with the missing word

a. Es _____ fünf Personen. — *There are five people.*

b. Mein _____, Nico, ist fünfzig Jahre alt. — *My father, Nico, is 50.*

c. Ich _____ mich gut mit ihm. — *I get on well with him.*

d. Ich verstehe mich _____ gut … — *I don't get on well …*

e. Mein Onkel Ben ist _____ Jahre alt. — *My uncle Ben is 41.*

f. Er ist _____ Jahre alt. — *He is 17 years old.*

g. _____ ist sechsunddreißig Jahre alt. — *She is 36 years old.*

h. Meine _____ Liese ist achtzig Jahre alt. — *My nan Liese is 80.*

3. Translate into English

a. Er ist zehn Jahre alt.

b. Sie ist fünfundzwanzig Jahre alt.

c. Meine Mutter ist achtunddreißig Jahre alt.

d. Ich verstehe mich gut mit meinem Opa.

e. Ich verstehe mich gut mit meiner Tante.

f. Meine kleine Schwester ist drei Jahre alt.

g. Es gibt sechs Personen in meiner Familie.

h. Ich verstehe mich nicht so gut mit meinen Eltern.

4. Complete with the missing letters

a. Ich habe einen gr_ _en Bruder.
I have a big brother.

b. In meiner Fa_ _lie g_bt e_ drei Personen.
In my family there are 3 people.

c. Meine C_ _ sine ist s_ _bzehn Jahre alt.
My cousin is 17.

d. Ich ver_ _ehe mich g_t mit meiner Oma.
I get on well with my nan.

e. Meine T_ _te ist vierzig J_ _ re a_t.
My aunt is 40 years old.

f. Ich verstehe m_ _h gu_ mit mein_ _ Vater.
I get on well with my father.

g. Meine S_ _ _ester ist f_nf_ehn Ja_re a_t.
My sister is 15 years old.

5. Translate into German

a. in my family there are

b. four people

c. there is my father

d. he is 40 years old

e. I get on well

f. with him

6. Spot and correct the errors

a. In meine Familie gibt es vier Personen.

b. Es gibt mein Vater.

c. Meine Bruder ist vierzehn Jahre alt.

d. Ich verstehe mich gut mit meine Bruder.

e. Mein Cousine ist sieben Jahre alt.

f. Ich verstehe mich nicht gut mit mein Schwester.

Unit 5. Talking about my family + Counting to 100: TRANSLATION

1. Match up

dreißig	100
fünfzig	30
vierzig	60
sechzig	70
achtzig	90
neunzig	50
einhundert	80
zwanzig	20
siebzig	40

3. Write out in German

a. 63   d

b. 89   n

c. 100   h

d. 74   v

e. 17   s

f. 36   s

g. 52   z

h. 25   f

i. 98   a

2. Write out with the missing number

a. Ich bin einund_____ Jahre alt.
I am 21.

b. Mein Vater ist sechsund_____ Jahre alt.
My father is fourty-six.

c. Meine Mutter ist neunund_____ Jahre alt.
My mother is thirty-nine.

d. Mein Opa ist einhundertund_____ Jahre alt.
My grandfather is one-hundred and eight years old.

e. Mein Onkel ist _____undfünfzig Jahre alt.
My uncle is fifty-five years old.

f. Sie sind _____ Jahre alt.
They are ninety years old.

g. Meine Cousins sind _____undzwanzig Jahre alt.
My cousins are twenty-four.

h. Ist er _____ Jahre alt?
Is he seventy years old?

4. Correct the translation errors

a. My father is forty.   Mein Vater ist fünfzig Jahre alt.

b. My mother is fifty-two.   Meine Mutter ist dreiundfünfzig Jahre alt.

c. We are forty-two.   Wir sind vierundzwanzig Jahre alt.

d. I am forty-one.   Ich bin einundachtzig Jahre alt.

e. They are thirty-four.   Wir sind dreiundvierzig Jahre alt.

5. Translate into German (please write out the numbers in letter)

a. In my family there are 5 people.

b. My mother is called Julia and she is 41.

c. My father is called Hannes and he is 39.

d. There is also my big brother Max, he is 14.

e. My little brother is called Jens and he is 10.

f. I am called Annemarie and I am 27.

g. My grandad is called Alexander and he is 77.

Unit 5. Talking about my family + Counting to 100: WRITING

1. Spot and correct the spelling mistakes

a. veirzehn   *vierzehn*

b. sechsehn

c. einsundzwanzig

d. achtundreißig

e. siebenzehn

f. funfzehn

g. nineundfünzig

h. seiben

2. Complete with the missing letters

a. Mein V__ter i__t f__nfzig Ja__re a__t.

b. Mein__ Sch__ester is__ vi__rzehn __ahre al__.

c. M__ine E__tern sin__ achtund__reißig Jahr__ __lt.

d. M__in kl__iner Br__der i__t n__un J__hre a__t.

e. M__ __n __pa __st s__ __benunda__ht__ig J__ __re __ __t.

f. Mei__ __ kl__ __ne__ Sc__ __est__ __ is__ v__ __r J__ __re a__ __.

3. Rearrange the sentences below in the correct word order

a. vier In Familie Personen meiner es gibt
In my family there are four people.

b. mit meinem Ich Bruder mich nicht verstehe gut
I don't get on well with my brother.

c. Jahre Vater alt und heißt ist er fünfundfünfzig Mein Michael
My father is called Michael and he is fifty-five years old.

d. Vater meinen meine mich Familie gibt In es meiner und drei Personen Mutter
In my family there are three people: my mother, my father and I.

e. Cousin heißt Jahre er und alt ist siebenundreißig Mein Benjamin
My cousin is called Benjamin and he is thirty-seven years old.

4. Complete

a. in my family there are
i__ m__ F_____ g____ e__

b. there are 4 people
e_____ g_____ v____ P_____

c. my sister is called
m_____ S_____ h_____

d. there is also my granny…
e_ g____ a___ m_____ O____…

e. …and my grandad
…u__ m_____ O____

f. he is sixty-six
e__ i____ s_____

g. I am thirty-two
i____ b_____ z_____

h. she is forty-one
s____ i____ e_____

5. Write a brief statement for each person as shown in the example

e.g. Mein bester Freund heißt Jens und er ist dreizehn Jahre alt. Ich verstehe mich sehr gut mit ihm.

Name	Relationship to me	Age	How I get along with them
e.g. Jens	*best friend*	*15*	*very well*
Martin	father	47	well
Laura	mother	45	not at all [gar nicht]
Daniela	aunt	60	very well [sehr gut]
Andreas	uncle	67	not well
Bernhard	grandad	75	very well

*mit ihm = with him / mit ihr = with her

Revision Quickie 1:
Numbers 1-100, dates and birthdays, hair and eyes, family

1. Match up

11	zwölf
12	fünfzehn
13	siebzehn
14	sechzehn
15	achtzehn
16	zwanzig
17	elf
18	dreizehn
19	vierzehn
20	neunzehn

2. Translate the dates into English

a. am vierten März

b. am ersten April

c. am vierundzwanzigsten Dezember

d. am einunddreißigsten Juli

e. am neunten November

f. am achten Mai

g. am dritten Oktober

h. am siebzehnten Juni

3. Complete with the missing words

a. Mein Geburtstag _____ am fünfzehnten Mai.

b. Ich bin vierzehn _____ alt.

c. Mein Bruder hat blonde _____.

d. Woher _____ du?

e. In meiner Familie _____ es drei Personen.

f. _____ Mutter hat blaue _____.

g. Ich komme _____ Berlin.

h. _____ Bruder _____ Sascha.

Haare	ist	Meine	gibt	aus
Augen	Mein	Jahre	kommst	heißt

4. Write out the solution in words as shown in the example

a. vierzig – dreißig   = zehn

b. dreißig – zehn   =

c. vierzig + dreißig   =

d. zwanzig x drei   =

e. achtzig – fünfzig   =

f. neunzig – vierzig   =

g. dreißig x drei   =

h. zwanzig + fünfzig   =

i. zwanzig + zwanzig =

5. Complete the words

a. mein O_ _   *my grandad*

b. meine Cou_ _ _ _   *my female cousin*

c. die Aug_ _   *the eyes*

d. gr_ _   *green*

e. der B_ _ _   *the beard*

f. die Bri_ _ _   *the glasses*

g. meine Schw_ _ _ _ _   *my sister*

h. ic_ h _ _ _   *I have*

6. Translate into English

a. Meine Mutter hat braune Haare.

b. Ich habe grüne Augen.

c. Ich bin einundvierzig Jahre alt.

d. Mein Opa ist neunzig Jahre alt.

e. Mein Onkel trägt eine Brille.

f. Mein Bruder hat Sommersprossen.

g. Mein Bruder hat lange schwarze Haare.

h. Meine Schwester hat graublaue Augen.

UNIT 6 (Part 1/2)
Describing myself and another family member (physical and personality)

Grammar Time 1: SEIN (Part 1)

Grammar Time 2: HABEN (Part 1)

Unit 6a: Talking about skills

In this unit you will learn:

- What your immediate family members are like
- Useful adjectives to describe them
- Adverbs of intensity and frequency to add interest to your sentences
- All the persons of the verbs 'sein' (to be) and 'haben' (to have) in the present tense
- How to use the modal verb 'können' to talk about what someone can do well

You will also revisit
- Numbers from 1 to 31
- Hair and eyes description

UNIT 6 (Part 1/2)
Intro to describing myself and another family member

Ich bin
I am

... und ich bin auch
... and I am also

Außerdem bin ich
Furthermore, I am

..., aber ich bin
... but I am

Meine kleine Schwester ist
My little sister is

Mein kleiner Bruder ist
My little brother is

... und sie ist auch
... and she is also

... und er ist
... and he is

Außerdem ist er ...
Furthermore, he is ...

..., aber sie ist
... but she is

sehr	*very*
ziemlich	*quite*
ein bisschen	*a bit*
nicht	*not*
gar nicht	*not at all*

immer	*always*
meistens	*mostly, usually*
oft	*often*
manchmal	*sometimes*
selten	*rarely*
nie	*never*

groß	*tall*
hässlich	*ugly*
hübsch	*pretty*
klein	*short*
muskulös	*muscular*
pummelig	*chubby*
schlank	*slim*
schön	*beautiful*
stark	*strong*
faul	*lazy*
fleißig	*hard-working*
frech	*cheeky*
freundlich	*friendly*
gemein	*mean*
langweilig	*boring*
lustig	*funny*
nervig	*annoying*
nett zu mir	*nice to me*
schlau	*smart*
stur	*stubborn*

Unit 6. Vocabulary building

1. Match

ich bin hübsch	I am strong
ich bin stur	I am slim
ich bin lustig	I am lazy
ich bin gemein	I am pretty
ich bin faul	I am funny
ich bin stark	I am mean
ich bin frech	I am stubborn
ich bin schlank	I am cheeky
ich bin groß	I am tall

2. Complete

a. Mein kleiner Bruder ist ein bisschen n_____.
My younger brother is a bit annoying.

b. Mein Vater ist sehr f_____.
My father is very friendly.

c. Meine große Schwester ist ziemlich s_____.
My older sister is quite stubborn.

d. Meine Oma ist immer l_____.
My gran is always funny.

e. Mein Freund Mo ist sehr s_____.
My friend Mo is very strong.

3. Categories – sort the adjectives below in the categories provided

a. lustig; b. stur; c. nett; d. muskulös; e. schön; f. schlau;
g. geduldig; h. gemein; i. pummelig; j. langweilig; k. nervig;
l. hässlich; m. stark; n. hübsch

das Aussehen	die Persönlichkeit

4. Complete the words

a. Ich bin langwei_ _ _ .

b. Ich bin sch_ _ _ .

c. Ich bin musk_ _ _ _ .

d. Ich bin st _ _ .

e. Ich bin n_ _ _ _ .

f. Ich bin fle_ _ _ _ _ .

g. Ich bin kl_ _ _ .

h. Ich bin schl_ _ .

5. Translate into English

a. Meine große Schwester ist immer nett.

b. Mein großer Bruder ist ein bisschen pummelig.

c. Mein Vater ist immer nett zu mir, ...

d. ... aber meine Mutter ist oft nervig.

e. Ich bin total hübsch, ...

f. ... aber ein bisschen stur.

g. Außerdem bin ich sehr kreativ.

h. Mein Freund Karl ist superstark.

6. Spot and correct the translation mistakes

a. Ich bin sehr stark.   *He is very strong.*

b. Er ist ziemlich schlank.   *He is quite chubby.*

c. Ich bin nicht so hässlich.   *I am not very ugly.*

d. Meine Mutter ist sehr groß.   *My mother is tall.*

e. Mein Bruder ist meistens nervig.   *My brother is never annoying.*

f. Meine Schwester ist total stur.   *My sister is really boring.*

g. Mein Vater ist manchmal gemein.   *My father is always mean.*

7. Complete

a. Mei_ Br_ _ _ _r is_ of_ fr_ _h.

b. Me_ _ _ _ Sc_ _ _ _ _ _ _ _ i_ _ ne_t.

c. M_ _ _n Va_ _ _ _ i_ _ ni_ _ _ _ st_ _, ...

d. ... ab_ _ e_ i_ _ _ im_ _ _ _ fa_ _.

e. M_ _ _ _ _ Mu_ _ _ _ _ i_ _ se _r lu_ _ _ _ _ ...

f. ... u_d s_ _ i_ _ ga_ ni_ _ _ g_m_ _ _ _.

8. Translate into German

a. I am quite strong.

b. I am also really pretty.

c. My little brother is a bit annoying ...

d. ..., but he is very smart.

e. My big sister is very kind.

f. She is also always hard-working.

g. My father is a bit lazy.

h. Furthermore, he is quite stubborn.

Grammar Time 1: SEIN - To be (Part 1)

ich	*I*	**bin**	*am*	**groß**	*tall*
				gutaussehend	*good-looking*
du	*you*	**bist**	*are*	**hässlich**	*ugly*
				hübsch	*pretty*
				klein	*short*
er	*he*			**muskulös**	*muscular*
mein Bruder				**pummelig**	*chubby*
mein Vater				**schlank**	*slim*
...				**schön**	*beautiful*
sie	*she*			**stark**	*strong*
meine Mutter		**ist**	*is*	--	
meine Schwester				**ehrlich**	*honest*
...				**entspannt**	*relaxed*
es	*it*			**faul**	*lazy*
das Kind	*the child*			**fleißig**	*hard-working*
das Baby	*the baby*			**frech**	*cheeky*
mein Brüderchen	*my baby brother*			**freundlich**	*friendly*
mein Schwesterchen	*my baby sister*			**geduldig**	*patient*
...				**geizig**	*stingy*
wir	*we*	**sind**	*are*	**gemein zu mir**	*mean to me*
mein Vater und ich				**geschwätzig**	*talkative*
meine Freundin Maria und ich				**großzügig**	*generous*
...				**gut gelaunt**	*in a good mood*
ihr	*you guys*	**s<u>ei</u>d**	*are*	**hilfsbereit**	*ready to help*
				intelligent	*intelligent*
				langweilig	*boring*
sie	*they*			**lustig**	*funny*
meine Eltern				**nervig**	*annoying*
meine Freunde				**nett**	*nice*
meine Geschwister	*my siblings*	**sind**	*are*	**schlau**	*smart*
meine Großeltern	*my grandparents*			**schüchtern**	*shy*
...				**stur**	*stubborn*
Sie	*you, Mr/Ms*			**streng**	*strict*
Frau Direktorin, Sie				**zuverlässig**	*reliable*
Mrs Headteacher, you					
Herr Lehrer, Sie					
Mr Teacher, you					
...					

Present tense of "sein" (to be) – Drills 1

1. Match up

wir sind	I am
sie sind	you are
ich bin	he is
du bist	they are
ihr seid	we are
er ist	you guys are

2. Complete with the missing forms of 'sein'

a. Ich _____ sehr geschwätzig. *I am very talkative.*

b. Meine Mutter _____ superlustig. *My mother is super-funny.*

c. Meine Schwestern _____ total frech. *My sisters are really cheeky.*

d. Mein Bruder _____ sehr geduldig. *My brother is very patient.*

e. Meine Eltern _____ gar nicht streng. *My parents are not at all strict.*

f. Wie _____ du? *What are you like?*

g. Wie _____ deine Haare? *What is your hair like?*

h. Ihr _____ total stark! *You guys are really strong*

3. Translate into English

a. Mein Vater ist supernett.

b. Meine Mutter ist immer entspannt.

c. Meine Cousine ist schüchtern.

d. Meine Tante ist sehr groß.

e. Mein bester Freund ist sehr nett.

f. Mein Opa ist immer gut gelaunt.

g. Mein Opa ist immer gut gelaunt.

h. Ihr seid immer gemein zu mir!

4. Complete with the missing letters

a. Wir s__ __ __ sehr fleißig. *We are very hard-working.*

b. Meine Mutter i__ __ superstreng. *My mother is super-strict.*

c. Meine Eltern s__ __ __ ein bisschen stur. *My parents are a bit stubborn.*

d. Meine Geschwister s__ __ __ total gemein zu mir. *My siblings are really mean to me.*

e. Meine Schwester i__ __ pummelig. *My sister is chubby.*

f. Ihr s__ __ __ sehr freundlich! *You guys are very friendly.*

g. Du b__ __ __ ein bisschen schüchtern. *You are a bit shy.*

h. Mein Opa und meine Oma s__ __ __ immer großzügig. *My grandad and my granny are always generous.*

i. Wie b__ __ __ du? *What are you like?*

j. Herr Direktor, Sie s__ __ __ sehr gemein! *Mr Headteacher, you are very mean!*

5. Translate into German

a. you are = du __ __ __ __

b. he is = er __ __ __

c. you guys are = ihr __ __ __ __

d. they are = sie __ __ __ __

e. we are = wir __ __ __ __

f. she is = sie __ __ __

6. Spot and correct the errors

a. Meine Mutter is sehr nett.

b. Meine Eltern sein total streng.

c. Meine Schwester est ziemlich intelligent.

d. Mein Bruder und ich bin sehr groß.

e. Wie ist du?

Present tense of "sein" (to be) – Drills 2

7. Complete with the missing letters

a. W__r s__nd sehr groß.   *We are very tall.*

b. D__ b__st ziemlich klein.   *You are quite short.*

c. Meine Mutter i__t ein bisschen pummelig. *My mother is a little chubby.*

d. Meine Lehrer si__d sehr gut.   *My teachers are very good.*

e. __u __ist sehr hübsch.   *You are very pretty.*

f. I__h __in nicht schüchtern.   *I am not shy.*

g. Mein Bruder und ich si__d sehr fleißig.   *My brother and I are very hard-working.*

8. Complete with the missing forms of the verb SEIN

a. Meine Mutter_____   f. Mein Bruder _____

b. Meine Eltern _____   g. Ihr _____

c. Ich _____   h. Du _____

d. Sie (they) _____   i. Frau Direktorin, Sie _____

e. Meine Mutter und ich _____

9. Complete with the missing forms of SEIN

a. Ich _____ achtzehn Jahre alt.   e. Ich _____ ein bisschen pummelig.

b. Meine Mutter _____ sehr groß und schön. f. Sie (they) _____ klein.

c. Meine Eltern _____ sehr streng.   g. Meine Schwester und ich _____ muskulös.

d. Mein Bruder _____ ziemlich nervig.   h. Mein Freund Marco _____ Italiener.

10. Translate into German

a. My mother is very tall.   e. My grandfather is really strict.

b. My father is quite short.   f. My grandmother is super-patient.

c. My little brother is a bit shy.   g. My mother is not at all lazy.

d. My little sister is not very friendly. h. My aunt is usually very nice.

11. Translate into German

a. My mother and my sister are very tall.   e. My brother and I are not at all tall.

b. My sisters are always nice to me.   f. My mother and my sister are quite pretty.

c. I am very friendly.   g. My girlfriend and her (=ihre) sister are very short.

d. You are always talkative and very lazy.   h. You all are really mean!

 **THE LANGUAGE GYM**

Grammar Time 2: HABEN – To have (Part 1)

ich	I	habe	have	keine Haare	no hair
du	you	hast	have	kurze Haare	short hair
				lange Haare	long hair
er	he			mittellange Haare	mid-length hair
mein Bruder mein Vater					
sie	she			glatte Haare	straight hair
				lockige Haare	curly hair
meine Mutter meine Schwester		hat	has	wellige Haare	wavy hair
es	it			blonde Haare	blonde hair
das Kind das Baby				dunkelblonde Haare	dark blonde hair
mein Brüderchen	my baby brother			braune Haare	brown hair
mein Schwesterchen	my baby sister			graue Haare	grey hair
				rote Haare	red hair
wir	we			rotblonde Haare	sandy hair
mein Vater und ich meine Freundin Maria und ich		haben	have	schwarze Haare	black hair
ihr	you guys	habt	have	weiße Haare	white hair
				einen/keinen Bart	a/no beard
sie	they			blaue Augen	blue eyes
meine Eltern meine Freunde meine Geschwister				braune Augen	brown eyes
		haben	have	hellbraune Augen	light brown eyes
Sie	you, Mr/Ms			dunkelbraune Augen	dark brown eyes
Frau Direktorin, Sie Herr Lehrer, Sie				graublaue Augen	grey-blue eyes
				grüne Augen	green eyes

Drills

1. Translate into English

a. Wir haben lange schwarze Haare.

b. Er hat kurze blonde Haare.

c. Ihr habt wellige braune Haare.

d. Du hast kurze rote Haare.

e. Sie haben lockige rotblonde Haare.

f. Ich habe lange weiße Haare.

g. Sie hat mittellange, wellige blonde Haare.

2. Spot and correct the mistakes (note: not all sentences are wrong)

a. Meine Mutter hat kurze schwarze Haare.

b. Meine Schwestern habe lange blonde Haare.

c. Ich hat kurze braune Haare.

d. Sie (=she) hast mittellange rote Haare.

e. Wir habe kurz Haare.

f. Meine Mutter und ich hat glatte braune Haare.

3. Complete with the missing part of the verb

a. Ich ha____ blonde Haare.

b. Meine Mutter ha____ blaue Augen.

c. Meine Schwestern ha___ rote Haare.

d. Mein Vater ha___ graue Haare.

e. Wir ha_____ schwarze Haare.

f. Mein Opa ha___ weiße Haare.

g. Maria und ich ha____ blonde Haare.

h. Mein Cousin ha___ braune Haare.

i. Ha___ ihr lange Haare?

j. Mein Bruder und ich ha____ lockige Haare.

k. Mein Freund Jonas ha____ grüne Augen.

l. Meine Geschwister hab___ kurze Haare.

m. Ich ha___ mittellange blonde Haare.

n. Ha___ du auch blonde Haare?

4. Complete with the missing forms of HABEN

a. Du und deine Mutter, ihr _____ blonde Haare.

b. Meine Eltern _____ braune Augen.

c. Meine Schwester und ich _____ rote Haare.

d. Meine Großeltern _____ schwarze Haare.

e. Du _____ einen Bart.

f. Herr Direktor, Sie _____ graue Haare.

g. Mein Bruder _____ kurze glatte Haare.

h. Mein Cousin _____ rotblonde Haare.

i. Meine zwei Schwestern _____ glatte Haare.

j. Meine Freundin und ich _____ blaue Augen.

5. Translate into German

a. We have long hair.

b. You have blonde hair.

c. You guys have dark brown hair.

d. She has green eyes.

e. My father has long curly hair.

f. My sister has short straight hair.

g. My grandad has grey hair.

h. My uncle has no hair.

i. My granny and I have blonde hair.

j. My uncle Tim has green eyes.

6. Guided writing – Write a text in the first person singular (I) including the details below:

a. Say you are 11 years old

b. Say you have a brother and a sister

c. Say your sister is 14

d. Say she has mid-length, wavy, blonde hair and blue eyes

e. Say she is tall, pretty and always friendly

f. Say your brother is 8

g. Say he has short, curly, black hair and brown eyes

h. Say your parents are short, have dark blonde hair and brown eyes

7. Write an 80 to 100 words text in which you describe four people you know very well, relatives, or friends. You must include their:

a. Name

b. Age

c. Hair (length, type, and colour)

d. Eye colour

e. If they wear glasses or not

f. Their physical description

g. Their personality description

UNIT 6 (Part 2/2)
Describing my family and saying why I like/dislike them

Es gibt vier Personen in meiner Familie. *There are 4 people in my family.*				

In meiner Familie gibt es ... *In my family there is ...*	**meine Oma Leni** *my granny Leni* **meine Mutter Angela** *my mother Angela* **meine Tante Barbara** *my aunt Barbara* **meine kleine/große Schwester Mia** *my big/little sister Mia* **meine Cousine Lisa** *my cousin Lisa*	**Ich mag meine Oma (nicht), denn sie ist ...** *I (don't) like my granny because she is ...* **Sie ist auch nicht/sehr/total...** *She is also not/very/really ...* **Außerdem ist meine Oma nie/oft/immer ...** *Besides, my granny is never/often/always ...*	**groß** *tall* **gutaussehend** *good-looking* **hässlich** *ugly* **hübsch** *pretty* **klein** *short* **muskulös** *muscular* **pummelig** *chubby* **schlank** *slim* **schön** *beautiful* **stark** *strong* **ehrlich** *honest* **entspannt** *relaxed* **faul** *lazy* **fleißig** *hard-working* **frech** *cheeky*	
Außerdem gibt es ... *Furthermore, there is ...*			**freundlich** *friendly* **geduldig** *patient*	
Es gibt auch ... *There is also ...*	**meinen Opa Karl** *my grandad Carl* **meinen Vater Johannes** *my father John* **meinen Onkel Moritz** *my uncle Moritz* **meinen großen/kleinen Bruder Max** *my big/little brother Max* **meinen Cousin Sinan** *my cousin Sinan*	**Ich mag meinen Opa (nicht), denn er ist ...** *I (don't)like my grandad because he is ...* **Er ist auch nicht/sehr/total ...** *He is also not/very/really ...* **Außerdem ist mein Opa nie/oft/immer ...** *Besides, he is never/often/always ...*	**geizig** *stingy* **gemein** *mean* **geschwätzig** *talkative* **großzügig** *generous* **gut gelaunt** *in a good mood* **hilfsbereit** *ready to help* **langweilig** *boring* **lustig** *funny* **nervig** *annoying* **nett** *nice* **schlau** *smart* **schüchtern** *shy* **stur** *stubborn* **streng** *strict* **zuverlässig** *reliable*	

Ich verstehe mich gut mit meinem Opa! *I get on well with my grandad!*	**Ich verstehe mich gut mit meiner Oma!** *I get on well with my nan!*

Author's note: *Well done for keeping to look out for those different ways the word "my" is written in German! Did you think about possible patterns back in Unit 5? Can you spot the patterns again on this page?*

THE LANGUAGE GYM

Unit 6. Describing my family: VOCABULARY BUILDING

1. Complete with the missing word

a. In meiner Familie g_____ es ...
In my family there is/are ...

b. Es gibt _____ Personen.
There are four people.

c. meine _____, die Leonie heißt
my mother, who is called Leonie

d. Mein Onkel ____ sehr groß.
My uncle is very tall.

e. Meine _____ ist total nett.
My aunt is totally nice.

f. Meine Cousine Olivia ist _____.
My cousin Olivia is funny.

g. Ich mag meinen kleinen _____.
I like my little brother.

2. Match up

Meine Tante	My cousin [f]
Mein Opa	My sister
Meine Mutter	My mum
Mein Vater	My cousin [m]
Mein großer Bruder	My dad
Mein Cousin	My grandad
Mein kleiner	My aunt
Bruder	My little bro
Mein Onkel	My big bro
Meine Schwester	My uncle
Meine Cousine	

3. Translate into English

a. Ich mag meinen Onkel.

b. Meine Cousine ist immer gut gelaunt.

c. Er hat lange braune Haare.

d. Ich verstehe mich nicht gut mit ...

e. Ich mag meine Tante nicht.

f. Ich verstehe mich gut mit ...

g. Sie ist total nervig.

h. Er ist nie nett.

4. Add the missing letter

a. st_r
b. gro__
c. _ett
d. s_hlank

e. gei_ig
f. s_ark
g. fle_ßig
h. hü__sch

i. f_ul
j. ge_ein
k. fr_undlich
l. zu_erlässig

5. Broken words

a. I__ m_____ Fam____ g_____ e__ ...
In my family there are ...

b. v_____ P_____
four people

c. M_____ M_____ i_ s_____ n___.
My mother is very nice.

d. I___ v_____ m____ g___ m____ ...
I get on well with my ...

e. M____ O_____ i___ s_____ g_____.
My uncle is very stingy.

f. I___ v_____ m____ n____ g__ m___ m_____ S_____.
I don't get on well with my sister.

g. M_____ B_____ h_____ k_____ l_____ H_____.
My brother has short curly hair.

h. M_____ V_____ i___ z_____ s_____.
My father is quite smart.

6. Complete with a suitable word

a. Es gibt _____ Personen.

b. Ich verstehe mich _____ mit ...

c. Meine Mutter ist _____ nett.

d. Sie ist sehr _____.

e. Er hat _____ Haare.

f. Ich _____ meinen Vater.

g. Ich _____ mich nicht gut mit ...

h. Sie hat lange _____ Haare.

i. Mein Opa hat _____Augen.

j. Mein Cousin ist _____ lustig.

k. Meine _____ ist sehr schlau.

l. Meine Oma ist _____ Jahre alt.

Unit 6. Describing my family: READING

Servus, ich bin Charly. Ich bin zehn Jahre alt und ich wohne in Wien, in der Hauptstadt von Österreich. In meiner Familie gibt es fünf Personen: meinen Vater Johannes, meine Mutter Andrea, meine Brüder Alex und Ben, und mich. Ich verstehe mich gut mit Alex, denn er ist nett und immer gut gelaunt. Aber ich mag Ben nicht. Er ist total gemein!

Guten Tag! Ich heiße Fatima. Ich bin vierzehn Jahre alt und ich wohne in Hamburg, im Norden von Deutschland. Ich mag meinen Opa sehr, denn er ist total lustig. Er ist auch sehr intelligent, aber ziemlich schüchtern.
Jedoch mag ich meinen Vater nicht. Er ist immer launisch und total faul, stell dir vor! Er hat kurze braune Haare und grüne Augen.

Ciao Freunde! Ich heiße Marco. Ich bin fünfzehn Jahre alt und ich wohne in Südtirol. Ich habe kurze blonde Haare. In meiner Familie gibt es sechs Personen. Ich verstehe mich nicht gut mit meiner Schwester. Sie ist total stur. Aber ich verstehe mich sehr gut mit meinen Cousinen. Sie sind alle sehr nett. Meine LieblingsCousine heißt Maria, denn sie ist nicht nur groß und stark, sondern auch sehr lustig und immer gut gelaunt. Sie hat kurze braune Haare und sie trägt eine Brille.

Hoi zäme! Ich heiße Angelo. Ich bin zehn Jahre alt und ich wohne in Luzern, in der Schweiz. Ich bin ziemlich gutaussehend! In meiner Familie gibt es viele Personen, insgesamt acht! Ich mag meinen Onkel, jedoch mag ich meine Tante nicht.
Ich verstehe mich gut mit meinem Onkel Carl, weil er total nett ist. Jedoch ist meine Tante Susi immer unfreundlich und gemein zu mir. Ich verstehe mich nicht gut mit ihr!
Susi hat lange, lockige blonde Haare und blaue Augen, so wie ich. Ihr Geburtstag ist am elften Mai.

Hi Leute, ich heiße Jonas. Ich bin neun Jahre alt und ich wohne in Bonn, in Deutschland. In meiner Familie gibt es vier Personen. Ich verstehe mich nicht gut mit meinem Vater. Er ist sehr streng und gar nicht nett. Jedoch mag ich meine Oma, denn sie ist immer großzügig.

1. Find the German for the following items in Fatima's text

a. I am called

b. in the north

c. I like ... very much

d. quite

e. but

f. however

g. imagine!

h. short brown hair

2. Answer the following questions about Angelo's text

a. How old is he?

b. Where is he from?

c. How many people are there in his family?

d. Who does he get on well with?

e. Why does he like Carl?

f. Who does he not like and why?

BONUS. Can you find another word for "because" in this text? What do you notice about the word order?

3. Complete with the missing words

Hallo! Ich heiße Alex. Ich _____ zehn Jahre alt und ich wohne _____ Berlin. In meiner _____ gibt es vier Personen. Ich _____ mich gut mit meinem Opa, denn ____ ist immer nett und entspannt. Er hat kurze graue _____ und graublaue _____. Aber ich verstehe mich nicht gut _____ meiner Tante, denn sie ____ total langweilig.

4. Find someone who? – answer the questions below about all 5 texts

a. Who has a granny who is always generous?

b. Who is fifteen years old?

c. Who celebrates their birthday on 11 May?

d. Who has a favourite cousin?

e. Who is from the north of Germany?

f. Who only gets on well with one of his brothers?

g. Who is a little shy?

h. Who is a always in a good mood?

i. Who has long, curly hair?

 THE LANGUAGE GYM

Unit 6. Describing my family: TRANSLATION

1. Bad translation: spot and correct any translation mistakes (in the English) you find below

a. In meiner Familie gibt es vier Personen.
In my family there are fourteen people.

b. Es gibt meine Mutter, Rita und meinen Bruder Ben.
There is my mother, Rita and my cousin Ben.

c. Ich verstehe mich nicht gut mit meinem Vater.
I get on very well with my father.

d. Mein Onkel heißt Carl.
My father is called Carl.

e. Carl ist superlustig und immer nett zu mir.
Carl is super-funny and always mean to me.

f. Carl hat kurze, lockige schwarze Haare.
Carl has short, curly brown hair.

2. From German to English

a. Ich mag meine Oma.

b. Meine Schwester ist immer gut gelaunt.

c. Meine Cousine ist superlustig und entspannt.

d. Ich verstehe mich gut mit meiner Tante.

e. Ich mag meinen Cousin sehr, …

f. … denn er ist immer nett zu mir.

g. Ich verstehe mich super mit meinem Vater, …

h. … aber ich mag meinen Onkel nicht, …

i. weil er immer gemein zu mir ist.

3. Phrase-level translation

a. He is very nice.

b. She is always generous.

c. I get on well with …

d. I don't get on well with …

e. My uncle is super-funny.

f. I like my little brother.

g. I don't like my cousin Mary.

h. She has short black hair.

i. He has blue eyes.

j. I don't like my grandad.

k. He is very stubborn and always mean to me.

4. Sentence-level translation

a. I'm called Stefan. I am nine years old. In my family I have four people.

b. My name is Carla. I have blue eyes. I get on well with my brother.

c. I don't get on well with my brother because he is not nice to me.

d. My name is Frank. I live in Austria. I do not like my uncle David because he is always mean to me.

e. I like my cousin a lot because she is very funny.

f. In my family there are five people. I get on well with my father, but I do not like my mother.

(NOTE: you can use "denn" or "weil" for "because", but be mindful of the word order!)

Unit 6. Describing my family: WRITING

1. Split sentences

Ich verstehe mich gut	sie total kreativ.
Sie ist immer gut	ziemlich klein.
Meine Oma ist	mit meiner Oma.
Sie hat	lockige weiße Haare.
Außerdem ist	meine Oma.
und sie ist immer	gelaunt.
Ich mag	nett zu mir.

2. Rewrite the sentences in the correct order (start each sentence with the underlined word)

a. habe sechs in Familie meiner Personen ich

b. ich gut mit Bruder verstehe meinem mich

c. Onkel mag nicht ich meinen

d. Mutter hat meine Augen blaue

e. meine immer ist Oma zu mir nett

3. Spot and correct the grammar and spelling errors

a. In meiner Familie es gibt ...

b. Ich verstehen mich gut mit ...

c. Ich nicht mag meine Tante.

d. Mein Bruder ist immer gemien.

e. Ich verstehst mich nicht gut mit ...

f. Miene Mutter ist großzügig.

g. Sie hat blau Augen.

h. Meine Schwester sein sehr faul.

i. Er hat rot Haare.

j. Ich mag mein Oma sehr.

4. Anagrams

a. tnet

b. ßigflei

c. ligpumme

d. luaf

e. mienge

f. ustr

g. tiglus

h. ternchschü

5. Guided writing – write 3 short paragraphs describing the people below in the first person:

Name	Age	Family	Likes	Likes	Dislikes
Luzi	13	4 people	mother – very hard-working – long blonde hair	older brother – because very funny and always nice to him	cousin Laura – because very mean and lazy
Leo	12	5 people	father –very relaxed – short black hair	grandmother – because super creative and often in a good mood	uncle Franz – because always stubborn and very ugly
Jonas	15	3 people	grandfather –very funny– very short white hair	younger sister– because very kind and always relaxed	cousin Kathrin – very strong but super talkative and mean to him

6. Describe this person in the third person:

Name & age:
Alex, 14

Family:
4 people

Likes:
his aunt Inge, always relaxed and funny, blonde hair

Dislikes:
his uncle Paul, not nice and never in a good mood

Unit 6a. Talking about skills

Kannst du Gitarre spielen? – *Can you play the guitar?*

Subject-Verb	Adverb	Activity with infinitive		Emotive comment
ich kann *I can*	**sehr gut** *very well*	**Deutsch sprechen** *speak German*		**Das ist ja fantastisch!** *That's fantastic!*
du kannst *you can*	**gut** *well*	**Einrad fahren** *ride the unicycle* **Gitarre spielen** *play the guitar* **Handstand machen** *do a handstand* **im Team arbeiten** *work in a team*		**Alter Falter!** *Blimey!*
er / sie kann *he / she can*	**ein bisschen** *a bit*	jonglieren *juggle* klettern *do rock-climbing* kochen *cook*		**Stell dir vor!** *Imagine!*
wir können *we can*	**nicht so gut** *not so well*	malen *paint* rechnen *do sums*		**Wie peinlich!** *How embarrassing!*
ihr könnt *you guys can*	**nicht** *not*	schreiben *write* schwimmen *swim* **singen** *sing*		**Wie schade!** *What a shame!*
sie / Sie können *they / you (formal) can*	**gar nicht** *not at all*	tanzen *dance* tauchen *do scuba-diving* **Yoga** *yoga*		**Oje!** *Oh dear!*

Author's note:
'können' = 'to be able to' is one of 6 modal verbs in German. Just like their English counterparts, German modal verbs need a second verb to go with them in order to make a complete sentence. This 2nd verb does not need to be conjugated: it stands in its infinitive form at the end of the sentence. This SB shows you again how different German word order can be from the English. But fear not: Du kannst es lernen! – You can learn it! Auf geht's!! ☺

Unit 6a. VOCABULARY BUILDING

1. Match German and English

sehr gut	to dance
klettern	very well
Wie schade!	We can
tanzen	My grandad can
Wir können	to do rock-climbing
Mein Opa kann	What a shame!

2. Complete with the missing form of KÖNNEN

a. Meine Schwester _____ gut jonglieren.

b. Mein Bruder und ich _____ sehr gut schwimmen.

c. Ich _____ nicht so gut singen.

d. Mein Onkel _____ supergut rechnen.

e. _____ du Salsa tanzen?

f. Nein, ich _____ nicht tauchen.

g. Ihr _____ nicht jonglieren? Oje!

3. Complete with the missing word

a. Ich kann sehr gut _____.   I can cook very well.

b. Meine Mutter kann ein _____ Klavier spielen.   My mother can play the piano a bit.

c. _____ du Spanisch sprechen?   Can you speak Spanish?

d. Meine Cousins _____ gut Einrad fahren.   My cousins can ride the unicycle well.

e. Ich kann nicht so gut _____. Wie schade!   I can't sing so well. What a shame!

f. Meine Oma kann Motorrad _____, stell dir vor!   My gran can ride the motorbike, imagine!

g. Mein kleiner _____ kann Handstand machen.   My little brother can do a handstand.

h. Meine große Schwester kann _____ gut schwimmen.   My big sister can swim very well.

4. Translate into English

a. Ich kann kochen.   e. Ich kann gut rechnen.   i. ein bisschen

b. Du kannst singen.   f. Mein Freund kann gut malen.   j. Stell dir vor!

c. Er kann tanzen.   g. Ihr könnt Deutsch sprechen.   k. Oje!

d. Sie kann schwimmen.   h. Wir können gut im Team arbeiten.   l. Alter Falter!

5. Spot and correct any English translation mistakes

a. Ich kann gut kochen.   I can't cook so well.

b. Sie kann sehr gut rechnen.   She can do sums very well.

c. Mein Onkel kann nicht singen.   My grandad can't sing.

d. Ich kann ein bisschen Gitarre spielen.   I can play the piano a bit.

e. Sie können gut malen.   They can paint very well.

f. Wir können gut klettern.   We can cook well.

g. Ich kann gar nicht im Team arbeiten.   I can't work in a team at

6. Anagrams (infinitives): write out the word and its English translation

a. chenko - <u>kochen</u> - <u>to cook</u>

b. ztanen - _____ - _____

c. beiarten - _____ - _____

d. lenma - _____ - _____

e. eisplen - _____ - _____

f. hafrne - _____ - _____

7. Broken words

a. I____ k_____ s_____ g____ D_____ s_____.
I can speak German very well.

b. E___ k_____ n_____ s_____.
He cannot swim.

c. M_____ O_____ k_____ E_____ f_____, s_____ d___ v____!
My granny can ride the unicycle, imagine!

d. K_____ d___ g____ t_____?
Can you dance well?

e. M_____ g_____ B_____ k_____ j_____.
My big brother can juggle.

f. M_____ F_____ Marie k_____ s_____ g_____ k_____.
My friend Marie can cook very well.

8. Complete with a suitable word

a. Mein _____ kann kochen.

b. Ich kann _____ schwimmen.

c. Kannst du _____ ?

d. Meine _____ kann Judo!

e. Mein Freund kann ____ tanzen.

f. Wie _____ !

g. _____ können Gitarre spielen.

h. Ich kann gar nicht _____, ...

i. ... aber ich kann _____.

Unit 6a. Talking about Skills: READING

Hallo, ich heiße Markus. Ich bin elf Jahre alt und ich wohne in München. Mein Lieblingsonkel heißt Matthias. Ich mag ihn sehr! Er ist nicht nur superlustig, sondern auch immer nett zu mir. Außerdem kann er sehr gut Klavier und Gitarre spielen. Ich finde das super! Und du, hast du einen Lieblingsonkel?

Moin moin! Ich heiße Olli und ich komme aus Oldenburg. Ich bin total cool, denn ich kann echt gut Basketball spielen! Ich habe keinen Lieblingsonkel. Aber ich habe einen Opa, der supersportlich ist. Stell dir vor, er kann total gut Judo und Karate! Leider kann er nicht Englisch sprechen. Wie schade! Aber vielleicht kann er es noch lernen. Und du, was kannst du?

Hola amigos! Ich bin Lisa und ich wohne in Bueno Aires. Ich habe eine Lieblingsschwester! Sie heißt Maria und sie ist zweiundzwanzig Jahre alt. Ich finde sie super, denn sie kann Spanisch, Englisch und Chinesisch sprechen. Das ist ja fantastisch, oder? Alter Falter, sie kann mit so vielen Leuten auf der Welt kommunizieren! Jedoch kann sie nicht Deutsch sprechen - aber ich kann das, ha!

Hallo Freunde, ich heiße Tom und ich wohne im Norden von London. Ich bin dreizehn Jahre alt. Ich habe einen Lieblingsonkel. Er heißt Louis und er kann sehr gut malen. Er malt immer Schildkröten, stell dir vor! Ich habe auch eine Lieblingstante. Sie heißt Mary. Ich mag sie, weil sie immer entspannt und gut gelaunt ist. Mary kann super singen und tanzen. Aber das Beste ist: Mary kann mit sechs Bällen jonglieren! Das ist der Hammer! Leider kann ich meinen Onkel und meine Tante nicht so oft sehen. Das ist soooo schade!

Hi Leute, ich heiße Jana. Ich bin zwölf Jahre alt und ich wohne in Luzern in der Schweiz. Ich habe eine Lieblingstante! Sie heißt Ellie und sie kann supergut Motorrad fahren. Ich mag Ellie sehr, sie ist immer nett zu mir und sie ist total lustig. Und du, hast du eine Lieblingstante?

1. Find the German for the following items in Olli's text

a. I come from

b. I can ... really well

c. favourite uncle

d. who is super-sporty

e. imagine

f. unfortunately, he cannot

g. What a shame!

h. But perhaps ...

i. ... he can still learn it

2. Answer the following questions about Tom's text

a. Where does Tom live?

b. What can his favourite uncle do (2 details)?

c. Why does he like his favourite aunt?

d. What is she really good at?

e. But what is the best thing?

f. Why is Tom a bit sad?

3. Complete with the missing words

Hallo! Ich _____ Mia. Ich bin zehn Jahre alt und ich _____ in Basel. Mein Lieblings_____ heißt Alexander. Ich_____ ihn sehr, denn _____ ist immer nett und gut gelaunt. Mein Onkel kann sehr gut Trompete _____ und er kann sehr gut Handstand _____, cool, ne? Und du, _____ du einen Lieblingsonkel?

4. Find someone who: answer the questions below about all 5 texts

a. Who has a grandad that can do martial arts really well?

b. Who has an aunt that likes motorbikes?

c. Who is good at painting?

d. Who has got a favourite sister?

e. Who can juggle with six balls?

f. Who hasn't got a favourite uncle?

g. Who can communicate with many people?

h. Who has got an aunt that is always nice to them?

Unit 6a. Talking about Skills: TRANSLATION/WRITING

1. Bad translation: spot and correct any translation mistakes (in the English) you find below

a. Mein Onkel kann sehr gut kochen.
My uncle cannot cook at all.

b. Meine Tante kann sehr gut tanzen und singen.
My aunt can dance and swim very well.

c. Mein Bruder und ich können gut Karate.
My brother and I can do Karate very well.

d. Ich kann sehr gut im Team arbeiten.
He can work in a team very well.

e. Ich mag ihn, denn er kann gut singen.
I like her, because he can sing well.

f. Sie können Deutsch und Spanisch sprechen.
She can speak German and Spanish.

2. From German to English

a. Mein Opa kann Handstand machen.

b. Ich habe einen Lieblingsonkel. Er heißt Max.

c. Ich mag ihn. Er kann tanzen und singen!

d. Ich verstehe mich gut mit meinem Onkel.

e. Ich habe eine Lieblingstante.

f. Ich mag sie sehr.

g. Sie kann <u>nicht nur</u> Yoga, <u>sondern auch</u>* Karate.

3. Rewrite the sentences in the correct order. Start each sentence with the underlined word.

a. <u>Mein</u> kann Onkel und kochen tanzen

b. können malen <u>Meine</u> Cousinen sehr gut

c. mag <u>Ich</u> Tante meine sehr

d. Bruder kann gut sprechen Deutsch <u>Mein</u>

e. <u>Ich</u> kann tauchen sehr gut, du und?

f. Schwester <u>Meine</u> kann fahren Einrad

g. ist ja <u>Das</u> fantastisch!

4. Spot and correct the grammar and spelling errors

a. Mein Lieblingsonkel kann kochen gut.

b. Mein Tante kann nicht so gut tanzen.

c. Wir konnen gut singen.

d. Du kannst sehr gut fußball spielen.

e. Ich mag meine Onkel, er kann jonglieren!

f. Kannst du joglieren?

g. Sie kann supergut deutsch sprechen!

5. Linking words match up

und	however
aber	furthermore
leider	unfortunately
jedoch	and
außerdem	because (1)
weil	but
auch	because (2)
denn	also

6. Guided writing – write 3 short paragraphs describing the people below in the first person:

Name	Age	Lives in	Favourite ...	Can do well	Can't do so well
Johann	15	Hamburg	uncle Adam	play Basketball	speak Spanish
Leonie	13	Lucerne	aunt Eva	ride motorbike	cook
Deniz	11	Linz	brother Yasim	draw and dance	play football

*nicht nur... sondern auch... = *not only...but also ...*

 **THE LANGUAGE GYM**

UNIT 7
Talking about pets

Grammar Time 3: HABEN (Part 2) - Pets and description
Grammar Time 4: A, THE, and MY in the nominative and accusative cases
Question Skills 1: Age / descriptions / pets

In this unit will learn how to say in German

- what pets you have at home
- what pet you would like to have
- what their name is
- some more adjectives to describe appearance and personality
- the articles "a", "the" and "my" in the nominative and accusative cases
- key question words

You will also learn how to ask questions about
- Name   / age / appearance / quantity

You will revisit the following
- Introducing oneself
- Family members
- Describing people
- The verb 'haben' (to have) in the present tense

UNIT 7
Talking about pets

Zu Hause habe ich ... *At home I have ...*	**ein<u>en</u> Fisch** **einen Frosch** **einen Hamster** **einen Hund** **einen Papagei** **einen Wellensittich**	*a fish* *a frog* *a hamster* *a dog* *a parrot* *a budgie*	**, <u>der</u> Walter heißt.** *that is called Walter.* **<u>Er</u> ist...** *He/It is*	**klein** **groß** **gefährlich** **hässlich** **faul** **frech**	*small* *big* *dangerous* *ugly* *lazy* *cheeky*
Ich habe auch ... *I also have ...*	**ein<u>e</u> Ente** **eine Katze** **eine Maus** **eine Schildkröte** **eine Schlange** **eine Spinne**	*a duck* *a cat* *a mouse* *a turtle* *a snake* *a spider*	**, <u>die</u> Susi heißt.** *that is called Susi.* **<u>Sie</u> ist...** *She/It is*	**langsam** **langweilig** **lebhaft** **lieb** **lustig** **neugierig** **ruhig** **schlau** **schnell** **schön** **stur** **süß** **verspielt**	*slow* *boring* *lively* *kind* *funny* *curious* *calm* *clever* *fast* *beautiful* *stubborn* *cute, sweet* *playful*
Mein Freund Max hat ... *My friend Max has ...* **Ich hätte gern ...** *I'd like to have ...*	**ein Huhn** **ein Kaninchen** **ein Pferd** **ein Schwein** **ein Meerschweinchen**	*a chicken* *a rabbit* *a horse* *a pig* *a guinea pig*	**, <u>das</u> Camillo heißt.** *that is called Camillo.* **<u>Es</u> ist...** *It is...*	**blau** **gelb**	*blue* *yellow*
Ich hätte nicht gern ... *I wouldn't like to have ...*	**zwei Enten*** **zwei Fische** **zwei Hamster** **zwei Hühner** **zwei Hunde** **zwei Kaninchen** **zwei Katzen**	*two ducks* *two fish* *two hamsters* *two chicken* *two dogs* *two rabbits* *two cats*	**, <u>die</u> Max und Moritz heißen.** *that are called Max and Moritz.* **Sie sind...** *They are...*	**grün** **grau** **lila** **orange** **rosa** **weiß**	*green* *grey* *purple* *orange* *pink* *white*

Ich finde mein<u>en</u> Hamster/ mein<u>e</u> Ente/ mein Pferd/ mein<u>e</u> Hunde supercool!
I find my hamster/ my duck/ my horse/ my dogs super-cool!

Leider habe ich <u>keinen</u> Fisch, <u>keine</u> Ente, <u>kein</u> Kaninchen und <u>keine</u> Hühner. – Wie schade!
Unfortuntately, I have <u>no</u> fish, <u>no</u> duck, <u>no</u> rabbit and <u>no</u> chicken. - What a shame!

*Author's note:

There are many different ways of forming the plural for nouns in German! For example, some nouns just add an –e, others add –en, sometimes they add an "Umlaut" in the middle, plus something at the end. Some even don't change at all! Ask your teacher about how you can look up the plural form of a noun. ☺

Unit 7. Talking about pets: VOCABULARY BUILDING

1. Complete with the missing word

a. Zu Hause habe ich einen W_____. *At home I have a budgie.*

b. Ich habe auch eine S_____. *I also have a turtle.*

c. Ich habe keine K_____. *I don't have a cat.*

d. Ich hätte gern einen H_____. *I'd like to have a dog.*

e. Zu H_____ habe ich zwei H_____. *At home I have 2 chicken.*

f. L____ habe ich keine S_____. *Unfortunately, I don't have a snake.*

g. Ich h_____ eine S_____ zu Hause. *I have a spider at home.*

h. Ich h_____ gern einen Hamster. *I'd like to have a hamster.*

2. Match up

Ich habe ...	I have ...
eine Katze	a pet
einen Hund	a hamster
ein Pferd	two fish
eine Spinne	a cat
keine Haustiere	a duck
eine Ente	no pets
einen Hamster	a frog
einen Papagei	a dog
zwei Fische	a parrot
ein Haustier	a spider
einen Frosch	a horse

3. Translate into English

a. Ich habe einen Hund.

b. Meine Freundin Luzi hat eine Ratte.

c. Ich habe fünf Fische.

d. Ich habe keine Haustiere.

e. Ich habe drei Hunde.

f. Ich hätte gern eine Schildkröte zu Hause.

g. Mein Bruder hat eine Schlange.

h. Mein Hund ist vier Jahre alt.

4. Add the missing letter

a. Ich ha__e ...

b. eine Schildkr__te

c. einen Papa__ei

d. zwei __atzen

e. einen Hu__d

f. Er ha__ einen Frosch.

g. ein Meersch__einchen

h. ein P__erd

5. Anagrams

a. Hndu   *Hund*

b. stremHa

c. rePdf

d. hsciF

e. ageiPap

f. lanSchge

g. nneiSp

h. zetaK

6. Broken words

a. Z__ H_____ h_____ i____ e_____ H_____. *At home I have a dog.*

b. M_____ F_____ Alex h_____ e_____ P_____. *My friend Alex has a parrot.*

c. M__ B_____ h_____ e____ S_____. *My brother has a turtle.*

d. I____ h_____ k_____ K_____. *I don't have a rabbit.*

e. I____ h_____ e_____ S_____. *I have a snake.*

f. M_____ K_____ i____ s____. *My cat is cute.*

g. I____ h_____ z____ H_____. *I have two pets.*

7. Complete with a suitable word

a. Mein Fisch _____ Nepomuk.

b. Mein _____ Jens hat einen Papagei.

c. Mein Bruder _____ eine Maus.

d. Mein Hund ist _____ und sehr süß.

e. Zu Hause habe ich _____ Haustiere.

f. Zu _____ habe ich einen Hund und ein _____.

g. Ich habe _____ Fisch zu Hause.

h. Zu Hause habe ich _____ Wellensittich.

Unit 7. Talking about pets: READING

Hallo, ich heiße Elena. Ich bin elf Jahre alt und ich wohne in Berlin. In meiner Familie gibt es vier Personen: meine Eltern, meinen kleinen Bruder Michael und mich. Ich mag Michael nicht, ich finde ihn ziemlich nervig. Wir haben zwei Haustiere: einen Hund, der Otto heißt, und eine Katze, die Mizi heißt. Otto ist total lieb, aber Mizi ist gar nicht nett. Genau wie mein Bruder!

Ich heiße Sandra. Ich bin zwölf Jahre alt. In meiner Familie gibt es fünf Personen: meine Eltern, mich und meine zwei großen Schwestern Svenja und Lotte. Svenja ist lustig und immer hilfsbereit. Aber Lotte ist stur und langweilig. Wir haben zwei Haustiere: ein Kaninchen, das Nick heißt, und ein Huhn, das Angela heißt. Ich finde Nick super, er ist total lieb! Aber Angela ist superlaut und ziemlich stur, genau wie Lotte!

Ich heiße Robert. Ich bin dreizehn Jahre alt und ich wohne in Salzburg. In meiner Familie gibt es vier Personen: meine Eltern, meinen großen Bruder Franz und mich. Franz ist zwölf Jahre alt. Ich mag ihn, weil er total lebhaft ist. Wir haben zwei Haustiere: einen Papagei, der Rico heißt, und eine Spinne, die Karate heißt. Rico ist ziemlich geschwätzig und Karate ist sehr lebhaft, so wie mein Bruder!

1. Find the German for the following in Elena's text

a. two pets

b. which is called (he)

c. a cat

d. a dog

e. quite annoying

f. like my brother

g. my parents

h. my name is

i. I find him

2. Find someone who: answer the questions below about Elena, Robert, Sandra and Julian

a. Who has a cat?

b. Who has parrot?

c. Who has a spider?

d. Who has a guinea pig?

e. Who has a rabbit?

f. Who has a dog?

Hi, ich heiße Julian. Ich bin zehn Jahre alt und ich wohne in Vaduz, in Liechtenstein. In meiner Familie gibt es meine Eltern, meine zwei Brüder Jörg und Manuel und mich. Jörg ist sehr geschwätzig und lustig. Manuel ist sehr ruhig und immer fleißig. Wir haben zwei Haustiere: ein Meerschweinchen, das Samuel heißt und eine Schildkröte, die Speedy heißt. Sie sind beide echt cool. Das Meerschweinchen ist total lustig und lebhaft, aber die Schildkröte ist sehr ruhig, genau wie mein Bruder Manuel!

3. Answer these questions about Julian's text

a. Where does Julian live?

b. What is his brother Manuel like?

c. Who is funny and lively?

d. Who is like Manuel?

e. Who is Jörg?

f. Who is Speedy?

g. Who is Samuel?

4. Complete with the missing words

Hallo Leute! Ich he_____ Yildiz. Ich bin zwölf J_____ alt und ich w_____ in Basel. In meiner F_____ gibt es fünf Personen: meine El_____, meine zwei Schwestern Fatima und Deniz, und mich. Ich fi_____ Fatima super, denn sie i_____ sehr fleißig und freundlich. Aber Deniz ist to_____ faul und oft gem_____ zu mir. Ich h_____ zwei Haustiere: eine Ratte, die Zorro heißt u___ eine Katze, die Lila h_____. Zorro ist superlebhaft und lu_____. Lila ist auch lebhaft, aber auch ein bisschen f_____, gen_____ w____ meine S_____ Deniz!

5. Fill in the table below

Name	Elena	Robert
Age		
City		
Pets		
Description of pets		

Unit 7. Talking about pets: TRANSLATION

1. Bad translation: spot and correct any translation mistakes you find below

a. In meiner Familie gibt es drei Personen und vier Haustiere.
In my family there are four people and three pets.

b. Zu Hause haben wir zwei Haustiere: einen Hund und eine kleine Katze.
At home we have two pets: a dog and a small rabbit.

c. Mein Freund Max hat eine kleine Schildkröte, die Rudi heißt. Rudi ist superlustig.
My friend Max has little spider called Rudi. Rudi is super-boring.

d. Meine Oma hat ein kleines Pferd, das Babsi heißt.
My granny has a small duck called Babsi.

e. Mein Opa hat einen Wellensittich, der Mo heißt.
My grandad has a parrot called Mo.

f. Ich habe zwei Hühner, die Kalle und Klaus heißen. Sie sind total süß!
I have two hens called Kalle and Klaus. They are really cute!

2. Translate into English

a. Ich habe ...

b. ... ein<u>en</u> groß<u>en</u> Hund   *a big dog*

c. ... einen kleinen Hamster

d. ... ein<u>e</u> lieb<u>e</u> Katze

e. ... eine kleine Schildkröte

f. ... ein süß<u>es</u> Kaninchen

g. Leider habe ich keinen Hund.

h. Wir haben keine Haustiere zu Hause.

i. Ich hätte gern einen kleinen Hund.

j. Ich hätte gern eine kleine Katze.

k. Ich habe ein kleines Kaninchen, aber ich hätte gern ein kleines Pferd. Ich liebe Pferde! *[I love horses!]*

3. Phrase-level translation [En to Ger]

a. I have a big dog

b. and a little cat

c. at home

d. and we have

e. a beautiful horse

f. two curious cats

g. I have

h. I don't have

i. I would like to have

4. Sentence-level translation [En to Ger]

a. My brother has a dog which* is called Mücke.

b. My sister has a turtle which is called Andy.

c. I have a horse which is called Gordito.

d. At home, we have three pets: a duck, a rabbit and a parrot.

e. I have a rat called Stuart.

f. At home, we have three pets: a cat, a dog and a hamster.

g. I have two fish which are called Nemo and Dory.

Here, 'which' translates into either 'der', 'die' or 'das', depending on the gender and number of the noun it stands for – have a look again at the sentence builder at the beginning of this unit if you need!

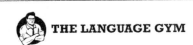

THE LANGUAGE GYM

Unit 7. Talking about pets: WRITING

1. Split sentences

Ich habe einen Hund,	hat zwei Hunde.
Ich habe auch ein	Katze.
Leider habe ich keine	der Konrad heißt.
Mein Onkel	kleines Pferd.
Ich hätte gerne einen	zu Hause.
Meine Oma hat zwei große	kleinen Frosch.
Ich habe keine Haustiere	Katzen.

2. Rewrite the sentences in the correct order (start each sentence with the underlined word)

a. wir drei <u>Zu</u> Hause haben Haustiere

b. <u>Ich</u> Ratte hätte gern eine

c. habe eine ein Katze und Kaninchen <u>Ich</u>

d. Ben <u>Mein</u> hat lustigen Papagei einen Freund

e. <u>Ich</u> das Schwein habe heißt ein Schnorchel

f. haben fünf Fische blaue <u>Wir</u>

g. Oma <u>Meine</u> einen der Lupo hat Hund heißt

3. Spot and correct the grammar and spelling [note: in several cases a word is missing]

a. Zu Hause habe ich ein Hund.

b. Ich habe ein Meershweinchen.

c. Ich gern eine große Spinne.

d. Meine Schwester habe zwei große Katzen.

e. Mein Freund Pedro hat vier Huhner.

f. Ich habe ein Pferd, Schnurrbart heißt.

g. Zu Hause ich habe einen kleinen Frosch.

h. Zu Hause wir drei Haustiere.

4. Anagrams

a. dnuH

b. Kztae

c. schchenMreewien

d. ihcFs

e. chenninKa

f. rePfd

g. Htierause

6. Describe this person in the third person:

Name:	Malte
Hair:	black, short
Eyes:	brown
Personality:	very nice
Physical:	short, fat
Pets:	a dog, a cat and two fish and would like to have a spider

5. Guided writing – write 3 short paragraphs (in 1st person) describing the pets below using the details in the box

Name	Animal	Age	Colour	Character or appearance
Tom	dog	4	white	cute
Leonie	duck	6	blue	funny
Moritz	horse	1	brown	beautiful

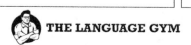

Grammar Time 3: HABEN (Part 2)
(Pets and description)

1. Translate

a. I have: i_ _ h_ _ _

b. You have: d_ h_ _ _

c. He/She/It has: e_/s_ _/e_ h_ _

d. We have: w_ _ h_ _ _ _

e. You guys have: i_ _ h_ _ _

f. They have: s_ _ h_ _ _ _

2. Translate into English

a. Ich habe ein großes Kaninchen.

b. Mein Bruder hat eine hässliche Katze.

c. Meine Mutter hat einen großen Hund.

d. Meine Cousins haben ein dickes Meerschweinchen.

e. Zu Hause haben wir eine sehr große Spinne.

f. Meine Freundin Luzi hat ein superschnelles Pferd.

3. Complete

a. I have a guinea pig ...   Ich _____ ein Meerschweinchen, ...

b. ... it has brown eyes.   ... es _____ braune Augen.

c. We have a turtle. It has red eyes.   Wir _____ eine Schildkröte. Sie _____ rote Augen.

d. My sister has a dog.   Meine Schwester _____ einen Hund.

e. My uncles have two cats.   Meine Onkel _____ zwei Katzen.

f. They have green eyes.   Sie _____ grüne Augen.

g. My brother and I have a snake.   Mein Bruder und ich _____ eine Schlange.

h. Do you guys have pets?   _____ ihr Haustiere?

i. What kind of animals do you guys have?   Was für Haustiere _____ ihr?

4. Translate into German

a. I have a guinea pig. It* has brown eyes.

b. We don't have pets at home.

c. My dog is three years old. It has long hair.

d. I have three sisters. They are very mean to me.

e. My cousins have a cat. It is very cute.

f. My auntie has long, curly blonde hair. She is very pretty.

g. My uncle and I have black hair and green eyes.

*Note: 'it' can translate into 'er', 'sie' or 'es', depending on whether the noun it stands for is masculine, feminine, or neuter – have a look again at the sentence builder at the beginning of this unit if you need!

THE LANGUAGE GYM

Grammar Time 4: A, THE, and MY
in the nominative and accusative cases

	NOMINATIVE CASE (Subject)	ACCUSATIVE CASE (direct object)
Example sentences	*(1) This is **a**...* *(2) **The** ... is ...* *(3) **My** ... is called ...* *(4) **He/she/it/they** is/are very ...*	*(1) I have **a** ...* *(2) I find **the** ...* *(3) I like **my** ...* *(4) I like **him/her/it/them**.*
Masculine singular der Hund *the dog*	(1) Das ist **EIN** Hund. (2) **DER** Hund ist groß. (3) **MEIN** Hund heißt Ben. (4) **ER** ist sehr groß.	(1) Ich habe **EINEN** Hund. (2) Ich finde **DEN** Hund cool. (3) Ich mag **MEINEN** Hund. (4) Ich mag **IHN**.
Feminine singular die Katze *the cat*	(1) Das ist **EINE** Katze. (2) **DIE** Katze ist süß. (3) **MEINE** Katze heißt Mizi. (4) **SIE** ist sehr süß.	(1) Ich habe **EINE** Katze. (2) Ich finde **DIE** Katze süß. (3) Ich mag **MEINE** Katze. (4) Ich mag **SIE**.
Neuter singular das Pferd *the horse*	(1) Das ist **EIN** Pferd (2) **DAS** Pferd ist schön. (3) **MEIN** Pferd heißt Rocky. (4) **ES** ist sehr schön.	(1) Ich habe **EIN** Pferd. (2) Ich finde **DAS** Pferd schön (3) Ich mag **MEIN** Pferd. (4) Ich mag **ES**.
Plural (all genders) die Hamster *the hamsters*	(1) Das sind (zwei) Hamster. (2) **DIE** Hamster sind klein. (3) **MEINE** Hamster heißen Taco und Jojo. (4) **SIE** sind sehr klein.	(1) Ich habe (zwei) Hamster. (2) Ich finde **DIE** Hamster klein. (3) Ich mag **MEINE** Hamster. (4) Ich mag **SIE**.

Author's notes:

(1) The table above shows you how 'a', 'the' and 'my' look depending on the gender, number, and case of the noun that they go with.

(2) Together with that noun (for example: 'dog'), these articles form a NOUN PHRASE, as in 'my dog'. Every noun phrase can be replaced by a pronoun like 'it', 'she' or 'him', 'her' etc. – I have included them in the table as well, so you can see.

(3) Take a look at the table. What patterns do you notice? Discuss with a partner and with your teacher. Use this table now and then to remind you of those patterns and what you have noticed.

Drills

1. Split sentences

Ich habe einen	ist superschnell!
Das ist ein	Hund.
Mein Pferd	sie fantastisch!
Ich mag meine	Mizi.
Sie heißt	Pferd.
Sie ist	Katze.
Ich finde	süß!

2. Complete the gap with a suitable word

a. Ich habe eine _____.

b. Ich finde meinen _____ nervig.

c. Das ist ein _____.

d. Mein _____ ist sehr gefährlich.

e. Ich mag meinen _____, er ist so cool!

f. Aber ich mag meine _____ nicht.

g. Die _____ ist sehr interessant.

h. Ich finde den _____ nicht so cool.

3. Underline the correct option

a. Ich habe **einen/eine/ein** Bruder.

b. Ich finde **meinen/meine/mein** Onkel cool.

c. Das ist **mein/meine** Vater ...

d. ...ich mag **ihn/sie/es**!

e. **Mein/Meine** Mutter ist so cool, ...

f. ... ich finde **ihn/sie/es** sehr lustig.

g. Ich mag **meinen/meine/mein** Eltern.

h. Das sind **mein/meine** Brüder.

i. **Der/Die/Das** Hamster ist zehn Jahre alt.

j. Ich finde **meinen/meine/mein** Pferd cool.

k. Hast du **einen/eine/ein** Schwester?

l. Ja, **er/sie/es** ist total cool!

4. Add the ending to 'ein', 'mein' und 'kein', if there is one

a. Ich habe leider kein__ Katze.

b. Mein__ Onkel ist zweiundzwanzig Jahre alt.

c. Ich finde mein__ Bruder cool.

d. Ich finde mein__ Oma nett.

e. Mein__ Schwester hat ein__ Spinne!

f. Hast du ein__ Pferd oder ein__ Hamster?

g. Mein__ Hamster und mein__ Katze sind total süß.

h. Mein__ Haustiere sind ein__ Hund und ein__ Fisch.

5. Translate into German

a. I have an uncle.

b. I find him cool.

c. My uncle is called Otto and he is very nice.

d. This is my dog! He is big!

e. I have a cat. It/she is called Mizi.

f. I find my cat very cute.

g. Do you have a horse?

h. I like it (my horse).

 **THE LANGUAGE GYM**

Question Skills 1: Age / Descriptions / Pets

1. Match question and answer

Wie alt bist du?	Sie ist zweiundsechzig und er ist einundsechzig Jahre alt.
Warum magst du deine Mutter nicht?	Es geht mir gut, danke!
Wie sind deine Haare?	Ich mag sie nicht, weil sie zu streng ist!
Wie alt sind deine Oma und dein Opa?	Blau, definitiv!
Welche Farbe haben deine Augen?	Ich bin vierzehn Jahre alt.
Was ist deine Lieblingsfarbe?	Drei, stell dir vor! Einen Hund, eine Katze und ein Huhn.
Wie geht es dir?	Ich bin hilfsbereit und sehr zuverlässig.
Hast du ein Haustier?	Nein. Er ist total stur und nie gut gelaunt. Ich mag ihn nicht.
Was ist dein Lieblingstier?	Am zwölften Mai.
Wie viele Haustiere hast du?	Meine Haare sind mittellang, lockig und dunkelbraun.
Wie ist dein Charakter?	Meine Augen sind blau.
Wie siehst du aus?	Ich habe zwei Lieblingstiere: Pferde und Katzen!
Verstehst du dich gut mit deinem Vater?	Nein, ich habe leider kein Haustier. Wie schade!
Wann hast du Geburtstag?	Ich bin klein, aber ziemlich muskulös!

2. Complete with the missing words

a. _____ kommst du?
Where are you from?

b. _____alt ist dein Vater?
How old is your father?

c. _____ ist Julia (vom Charakter her)?
How is Julia (personality-wise)?

d. _____ du dich mit deiner Mutter?
Do you get on with your mum?

e. _____ ist dein Geburtstag?
When is your birthday?

f. _____ ist dein Hund?
What is your dog like?

g. _____ _____ Haustiere hast du?
How many pets do you have?

3. Translate the following question words into English

a. Welche?

b. Wann?

c. Wo?

d. Wie?

e. Woher?

f. Wer?

g. Wie viele?

h. Was?

i. Warum?

4. Complete

a. Wi____ al_____ bi_____ d___?

b. Wo_____ ko_____ d__?

c. Wi____ si____ de_____ Ha_____?

d. Wa_____ is__ de_____ Ge_____?

e. W___ vi_____ Hau_____ hast du?

f. W___ wo_____ d___?

g. Ve_____ d__ di___ g__ mi___ de_____ V_____?

5. Translate into German

a. What is your name?

b. How old are you?

c. How is your hair?/What is your hair like?

d. What is your favourite animal?

e. Do you get on well with your father?

f. Why don't you like your mother?

g. How many pets do you have?

h. Where are you from?

UNIT 8
Saying what jobs people do, why they like/dislike them and where they work

Grammar Time 5: WOHNEN & ARBEITEN
and other regular verbs in the present tense

Grammar Time 6: SEIN (Part 2) - Jobs

Unit 8a. Using 'finden' (to find) to express an opinion

In this unit you will learn how to say:

- What jobs people do
- Why they like/dislike those jobs
- Where they work
- Adjectives to describe jobs
- Words for jobs
- Words for types of buildings
- The present tense conjugation of 'arbeiten' (to work), 'wohnen' (to live)
- "Ich finde" + accusative to give an opinion about something or someone

You will revisit the following:
- Family members
- The full conjugation of the verb 'sein' (to be)
- Description of people and pets

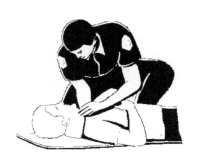

UNIT 8
Saying what jobs people do, why they like/dislike them and where they work

Mein Vater *My father* **Mein großer Bruder** *My big brother* **Mein Onkel** *My uncle*	**ist** *is* **arbeitet als** *works as a*	**Arzt** *doctor* **Anwalt** *lawyer* **Bauer** *farmer* **Buchhalter** *accountant* **Friseur** *hairdresser* **Geschäftsmann** *businessman* **Ingenieur** *engineer* **Hausmann** *house-husband* **Koch** *chef* **Krankenpfleger** *nurse* **Lehrer** *teacher* **Mechaniker** *mechanic* **Schauspieler** *actor*	**Er mag seine Arbeit (nicht), denn sie ist …** *He likes his work (not), because it is …* **Er findet seine Arbeit …** *He finds his work …*	**aufregend** *exciting* **anstrengend** *exhausting* **bereichernd** *rewarding* **einfach** *easy* **gut bezahlt** *well-paid* **interessant** *interesting* **langweilig** *boring* **schwierig** *difficult* **spannend** *exciting* **stressig** *stressful* **vielfältig** *varied*
Meine Mutter *My mother* **Meine große Schwester** *My big sister* **Meine Tante** *My aunt*	**ist** *is* **arbeitet als** *works as a*	**Ärztin** *doctor* **Anwältin** *lawyer* **Bäuerin** *farmer* **Buchhalterin** *accountant* **Friseurin** *hairdresser* **Geschäftsfrau** *businesswoman* **Ingenieurin** *engineer* **Hausfrau** *housewife* **Köchin** *chef* **Krankenpflegerin** *nurse* **Lehrerin** *teacher* **Mechanikerin** *mechanic* **Schauspielerin** *actress*	**Sie mag ihre Arbeit (nicht), denn sie ist …** *She likes her work (not), because it is …* **Sie findet ihre Arbeit …** *She finds her work …*	

Er arbeitet … *He works …* / **Sie arbeitet …** *She works …*

auf einem Bauernhof	*on a farm*	**in einem Restaurant**	*in a restaurant*
auf einer Baustelle	*on a building site*	**in einem Theater**	*in a theatre*
in der Stadt	*in the city*	**in einer Fabrik**	*in a factory*
in einem Büro	*in an office*	**in einer Schule**	*in a school*
in einem Hotel	*in a hotel*	**in einer Werkstatt**	*in a garage*
in einem Krankenhaus	*in a hospital*	**zu Hause**	*at home*

Er liebt/hasst <u>seine Arbeit</u>, weil sie … ist. *He loves/hates <u>his work</u>, because it is …*	**Sie liebt/hasst <u>ihre Arbeit</u>, weil sie … ist.** *She loves/hates <u>her work</u>, because it is …*

 **THE LANGUAGE GYM**

Unit 8. Saying what jobs people do: VOCABULARY BUILDING

1. Complete with the missing word

a. Mein Vater ist K_____.   *My father is a nurse.*

b. Meine Tante ist F_____.   *My aunt is a hairdresser.*

c. Mein großer Bruder arbeitet als M_____.   *My big brother works as a mechanic.*

d. Meine Mutter ist Ä_____.   *My mother is a doctor.*

e. Meine große S_____ arbeitet als B_____.   *My big sister works as an accountant.*

f. Meine Tante ist I_____.   *My aunt is an engineer.*

g. Mein O_____ ist A_____.   *My uncle is a lawyer.*

2. Match up

Meine Arbeit ist ...   *My work is ...*

langweilig	stressful
vielfältig	exhausting
schwierig	difficult
anstrengend	well-paid
spannend	varied
stressig	rewarding
einfach	boring
bereichernd	interesting
interessant	easy
gut bezahlt	exciting

3. Translate into English

a. Meine Mutter ist Anwältin.

b. Sie mag ihre Arbeit nicht.

c. Er arbeitet in einer Werkstatt.

d. Mein Onkel ist Buchhalter.

e. Sie findet ihre Arbeit anstrengend.

f. Meine Cousine ist Friseurin.

g. Er liebt seine Arbeit ...

h. ..., weil sie spannend ist.

4. Add the missing letter

a. ein__ach

b. er li__bt

c. span__end

d. An__alt

e. stre__sig

f. er ar__eitet als

g. sie ist __rztin

h. mein On__el

5. Anagrams

a. erBau   *Bauer*   c. herLerin   e. rÄtinz   g. risFuer

b. altAwn   d. lerspieSchau   f. terhalBuch   h. uasfHrau

6. Broken words

a. M_____ O_____ i____ H_____.
My uncle is a house husband.

b. ..., d_____ s____ i____ v_____.
... because it is varied.

c. M_____ V_____ i____ A_____.
My father is a doctor.

d. E____ a_____ i____ d_____ S_____.
He works in the city.

e. E_____ l_____ s_____ A_____.
... He loves his job ...

f. ..., w_____ s____ s_____ i____.
... because it is exciting.

g. E___ f_____ s_____ b_____.
He finds it rewarding.

7. Complete with a suitable word

a. Meine Mutter ist_____.

b. Sie findet sie _____.

c. Mein Opa arbeitet als _____.

d. Er findet seine Arbeit _____.

e. Er mag seine Arbeit _____,

f. denn sie ist sehr _____.

g. Meine _____ ist Ärztin.

h. Sie _____ ihre Arbeit,

i. ..., weil sie _____ ist.

j. Meine Cousine arbeitet in einem
_____.

Unit 8. Saying what jobs people do: READING

Hi Leute! Ich heiße Olaf. Ich bin dreizehn Jahre alt und ich wohne in Rostock. In meiner Familie gibt es vier Personen. Ich habe auch einen Hund, der David heißt. Er ist sehr lustig! Mein Vater arbeitet als Arzt in der Stadt. Er mag seine Arbeit, weil sie sehr bereichernd ist. Jedoch ist sie manchmal sehr anstrengend. Mein Onkel Johannes ist Bauer und er liebt seine Arbeit. Er findet sie superhart und schwierig, aber er liebt die Tiere!

Hallo Leute, ich heiße Nils. In meiner Familie gibt es vier Personen. Mein Vater heißt Oliver und er ist Journalist. Er mag seine Arbeit, weil sie interessant ist. Jedoch ist sie manchmal sehr stressig. Meine Mutter ist Journalistin und sie mag ihre Arbeit sehr. „Die Arbeit ist total spannend", sagt sie. Zuhause habe ich einen Hund. Er heißt Rocky und er ist superlustig. Ich liebe Hunde, aber ich hasse Katzen.

Hi! Ich heiße Fatima. Ich wohne in Köln, in Westdeutschland. Ich verstehe mich super mit meiner Mutter – sie ist ein bisschen schüchtern, aber sehr nett. Sie ist Architektin, aber sie arbeitet im Moment nicht. Ich habe einen Onkel. Er wohnt in Bonn. Ich mag ihn nicht, weil er total stur und unfreundlich ist. Er arbeitet in einer Schule in der Stadt, aber er hasst Kinder, stell dir vor! Zu Hause habe ich eine Schildkröte, die Schumi heißt. Sie ist langsam, aber sehr lustig, genau wie meine Schwester Paula.

Hallo, ich heiße Maike. Ich bin dreizehn Jahre alt und ich wohne in Innsbruck, in Österreich. In meiner Familie gibt es drei Personen. Meine Mutter heißt Kathrin und arbeitet als Krankenschwester. Sie liebt ihre Arbeit, weil sie vielseitig ist. Mein Vater ist Hausmann. Er mag seine Arbeit überhaupt nicht! Er findet sie sehr schwierig und total langweilig. Ich habe leider kein Haustier, aber ich hätte gern ein Pferd! Meine Cousine hat ein Pferd, stell dir vor, es heißt Nikolaus und es ist sehr groß und stark! Wie cool!

1. Find the German for the following in Olaf's text

a. I am 13 years old

b. I also have a dog

c. my dad works …

d. as (a) doctor

e. in the city

f. he likes his work

g. because it is rewarding

h. however it is sometimes

i. he loves his work

j. super-hard and difficult

2. Answer the questions on ALL texts

a. Who is Nikolaus?

b. Whose mum is a journalist?

c. Whose uncle is in the wrong job?

d. Whose father is a doctor?

e. Who has a turtle?

f. Who has a dog?

3. Answer the following questions about Fatima's text

a. Where does Fatima live?

b. Who does she get on with really brilliantly?

c. What does her mum do [2 details]?

d. Why does she hate her uncle?

e. Why is her uncle a bad teacher?

f. Who is Schumi?

g. What is Paula like?

4. Fill in

Ich h_____ Jessica. Ich bin vierzehn J_____ alt und ich w_____ in Bern. In meiner F_____ gibt es fünf Personen. Mein Cousin Manu i____ ziemlich nett und sehr fleißig. Er ist dreißig Jahre alt und er arbeitet als Ko_____ in einem Re_____. Er wohnt in Barcelona, stell dir vor! Er mag seine A_____, weil sie supervielfältig und int_____ ist. Mein V_____ arbeitet im Moment nicht. Zu H_____ habe ich eine Schlange, die Lucky h_____. Sie ist nicht gefährlich, zum Glück!

5. Fill in the table below

Name	Jessica [Pets]	Manu [Jobs]
Age		
City		
Pets/Job		
Description pets/job		

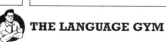

Unit 8. Saying what jobs people do: TRANSLATION

1. Bad translation: spot and correct [IN THE ENGLISH] any translation mistakes you find below

a. Mein Vater arbeitet als Schauspieler. Er mag seine Arbeit, denn sie ist sehr vielseitig. Er arbeitet in einem Theater.
My father works as a cook. He likes his job because it is very stressful. He works in a school.

b. Meine Tante arbeitet als Geschäftsfrau in einem Büro. Sie liebt ihre Arbeit, aber sie ist sehr anstrengend.
My cousin works as a businesswoman in a theatre. She hates it but it's very exhausting.

c. Mein Freund Maik arbeitet als Krankenpfleger. Er arbeitet in einem Krankenhaus und er mag seine Arbeit.
My uncle Maik works as a nurse. He lives in a hospital and likes his job.

d. Mein Onkel Gianfranco ist Koch in einem italienischen Restaurant und er liebt seine Arbeit.
My uncle Gianfranco is a lawyer in an Italian restroom and he hates his job.

e. Meine Mutter Angela ist Buchhalterin und sie arbeitet in einem Büro. Sie hasst ihre Arbeit, weil sie sehr langweilig ist.
My mother Angela is an actress and works in an office. She loves her work because it is very boring.

2. Translate into English

a. Mein Onkel arbeitet als …

b. Meine Tante arbeitet als …

c. Hausfrau

d. Krankenschwester

e. Friseurin

f. Mechanikerin

g. Sie liebt ihre Arbeit.

h. Sie arbeitet in einer Werkstatt.

i. Er arbeitet in einem Theater.

j. in einer Schule

k. Die Arbeit ist vielseitig.

l. Sie ist hart, aber vielseitig.

3. Phrase-level translation [En to Ger]

a. my brother works

b. as a farmer

c. as an accountant

d. he likes

e. his job

f. because* it is exciting

g. and varied

h. but it's hard

Note that you have 2 options that you can use for "because": 1) "denn" and 2) "weil". When you use "weil", you have to put the verb to the end.

4. Sentence-level translation [En to Ger]

a. My brother is a mechanic.

b. My sister is a businesswoman.

c. My uncle is a farmer and he loves his job.

d. My brother Peter works in an office.

e. At home, I have a spider called Tim.

f. At home, I have a big dog and a small cat.

g. My aunt is a nurse. She likes her job …

h. … because it is rewarding.

i. She works in a hospital.

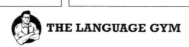

Unit 8. Saying what jobs people do: WRITING

1. Split sentences

Mein Bruder hat	vielseitig ist.
Meine Tante ist	als Mechaniker.
Mein Onkel arbeitet	Lehrerin.
Er mag	einer Schule.
weil sie	einer Werkstatt.
Er arbeitet in	seine Arbeit.
Sie arbeitet in	eine kleine Katze.

2. Rewrite the sentences in the correct order [note: start each sentence with the underlined word]

a. mag <u>Er</u> seine sehr Arbeit

b. arbeitet als <u>Er</u> Buchhalter Büro in einem

c. <u>Sie</u> ihre Arbeit super findet

d. Onkel ist <u>Mein</u> Bauer

e. arbeitet <u>Mein</u> Bruder einem Theater in

f. <u>Mein</u> hasst Opa seine Arbeit

g. Freundin Ärztin ist Krankenhaus in einem <u>Meine</u>

3. Spot and correct the grammar and spelling [note: in several cases a word is missing]

a. Meine Mutter ist Hausmann.

b. Sie ihre Arbeit sehr interessant.

c. Meine Schwester arbeitet Ärztin.

d. Sie hasst ihre Arbeit, weil sie ist langweilig.

e. Sie arbeitet in Krankenhaus in Stadt.

f. Er mag ihre Arbeit, denn sie spannend.

g. Meine Vater findet seine Arbeit bereichernd.

h. Er mag sein Arbeit, weil sie gut bezahlt ist.

4. Anagrams

a. trAz

b. cherndreibe

c. weiliglang

d. nnendspa

e. ohfBauern

f. hasuKkranen

g. herLerin

6. Describe this person in German in the 3rd person

Name:
Hanna

Hair/eyes:
blonde + green eyes

Physique:
tall and pretty

Personality:
hard-working

Job:
nurse

Opinion:
loves her job

Reason:
stressful but rewarding

5. Guided writing – write 3 short paragraphs describing the people below using the details in the box [in 1st person]

Person	Relation	Job	Like/ Dislike	Reason
Anna	My mother	Lawyer	Loves	Varied and exciting
Luciano	My brother	Chef	Hates	Boring and exhausting
Marta	My aunt	Engineer	Likes	Difficult but well-paid

Grammar Time 5: WOHNEN & ARBEITEN
and other regular verbs in the present tense

wohnen		to live				
ich *I*	**wohne** *live*	**in Berlin**	*in Berlin*	**im Norden** **im Süden**	*in the north* *in the south*
du *you*	**wohnst** *live*	**in Bern**	*in Bern*	**im Westen** **im Osten**	*in the west* *in the east*
er/sie/es *he/she/it*	**wohnt** *lives*	**in Wien** **in Vaduz**	*in Vienna* *in Vaduz*	**im Zentrum**	*in the centre*
wir *we*	**wohnen** *live*				
ihr *you guys*	**wohnt** *live*	**in einem Haus** **in einer Wohnung** **in einem Gebäude**	*in a house* *in a flat* *in an building*	**an der Küste** **auf dem Land** **in der Stadt** **in den Bergen**	*on the coast* *in the countryside* *in the city* *in the mountains*
sie/Sie *they/you* *(formal)*	**wohnen** *live*				

Note: *Other verbs you have seen already in this book that have the same verb endings are:*
kommen [to come], lieben [to love], hassen [to hate].

arbeiten		to work		
ich *I*	**arbeite** *work*	**als** *as*	**Arbeiter / Arbeiterin** **Architekt / Architektin** **Arzt / Ärztin** **Bäcker / Bäckerin** **Bauer / Bäuerin** **Fußballprofi** **Geschäftsmann / Geschäftsfrau** **Hausfrau / Hausmann** **Koch / Köchin** **Lehrer / Lehrerin** **Schauspieler / Schauspielerin**	**auf dem Land** **auf einer Baustelle** **in der Stadt** **in einem Büro** **in einem Hotel** **in einem Krankenhaus** **in einem Restaurant**
du *you*	**arbeitest** *work*			
er/sie/es *he/she/it*	**arbeitet** *works*			
wir *we*	**arbeiten** *work*		**Arbeiter / Arbeiterinnen** **Architekten / Architektinnen** **Bäcker / Bäckerinnen** **Bauern / Bäuerinnen** **Fußballprofis** **Geschäftsleute** **Hausmänner / Hausfrauen** **Köche / Köchinnen** **Lehrer / Lehrerinnen** **Schauspieler / Schauspielerinnen**	**in einem Theater** **in einer Fabrik** **in einer Firma** **in einer Schule** **in einer Werkstatt** **zu Hause**
ihr *you guys*	**arbeitet** *work*			
sie/Sie *they/you* *(formal)*	**arbeiten** *work*			

Note: *'arbeiten' has the same verb endings as 'wohnen', apart from the extra '-e' before '-t' and '-st' endings. The '-e' appears because it makes the ending easier to pronounce. All regular verbs with the stem ending in '–t' or '–d' do this, and also a lot of irregular verbs, including 'finden'.*

 **THE LANGUAGE GYM**

Drills

1. Match up

you live	ich wohne
I live	er wohnt
he lives	sie wohnen
you guys live	du wohnst
they live	sie wohnt
she lives	ihr wohnt

2. Complete with the correct option

a. Mein Bruder und ich _____ in München.

b. Er _____ in einer kleinen Wohnung.

c. Du _____ in einem kleinen Haus.

d. Meine Eltern _____ an der Küste.

e. Meine Großeltern _____ in Berlin.

f. Wo _____ du?

g. Warum _____ ihr nicht in Köln?

h. Ich _____ im Stadtzentrum.

wohnen	wohne	wohnt	wohnen
wohnst	wohnen	wohnst	wohnt

3. Translate into English

a. Ich arbeite immer im Büro.

b. Meine Eltern arbeiten in einer Schule.

c. Mein Bruder und ich arbeiten nicht.

d. Sie arbeitet auf einem Bauernhof.

e. Was arbeitest du?

f. Arbeitet ihr in einem Restaurant?

4. Cross out the wrong option

	A	B
Mein Bruder	arbeitet	arbeite
Mein Cousin	arbeitest	arbeitet
Meine Omas	arbeiten	arbeitest
Meine Tante	arbeitet	arbeite
Meine Tanten	arbeiten	arbeitet
Du und ich	arbeitest	arbeiten
Wir	arbeiten	arbeite
Ihr	arbeite	arbeitet
Mein Opa	arbeitest	arbeitet
Sie und er	arbeitet	arbeiten

5. Complete the verbs

a. Meine Mutter und ich wohn_ __ in Köln.

b. Sie arbeit_ __ als Krankenschwester.

c. Mein Vater wohn_ in Leipzig.

d. Er arbeit_ __ als Mechaniker in der Stadt.

e. Ihr arbeit_ __ nie!

f. Meine Großeltern wohn_ __ in einer Wohnung.

g. Wohn_ __ du in der Stadt oder auf dem Land?

h. Meine Freundin arbeit_ __ im Krankenhaus.

i. Du arbeit_ __ __ nicht!

6. Complete with the correct form of WOHNEN or ARBEITEN

a. Meine Oma _____ in einem Haus am Stadtrand. *My granny lives in a house in the suburbs.*

b. Sie _____ nicht mehr. *She doesn't work any more.*

c. Meine Tante und ihr Mann _____ in Hannover. *My aunt and her husband live in Hanover.*

d. Sie _____ als Ingenieure in einem Büro. *They work as engineers in an office.*

e. Meine große Schwester und ich _____ in München. *My big sister and I live in Munich.*

f. Wir _____ zusammen in einem Restaurant. *We work together in a restaurant.*

g. Du _____ in Berlin, richtig? *You live in Berlin, right?*

h. _____ du in einem Büro oder in einer Fabrik? *Do you work in an office or in a factory?*

i. Ich _____ in einem Theater. *I work in a theatre.*

Other verbs like WOHNEN

gehen	*to go*
frühstücken	*to eat for breakfast*
hören	*to listen to*
lieben	*to love*
lernen	*to learn*
kommen	*to come*
machen	*to make*
spielen	*to play*
üben	*to practise*
tanzen	*to dance*
trinken	*to drink*

7. Complete the sentences using the correct form of the verbs in the grey box on the left

a. Ich lieb____ meine Großeltern.   *I love my grandparents.*

b. Er komm____ aus der Schweiz.   *He comes from Switzerland.*

c. Wir hör____ immer Popmusik.   *We always listen to pop music.*

d. Das mach____ Sinn!   *That makes sense!*

e. Was frühstück____ du?   *What do you eat for breakfast?*

f. Meine Schwester üb____ Gitarre.   *My sister is practising the guitar.*

g. Meine Freunde und ich tanz____ Salsa.   *My friends and I dance salsa.*

h. Sie trink____ keinen Kaffee.   *They don't drink coffee.*

i. Herr Schuldirektor, spiel____ Sie Tennis?   *Headmaster, do you play tennis?*

j. Heute lern____ ihr Deutsch!   *Today, you are learning German!*

k. Wir geh____ ins Kino.   *We are going to the cinema.*

Unit 8a. Using FINDEN + ACCUSATIVE
to express an opinion on something/someone

Subject - Verb	Direct Object		Adjective	
ich finde *I find* **du findest** *you find*	**den Job** **meinen* Onkel** **ihn**	*the job* *my uncle* *him, it*	**super** **sehr gut**	*great* *very good*
er/sie/es findet *he/she/it finds*	**die Arbeit** **meine Tante** **sie**	*the work* *my auntie* *her, it*	**gut**	*good*
wir finden *we find* **ihr findet** *you guys find*	**das Büro** **mein Brüderchen** **es**	*the office* *my baby brother* *it*	**nicht so gut** **schlecht**	*not so good* *bad*
sie/Sie finden *they/you (formal) find*	**die Kollegen** **meine Freunde** **sie**	*the colleagues* *my friends* *them*	**furchtbar**	*terrible*

Author's notes:

(1) Using 'finden' to express an opinion is very common in German. Make sure you pronounce the letter 'i' in finden like the 'i' in the word 'bin'. (2) After 'ich finde', the noun phrase is in the accusative case. Can you recognize the words for 'a', 'the' and 'my' from Grammar Time 4? (3) If you want to talk about someone else's job, you will need these words: **mein** *[my],* **dein** *[your],* **sein** *[his, its],* **ihr** *[her, its],* **unser** *[our],* **euer** *[your plural],* **ihr** *[their]. These are called possessive articles. For all of them, use the same endings as the ones you have seen for "my".*

THE LANGUAGE GYM

Drills

1. Match up

ich finde es	you find it
sehr gut	we find it
schlecht	I find it
wir finden es	bad
furchtbar	terrible
du findest es	very good

2. Complete with the correct form of FINDEN

a. Ich _____ meinen Job super.

b. Er _____ seinen Job sehr nervig.

c. Meine Schwester _____ ihren Job prima.

d. Wir _____ unseren Job sehr gefährlich.

e. Wie _____ du deinen Job?

f. Wie _____ ihr eure Arbeit?

g. Mein Bruder _____ seine Arbeit klasse.

h. Meine Tante_____ ihre Arbeit okay.

i. Meine Eltern _____ meine Arbeit super.

3. Choose the correct article or pronoun

a. Ich finde **den/die/das** Job cool.

b. Er findet **den/die/das** Arbeit toll.

c. Ich finde **meinen/meine/mein** Onkel nett.

d. Er findet **ihn/sie/es** *(him)* nicht nett.

e. Er findet **seinen/seine/sein** Arbeit prima.

f. Meine Oma findet **ihren/ihre/ihr** Job okay.

g. Ich finde **meinen/meine/mein** Eltern nett.

h. Sie findet **ihren/ihre/ihr** Spinne cool.

i. Ich finde **ihn/sie/es** *(her)* gefährlich!

j. Ich finde **meinen/meine/mein** Hund cool.

k. Wie findest du **meinen/meine/mein** Auto?

l. Ich finde **ihn/sie/es** *(it)* total cool!

4. Spot the errors and rewrite (check verb + noun phrase, max 2 errors per sentence)

a. Ich findest die Job langweilig.

b. Ich finde meine Onkel cool.

c. Meine Mutter finde ihren Arbeit super.

d. Wie finde du deinen Job?

e. Ich finde meine Vater nett.

f. Wie finde ihr meine Hund?

g. Ich finden dein Hund sehr lustig.

h. Meine Schwester find sein Arbeit toll.

5. Translate into German

a. I find my work interesting.

b. I find my uncle very cool.

c. He finds his work terrible.

d. She finds her work exciting.

e. I find my auntie funny.

f. My father finds her annoying.

g. How do you find your colleagues?

h. I find them fantastic!

Grammar Time 6: SEIN (Part 2)
(Present tense of SEIN and more jobs)

Present tense of SEIN			Jobs (nouns)	
SINGULAR				
ich	*I*	**bin** *am*	**Biologe / Biologin**	*biologist*
			Botschafter /Botschafterin	*ambassador*
du	*you*	**bist** *are*	**Chefkoch / Chefköchin**	*head chef*
			Elektriker / Elektrikerin	*electrician*
			Feuerwehrmann / Feuerwehrfrau	*firefighter*
er	*he*		**Finanzberater / Finanzberaterin**	*financial advisor*
mein Bruder			**Fitnesstrainer / Fitnesstrainerin**	*gym instructor*
mein Onkel			**Musiker / Musikerin**	*musician*
			Pilot / Pilotin	*pilot*
		ist *is*	**Politiker / Politikerin**	*politician*
sie	*she*		**Staranwalt / Staranwältin**	*star lawyer*
meine Schwester			**Umweltaktivist / Umweltaktivistin**	*environmental activist*
meine Tante			**Wissenschaftler / Wissenschaftlerin**	*scientist*
			YouTube-Influencer / YouTube-Influencerin	
PLURAL				
wir	*we*		**Biologen / Biologinnen**	*biologist*
mein Freund und ich		**sind** *are*	**Botschafter /Botschafterinnen**	*ambassadors*
meine Freundin und ich			**Chefköche / Chefköchinnen**	*head chefs*
			Elektriker / Elektrikerinnen	*electricians*
ihr	*you guys*	**seid** *are*	**Feuerwehrleute**	*firefighters*
			Finanzberater / Finanzberaterinnen	*financial advisors*
			Fitnesstrainer / Fitnesstrainerinnen	*gym instructors*
sie	*they*		**Musiker / Musikerinnen**	*musicians*
meine Eltern			**Piloten / Pilotinnen**	*pilots*
meine Geschwister			**Politiker / Politikerinnen**	*politicians*
meine Freunde		**sind** *are*	**Staranwälte / Staranwältinnen**	*star lawyers*
			Umweltaktivisten / Umweltaktivistinnen	*environmental activists*
Sie	*You (formal)*		**Wissenschaftler / Wissenschaftlerinnen**	*scientists*
			YouTube-Influencer / YouTube-Influencerinnen	

Drills

1. Match

ich	sind
wir	bin
du	seid
ihr	bist
sie	ist
sie	sind

2. Complete with the missing forms of SEIN

a. Meine Mutter und ich _____ Ärztinnen.

b. Meine Brüder _____ Piloten.

c. Meine Schwester _____ Musikerin.

d. Meine Eltern und ich _____ Journalisten.

e._____ du Anwältin?

f. Nein, ich _____ Feuerwehrfrau.

g. Ihr _____ Wissenschaftlerinnen.

h. Wir _____ YouTube-Influencer.

i. Ihr _____ Fußballprofis, richtig?

j. Meine Onkel _____ Sänger in einer Band.

3. Translate into English

a. Wir sind Elektriker.

b. Sie sind Polizistinnen.

c. Bist du Schauspielerin?

d. Hansi ist Politiker.

e. Sie sind Chefköche.

f. Ich bin Polizist.

g. Seid ihr Krankenpfleger?

h. Wir sind Feuerwehrleute.

i. Mein Vater und ich sind Bäcker.

j. Seid ihr Lehrer?

k. Ich bin Koch.

4. Translate into German (easier)

a. My father is a doctor.

b. My parents are teachers.

c. My uncle is a lawyer.

d. I am a mechanic.

e. My cousins are engineers.

f. My aunt is a singer.

g. My friend Hansi is an actor.

5. Translate into German (harder)

a. My brother is tall and handsome. He is an actor.

b. My sister is very intelligent and always hard-working. She is a businesswoman.

c. My little brother is very sporty and active. He is a gym instructor.

d. My mother is very strong and hard-working. She is a doctor.

e. My father is very patient, calm and organized. He is an accountant.

UNIT 9
Comparing people's appearance and personality

Revision Quickie 2: Family / Pets / Jobs

In this unit you will learn how to say in German:
- More ... than
- As ... as / not as ... as ...
- New adjectives to describe people

You will revisit the following:
- Family members
- Pets
- Describing animals' appearance and character

Unit 9 - Comparing people

a. more...than

ich bin	**aktiv<u>er</u>**	*more active*	**als**	ich
du bist	**<u>ä</u>lt<u>er</u>**	*older*	*than*	du
er/sie/es ist	**<u>besser</u>**	*better*		er, sie, das/dieses
wir sind	**entspannt<u>er</u>**	*more relaxed*		wir *[us]*
ihr seid	**faul<u>er</u>**	*lazier*		ihr
sie/Sie sind	**fleißig<u>er</u>**	*more hard-working*		sie, Sie
	freundlich<u>er</u>	*friendlier*		
meine beste Freundin ist	**grö<u>ß</u><u>er</u>**	*taller*		meine beste Freundin
meine Freundin <u>Mia ist</u>	**großzügig<u>er</u>**	*more generous*		meine Freundin <u>Mia</u>
meine Katze ist	**hässlich<u>er</u>**	*uglier*		meine Katze
meine Cousine ist	**hübsch<u>er</u>**	*prettier*		meine Cousine
meine Mutter ist	**intelligent<u>er</u>**	*more intelligent*		meine Mutter
meine Schwester ist	**jüng<u>er</u>**	*younger*		meine Schwester
meine Tante ist				meine Tante
meine Tochter ist	**klein<u>er</u>**	*shorter*		meine Tochter
meine Oma ist	**langweilig<u>er</u>**	*more boring*		meine Oma
	laut<u>er</u>	*noisier*		
mein Bruder ist	**lustig<u>er</u>**	*funnier*		mein Bruder
mein Cousin ist	**nett<u>er</u>**	*nicer, kinder*		mein Cousin
mein bester Freund ist	**nervig<u>er</u>**	*more annoying*		mein bester Freund
mein Freund <u>Max ist</u>	**schlank<u>er</u>**	*slimmer*		mein Freund <u>Max</u>
mein Hund ist	**schlau<u>er</u>**	*smarter*		mein Hund
mein Opa ist				mein Opa
mein Onkel ist	**sportlich<u>er</u>**	*sportier*		mein Onkel
mein Pferd ist	**stärk<u>er</u>**	*stronger*		mein Pferd
mein Sohn ist	**streng<u>er</u>**	*stricter*		mein Sohn
mein Vater ist				mein Vater
meine Geschwister sind				meine Geschwister
meine Eltern sind				meine Eltern
meine Großeltern sind				meine Großeltern

b. as...as / not as...as (less...than)

ich bin	**genauso**	**aktiv**	*active*	**wie**	ich
du bist	*as*	**alt**	*old*	*as*	du
er/sie/es ist		**doof**	*stupid*		er, sie, das/dieses
wir sind		**ernst**	*serious*		wir *us*
ihr seid		**faul**	*lazy*		ihr
sie/Sie sind	**nicht so**	**groß**	*tall*		sie, Sie
	not as	**klein**	*short*		
		launisch	*moody*		
		nett	*nice, kind*		
		sportlich	*sporty*		
		stark	*strong*		
		zuverlässig	*reliable*		

Unit 9. Comparing people: VOCABULARY BUILDING

1. Complete with the missing word

a. Mein Vater ist größer _____ mein Onkel Dieter. *My father is taller than my uncle Dieter.*

b. Meine Mutter ist _____ ___ sportlich wie meine _____. *My mother is not as sporty as my aunt.*

c. Mein _____ ist kleiner als _____ Vater. *My grandfather is shorter than my father.*

d. Meine Cousins _____ fauler als _____. *My cousins are lazier than us.*

e. Mein Hund ist _____ als meine _____ . *My dog is more noisy than my cat.*

f. Meine Tante ist nicht so _____ wie _____ Mutter. *My aunt is not as pretty as my mother.*

g. Mein _____ ist _____ als ich. *My brother is more hard-working than me.*

h. Meine Eltern sind _____ als meine Großeltern. *My parents are kinder than my grandparents.*

i. Mein großer Bruder ist _____ groß _____ ich. *My brother is as tall as me.*

2. Translate into English

a. meine Cousinen
b. netter
c. mein Onkel
d. meine Großeltern
e. meine Tante
f. mein bester Freund
g. fleißig
h. meine Freundin
i. groß
j. älter
k. zuverlässiger
l. faul

3. Match German and English

fleißig	strong
gutaussehend	sporty
nett	old
stark	stupid
sportlich	good-looking
alt	hard-working
doof	kind

4. Spot and correct any English translation mistakes

a. Er ist älter als du. *He is taller than you.*

b. Sie ist genauso fleißig wie ich. *She is as good-looking as me.*

c. Er ist ruhiger als ich. *He is stronger than me.*

d. Ich bin nicht so pummelig wie er. *I am as chubby as him.*

e. Sie sind kleiner als ihr. *They are shorter than us.*

f. Ich bin genauso alt wie er. *She is as old as him.*

g. Du bist genauso sportlich wie ich. *You are more sporty than me.*

5. Complete with a suitable word

a. Meine Mutter ist älter als meine _____.

b. _____ Vater _____ jünger als mein Onkel.

c. Meine Eltern _____ genauso _____ wie meine Großeltern.

d. _____ Brüder _____ sportlicher als meine Cousins.

e. Mein _____ ist nicht so laut _____ meine Katze.

f. Meine Oma _____ genauso großzügig wie mein _____.

g. Meine Freundin ist _____ hübsch wie meine _____.

h. Mein Onkel ist _____ so stark _____ mein _____.

6. Match the opposites

gutaussehend	klein
fleißig	gemein
jung	hässlich
groß	pummelig
nett	unsportlich
großzügig	faul
sportlich	alt
schlank	geizig

Unit 9. Comparing people: READING

Hallo, ich heiße Laura. Ich bin neunzehn Jahre alt und ich wohne in Zürich in der Schweiz. In meiner Familie gibt es vier Personen: meine Eltern, meine beiden Brüder Luis und Oskar und mich. Luis ist größer, stärker und hübscher als Oskar, aber Oskar ist netter, schlauer und fleißiger als Luis.

Meine Eltern heißen Toni und Anna. Beide sind sehr nett, aber mein Vater ist strenger als meine Mutter. Außerdem ist meine Mutter geduldiger und nicht so stur wie mein Vater. Ich bin genauso stur wie er!

Zu Hause haben wir zwei Haustiere: einen Papagei und eine Katze. Beide sind total süß, aber mein Papagei ist lauter. Genauso laut wie ich.

Hey, na? Ich heiße Miriam und ich bin zwanzig Jahre alt und ich wohne in Salzburg in Österreich. Ich wohne mit meinen Eltern und mit meinen beiden Schwestern Julia und Vero. Julia ist viel hübscher als Vero, aber Vero ist viel netter.

Meine Eltern sind total lieb, aber mein Vater ist lustiger als meine Mutter. Außerdem ist er ein bisschen entspannter als sie. Genauso entspannt wie ich!

Zu Hause haben wir zwei Haustiere: einen Hund und ein Kaninchen. Beide sind ziemlich pummelig, aber mein Hund ist fauler. Genauso faul wie ich.

Hallo, ich heiße Jan. Ich bin fünfzehn Jahre alt und ich wohne in Mainz in Deutschland. In meiner Familie gibt es fünf Personen: meine Eltern, meine beiden Brüder Stefan und Max und mich. Stefan ist schlanker und sportlicher als Max, aber Max ist größer und stärker.

Meine Eltern heißen Carmen und Peter. Ich mag meine Mutter mehr als meinen Vater, weil sie nicht so streng ist wie er. Außerdem ist meine Mutter viel aktiver als mein Vater – genauso aktiv wie ich! Zu Hause haben wir zwei Haustiere: einen Wellensittich und ein Meerschweinchen. Beide sind sehr lieb, aber mein Wellensittich ist viel frecher. Genauso frech wie ich.

1. Find the German for the following in Laura's text

a. I live in

b. my parents

c. prettier

d. more hard-working

e. both are

f. very nice

g. furthermore

h. not so stubborn

i. two pets

j. super-sweet

k. as loud as

l. at home we have

2. Complete the statements below based on Miriam's text

a. I am _____ years old.

b. Julia is a lot _____ than Vero.

c. Vero is a lot _____.

d. My parents are really _____.

e. I am as _____ as my father.

f. We have _____ pets.

g. Both are quite _____.

h. My dog is _____ than my rabbit.

i. I live in _____ (country).

3. Correct any of the statements below [about Jan's text] which are incorrect

a. Jan hat drei Haustiere.

b. Stefan ist nicht so pummelig wie Max.

c. Max ist nicht so klein wie Stefan.

d. Jan ist genauso frech wie sein Meerschweinchen.

e. Jan mag seinen Vater mehr als seine Mutter.

f. Jan ist aktiver als seine Mutter.

4. Answer the questions on the three texts above

a. Where does Jan live?

b. Who is stricter, his mother or his father?

c. Who is as loud as their parrot?

d. Who is as lazy as their dog?

e. Who has a stubborn father?

f. Who has a rabbit?

g. Who has a guinea pig?

h. Which one of Jan's brothers is sportier?

i. What are the differences between Jan's brothers?

 THE LANGUAGE GYM

Unit 9. Comparing people: TRANSLATION/WRITING

1. Translate into English

a. groß

b. schlank

c. klein

d. nervig

e. intelligent

f. stur

g. lustig

h. nicht so ... wie

i. ernst

j. größer als

k. nicht so fleißig

l. genauso ... wie

m. zuverlässig

n. netter als

2. Gapped sentences

a. Meine _____ ist _____ als mein _____.
My granny is taller than my grandad.

b. _____ Vater _____ nicht so _____ wie mein großer Bruder.
My father not as strong as my big brother.

c. Meine _____ sind _____ als wir.
My cousins are sportier than us.

d. _____ Schwester ist _____ als _____.
My sister is more hard-working than me.

e. Meine Mutter ist _____ nett _____ mein Vater.
My mother is as kind as my father.

f. Mein _____ ist viel _____ als _____.
My uncle is a lot more talkative than us.

g. Meine _____ ist nicht so _____ _____ ich.
My girlfriend is not as serious as me.

h. Mein _____ ist _____ ____ meine kleine _____.
My parrot is cheekier than my little sister.

3. Phrase-level translation [En to Ger]

a. my mother is

b. taller than

c. as slim as

d. not as stubborn as

e. I am shorter than

f. my parents are

g. my cousins are

h. as chubby as

i. they are as strong as

j. my grandparents are

k. I am as lazy as

4. Sentence-level translation [En to Ger]

a. My big sister is nicer than my little sister.

b. My father is as stubborn as my mother.

c. My girlfriend is more hard-working than me.

d. I am not as intelligent as my brother.

e. My best friend is stronger and sportier than me.

f. My boyfriend is not as pretty as me.

g. My cousins are uglier than we.

h. My budgie is noisier than my cat.

i. My turtle is funnier than my dog.

j. My rabbit is not as fat as my guinea pig.

Revision Quickie 2 : Family, Pets and Jobs

1. Match

Lehrerin	doctor
Anwältin	cook
Krankenpfleger	actor
Koch	nurse
Arzt	IT worker
Flugbegleiterin	flight attendant
Feuerwehrleute	lawyer
Informatiker	firefighters
Schauspielerin	teacher

2. Sort the words listed below in the categories in the table

a. Ingenieur; b. groß; c. Mechaniker; d. lustig; e. klein; f. Cousin;
g. Lehrer; h. Arzt; i. Onkel; j. Vater ; k. blau; l. schlank; m. Katze;
n. Architektin; o. Mutter; p. Bruder; q. Kaninchen; r. braun;
s. Schlange; t. hübsch

Beschreibungen [descriptions]	Tiere	Berufe	Familie

3. Complete with the missing adjectives

a. Mein Bruder ist _____ *chubby.*

b. Meine Schwester ist _____ *tall.*

c. Mein Onkel ist _____ *short.*

d. Meine Freundin ist _____ *pretty.*

e. Mein Opa ist _____ *annoying.*

f. Mein Sportlehrer ist _____ *boring.*

4. Complete with the missing nouns

a. Meine Mutter arbeitet als _____ *lawyer.*

b. Meine Tante ist _____ *nurse.*

c. Mein bester Freund ist _____ *journalist.*

d. Meine Cousine ist _____ *hairdresser.*

e. Mein Cousin ist _____ *student.*

f. Ich arbeite als _____ *doctor.*

g. Dieter arbeitet als _____ *financial advisor.*

h. Meine Oma ist _____ *singer.*

5. Match the opposites

groß	fleißig
hübsch	dumm
pummelig	klein
faul	ruhig
intelligent	hässlich
laut	ungeduldig
gemein	schlank
geduldig	nett

6. Complete the numbers below

a. vierz__ _ _   14

b. vier__ _ _   40

c. sech__ _ _   60

d. sieb__ _ _ _   17

e. einundz__ _ _ _ _ _   21

f. drei__ _ _   30   *tip: no „z"!*

7. Complete with the correct verb

a. Meine Mutter _____ sehr groß.
My mother is very tall.

b. Ich _____ schwarze Haare.
I have black hair.

c. Ich _____ als Klempner.
I work as a plumber.

d. Mein Vater _____ 40 Jahre alt.
My father is 40.

e. Wie viele Personen _____ es in deiner Familie?
How many people are there in your family?

f. Meine Brüder _____ groß.
My brothers are tall.

g. Mein Opa _____ nicht mehr.
My grandad doesn't work any more.

h. Meine Freundin _____ Mia.
My friend is called Mia.

UNIT 10
Saying what's in my school bag / classroom/ describing colour

Grammar Time 7: HABEN + indefinite article + noun

Grammar Time 8: HABEN + indefinite article + adjective + noun

In this unit will learn how to say:

- What objects you have in your school bag/pencil case/classroom
- Words for classroom equipment
- What you have and don't have
- The indefinite article "einen/eine/ein" with an adjective and a noun after "ich habe" *[I have]* and "es gibt" *[there is/are]*

You will revisit the following:

- Colours
- Introducing yourself (e.g. name, age, town, country)
- Pets

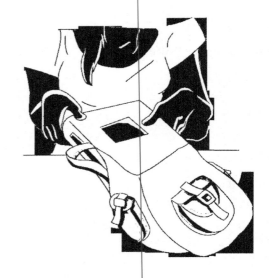

Ich bin ein Pinguin

UNIT 10.
Saying what's in my school bag/ classroom/describing colour

In meiner Tasche habe ich *In my bag, I have*	**einen** *a* **keinen** *no*	**Bleistift** **Computer** **Filzstift** **Füller** **Kalender** **Klebstift** **Kuli** **Spitzer** **Stuhl** **Taschenrechner** **Tisch**	*pencil* *computer* *felt tip pen* *fountain pen* *calendar* *glue stick* *pen* *pencil sharpener* *chair* *calculator* *table*	**Er ist** *It is*	**alt** **groß** **hässlich** **kaputt** **klein** **neu** **praktisch** **schmutzig**	*old* *big* *ugly* *broken* *small* *new* *practical* *dirty*
In meiner Klasse gibt es *In my class, there is/are*	**eine** *a* **keine** *no*	**Brotdose** **Schere** **Tafel** **Wasserflasche**	*a lunch box* *scissors* *whiteboard* *water bottle*	**Sie ist** *It is*	**sauber** **schön** **schwarz** **weiß**	*clean* *beautiful* *black* *white*
Ich habe auch *I also have* **Ich brauche** *I need*	**ein** *a* **kein** *no*	**Blatt Papier** **Buch** **Federmäppchen** **Heft** **Lineal** **Radiergummi** **Wörterbuch**	*sheet of paper* *book* *pencil case* *exercise book* *ruler* *rubber* *dictionary*	**Es ist** *It is*	**rot** **blau** **grün** **gelb** **lila** **rosa** **braun** **grau** **orange**	*red* *blue* *green* *yellow* *purple* *pink* *brown* *grey* *orange*
Mein Freund Max hat *My friend Max has* **Mein Freund Max braucht** *My friend Max needs*	**ein paar** *a few* **viele** *many* **keine** *no*	**Bleistifte** **Kulis** **Hefte** **Scheren** **Stühle** **Taschenrechner** **Tische** **Wörterbücher**	*pencils* *pens* *exercise books* *scissors* *chairs* *calculators* *tables* *dictionaries*	**Sie sind** *They are*	**hellblau** *light blue* **dunkelblau** *dark blue*	

 THE LANGUAGE GYM

Unit 10. Saying what's in my school bag: VOCABULARY BUILDING

1. Match up

Ich habe ...	a rubber
ein Radiergummi	a calendar
einen Kalender	I have ...
einen Kuli	no chair
einen Bleistift	no lunch box
eine Schere	a pen
kein Lineal	no ruler
keinen Stuhl	I need
ich brauche	a pencil
keine Brotdose	scissors

2. Add the missing letter

a. ich hab_   e. ein He_t

b. einen S_itzer   f. mein Fre_nd

c. ich brau_he   g. ke_ne Schere

d. einen Bl_istift h. eine Ta_el

3. Complete with the missing word

a. In meiner Schultasche habe ich ein _____.
In my school bag I have an exercise book.

b. Ich brauche ein _____.
I need a rubber.

c. Ich habe _____ Kuli.
I don't have a pen.

d. Mein Freund _____ ein Blatt Papier.
My friend has a paper.

e. Ich _____ einen Taschenrechner.
I have a calculator.

f. Ich brauche einen _____.
I need a chair.

g. Ich habe kein _____.
I don't have a ruler.

h. Mein Freund hat _____ Schere.
My friend doesn't have scissors.

4. Translate into English

a. Ich habe keine Schere.

b. Es gibt viele Tische.

c. Ich habe kein Heft.

d. Sie hat einen Bleistift.

e. Ich habe ein Radiergummi.

f. Ich brauche einen Kalender.

g. Mein Freund hat ein Wörterbuch.

h. Ich habe keinen Taschenrechner.

5. Anagrams

a. ftBlstiei *Bleistift*

b. iuKl

c. warschz

d. ürgn

e. ereSch

f. sackRuck

g. stlebKift

h. fteH

6. Broken words

a. I_ m_____ T_____ h_____ i___ e____ F_____.
In my bag I have a pencil case.

b. I____ h_____ a_____ e____ L_____.
I also have a ruler.

c. I____ h_____ k_____ R_____.
I don't have a rubber.

d. I___ b_____ e_____ S_____.
I need a pencil sharpener.

e. E____ g_____ e_____ T_____.
There is a whiteboard.

f. M_____ F_____ Max h_____ e____ W_____.
My friend Max has a dictionary.

g. I___ b_____ e_____ F_____.
I need a felt tip pen.

7. Complete with a suitable word

a. Ich habe ein _____.

b. Ich _____ einen Kuli.

c. _____ ist meine Lieblingsfarbe.

d. Ich habe keine _____.

e. Die Tasche ist _____.

f. Mein Kuli ist _____.

g. Meine _____ ist schön.

h. Meine _____ hat eine Brotdose.

i. Mein _____ hat kein Heft.

j. Die _____ sind rot.

k. Es gibt _____ Tafel.

Unit 10. Saying what's in my school bag: READING

Ich heiße Lisa. Ich bin zwölf Jahre alt und ich wohne in Luzern, in der Schweiz. In meiner Familie gibt es vier Personen. Ich habe auch eine weiße Katze! In meiner Tasche habe ich einen blauen Kuli, ein gelbes Heft, ein rotes Lineal und ein cooles weißes Radiergummi. Ich liebe mein Radiergummi! Meine Freundin Anne hat nur einen Bleistift in ihrer Tasche. Aber zu Hause hat sie ein graues Pferd, stell dir vor!

Ich heiße Peter. Ich bin fünfzehn Jahre alt und ich wohne in Innsbruck, in Österreich. In meiner Familie gibt es drei Personen. Ich habe ein sehr lustiges Meerschweinchen. In meiner Klasse gibt es viel: eine Tafel, einen Computer und dreißig Tische. Meine Klasse ist ziemlich groß. In meiner Tasche habe ich einen blauen Bleistift, ein gelbes Lineal, einen blauen Spitzer und ein weißes Radiergummi. Mein Freund Martin hat viele bunte Filzstifte.

Ich heiße Deniz. Ich bin achtzehn Jahre alt und ich wohne in Köln, im Westen von Deutschland. In meiner Familie gibt es fünf Personen. Mein Bruder heißt Ahmet. In meiner Klasse gibt es eine Tafel und zwanzig Tische. Es gibt auch zwanzig Stühle, für jede Person einen! Meine Klasse ist schön und mein Lehrer ist sehr lustig. Aber ich habe keinen Bleistift, kein Lineal und ich habe auch kein Radiergummi. Ich habe nichts und ich brauche alles! Das ist ein großes Problem! Zu Hause habe ich ein lustiges weißes Kaninchen.

Ich heiße Paul. Ich bin dreizehn Jahre alt und ich wohne in Stuttgart. In meiner Familie gibt es vier Personen. Ich liebe meine Mutter, aber ich mag meinen Vater nicht. Er ist immer gemein zu mir! Er ist Anwalt. In meiner Klasse gibt es nicht viel. Es gibt keine Tafel und es gibt auch keinen Computer. Es gibt achtundzwanzig Tische, aber nur siebenundzwanzig Stühle. Das ist ein Problem! Ich habe einen Bleistift, einen Taschenrechner und einen Kalender in meiner Tasche.

1. Find the German for the following in Lisa's text

a. I am 12 years old

b. I live in Lucerne

c. in my family there are

d. in my bag I have

e. a yellow exercise book

f. a red ruler

g. I love

h. my friend only has

i. in her bag

j. a grey horse

2. Find someone who: which person …

a. … has a blue pencil?

b. … has most tables in their class?

c. … has a class with one student always standing?

d. … has no school equipment?

e. … has a big pet?

f. … doesn't like their dad?

3. Answer the following questions about Deniz' text

a. Where does Deniz live?

b. Who is Ahmet?

c. How many tables and chairs are there in her class?

d. How does she describe her class?

e. What school equipment does she have?

f. What pet does she have?

g. How does she describe her pet?

4. Fill in the missing words

Ich h_____ Jens. Ich bin acht J_____ alt und ich wo_____ in Bern, in der Schweiz. In meiner Familie gi_____ es vier Personen. In meiner Kl_____ gibt es viele Sachen: einen Co_____, eine Taf_____ und viele Wö_____. In meiner Ta_____ habe ich einen Bl_____, einen ro_____ Kuli und ein Ra_____. Meine F_____ Marie hat viele Sac_____, aber sie hat kein L_____. Ich mag meinen Lehr_____, denn er ist sehr n_____ . Zu Hause habe ich e_____ grüne Schlange!

5. Fill in the table below

Name	Peter	Paul
Age		
City		
Items in bag		

Unit 10. Saying what's in my school bag: TRANSLATION

1. Bad translation: spot and correct [in the English] any translation mistakes you find below

a. In meiner Klasse gibt es zwei Tafeln und einen Computer. Ich mag meinen Lehrer nicht.
In my class there is a whiteboard and a computer. I like my teacher.

b. In meinem Federmäppchen habe ich einen grünen Bleistift, ein rotes Heft, aber kein Lineal.
In my pencil case, I have a red pencil, a green exercise book, but no rubber.

c. Mein Freund Dieter hat vier Personen in seiner Familie. Er braucht einen roten Kuli und einen Kalender.
My friend Dieter has five people in his family. He needs a black pen and a calendar.

d. Ich brauche ein Heft und einen Klebstift. Ich habe kein Lineal und keinen Kuli. Ich liebe meinen Lehrer!
I need paper and a rubber. I don't have a ruler or a pencil. I hate my teacher!

e. In meiner Klasse gibt es dreißig Stühle und dreißig Tische. Ich habe schon ein Wörterbuch, aber ich brauche einen Taschenrechner.
In my class there are thirty cats and thirty chairs. I already have a pen, but I need a calculator.

2. Translate into English

a. ich brauche

b. Ich habe einen roten Bleistift.

c. Ich habe einen blauen Kuli.

d. Ich habe ein grünes Lineal.

e. Ich habe einen Hund zu Hause.

f. Mein Freund hat ein Buch.

g. in meinem Federmäppchen

h. Ich mag meinen Lehrer.

i. Ich habe gelbe Bleistifte.

j. eine große Tafel

k. Ich habe viele Sachen.

l. Ich habe keinen Spitzer.

m. Ich brauche ein Wörterbuch.

3. Phrase-level translation [En to Ger]

a. I have ...

b. ... a red exercise book

c. ... a blue pencil

d. I need

e. I like

f. there are

g. thirty chairs

h. my friend has

4. Sentence-level translation [En to Ger]

a. There are 20 tables.

b. There is a whiteboard.

c. My teacher is nice.

d. I have a few blue pens.

e. I have many green pencils.

f. I need a rubber and a sharpener.

g. I need a chair and a book.

h. My class is very big and pretty.

i. My father is a teacher.

 THE LANGUAGE GYM

Unit 10. Saying what's in my school bag: WRITING

1. Split sentences

Ich habe eine	meinen Lehrer.
Ich habe keinen	rote Schere.
Meine Klasse	ich viele Sachen.
Es gibt dreißig	Taschenrechner.
Mein Freund braucht ein	ist sehr groß.
Ich mag	rotes Heft.
In meiner Tasche habe	Stühle.

2. Rewrite the sentences in the correct order [note: start each sentence with the underlined word]

a. <u>ich</u> einen Taschenrechner brauche

b. <u>ich</u> einen habe Lineal ein und Kuli

c. Klasse groß sehr ist <u>meine</u>

d. <u>mein</u> Freund ein Lineal weißes hat

e. <u>ich</u> keinen blauen habe Kalender

f. habe ich <u>zu</u> Hause Schildkröte eine

g. Vater ist <u>mein</u> Arzt und er arbeitet Krankenhaus in einem

3. Spot and correct the grammar and spelling [note: in several cases a word is missing]

a. In meiner Klasse gibt zwanzig Stühle.

b. Ich habe schwarzen Taschenrechner.

c. In mein Tasche habe ich nicht viele Sachen.

d. Mein Freund braucht ein rote Schere.

e. Ich braucht ein Heft und einen Kuli.

f. Mein Freund Mario hat viele bunte Filzstift.

g. Meine Mutter ist Mechaniker und sie arbeitet in der Stadt.

h. Ich bin sehr groß. Ich habe blond Haare und grüne Augen.

4. Anagrams

a. ieBlftist   *Bleistift*

b. felaT

c. iKul

d. chiTse

e. schTaenchnerre

f. rellüF

g. neLail

6. Describe this person in German:

Name:
Thomas

Pet:
A black rabbit

Hair/eyes:
brown hair + blue eyes

School equipment:
has pen, pencil, ruler, rubber, lunch box

Does not have:
sharpener, paper, chair

Favourite colour:
red

5. Guided writing – write 3 short paragraphs describing the people below using the details in the box [I]

Person	Lives	Has	Hasn't	Needs
Natalie	Bern	exercise book	pen	calendar
Anton	Graz	ruler	pencil	a piece of paper
Julia	Hamburg	felt tip pens	sharpener	a glue stick

Grammar Time 7:

HABEN + indefinite article + noun

Subject-Verb	Article	Noun	
ich habe *I have*	**einen** *a* **keinen** *no*	MASCULINE NOUNS (der …) **Bruder, Cousin, Onkel, Vater, …** **Bär, Hund, Hamster, Papagei, Tiger, …** **Bleistift, Kalender, Kuli, Taschenrechner, …** **Computer, Fernseher, Fußball, Laptop, …**	
du hast *you have* **er/sie/es hat** *he/she/it has*	**eine** **keine**	FEMININE NOUNS (die …) **Schwester, Cousine, Tante, Mutter, …** **Brotdose, Schere, Tasche, Wasserflasche, …** **Katze, Maus, Schildkröte, Schlange, …** **Gitarre, Trompete, PlayStation, Xbox, …**	
wir haben *we have* **ihr habt** *you guys have* **sie/Sie haben** *they/you (formal)* *have*	**ein** **kein**	NEUTER NOUNS (das …) **Brüderchen, Schwesterchen, Tantchen, …** **Blatt Paper, Buch, Heft, Lineal, …** **Haustier, Meerschweinchen, Pferd, Schaf, …** **Auto, Fahrrad, Smartphone, Souvenir, …**	
	viele *many* **keine**	PLURAL NOUNS (die …) **Geschwister, Eltern, Freunde, Großeltern, …** **Bücher, Hefte, Stifte, Tische, Stühle, …** **Haustiere, Kaninchen, Hunde, Katzen, …** **blonde Haare, blaue Augen, Sommersprossen, …**	

Present tense of HABEN + indefinite article: Drills (1)

1. Match up

ich habe	we have
wir haben	I have
du hast	they have
er/sie hat	you have
ihr habt	he/she has
sie haben	you guys have

2. Complete with the missing form of HABEN

a. Ich _____ keine Haustiere.   *I don't have any pets.*

b. Wir _____ eine graue Katze.   *We have a grey cat.*

c. Sie _____ zwei Schildkröten.   *They have two turtles.*

d. _____ du Geschwister?   *Do you have siblings?*

e. _____ ihr Haustiere?   *Do you guys have pets?*

f. Er _____ ein Meerschweinchen.   *He has a guinea pig.*

g. Oma _____ keine Haustiere.   *Nan doesn't have pets.*

h. Wir _____ keine Haustiere.   *We have no pets.*

3. Complete with the present tense form of HABEN

ich   _____

du   _____

er, sie, es   _____

wir   _____

ihr   _____

sie, Sie   _____

4. Add the correct form of HABEN

a. Meine Brüder _____ einen Hamster.

b. Mein Onkel _____ einen Papagei.

c. Ich _____ ein Buch.

d. _____ du ein Pferd?

e. _____ ihr Fische zu Hause?

f. Meine Eltern _____ eine Schlange, stell dir vor!

g. Ich _____ eine süße Katze.

h. Er _____ eine kleine Schwester.

5. Complete with the missing form of HABEN

a. Mein Bruder _____ blaue Augen.

b. Meine Mutter _____ lange blonde Haare.

c. Meine Eltern _____ braune Augen.

d. Mein Onkel Paul _____ keine Haare.

e. _____ du blaue oder braune Augen?

f. Ihr _____ sehr schöne Haare!

g. Ich _____ leider kein Haustier, aber mein

Bruder _____ ein Meerschweinchen.

6. Translate into German

a. My father has blue eyes.

b. I don't have any pets.

c. I don't have a brother.

d. In my pencil case I have a ruler.

e. Do you have any pens?

f. I have a dog at home.

g. My mother has blonde hair.

h. My father is 38.

i. How old are you?

Present tense of HABEN + indefinite article: Drills (2)

7. Translate the pronoun and verb into German as shown in the example

I have	*Ich habe*

You have

She has

He has

It has

We have

You guys have

They have

8. einen, eine, or ein?

a. Wir haben _____ Papagei (m).

b. Ich habe _____ Heft (n).

c. Mein Bruder hat _____ Katze (f).

d. Ich hätte gern _____ Kalender (m).

e. Wir haben _____ Schildkröte (f).

f. Ich habe _____ Haustiere. (pl)   *I have no pets.*

g. Hast du _____ Bruder oder eine Schwester?

9. Translate into German. Topic: family members

a. I don't have an uncle.

b. We have two brothers.

c. My mother has no sisters.

d. Do you have any grandparents?

e. Do you guys have any friends?

f. I don't have a brother.

10. Translate into German. Topic: Pets

a. I have a turtle.

b. We have a horse.

c. He has two dogs.

d. They have five fish.

e. Do you have a rabbit?

f. My mother has a frog.

11. Translate into German. Topic: Hair and eyes

a. I have black hair.

b. We have blue eyes.

c. She has curly hair.

d. My mother has blonde hair.

e. Do you have grey eyes?

f. They have green eyes.

g. My brother has brown eyes.

h. We have no hair.

i. You guys have beautiful eyes.

j. My parents have red hair.

k. You have no hair.

l. My sister has very long hair.

Grammar Time 8:
HABEN + indefinite article + adjective + noun

Subject-Verb	Direct object (Noun phrase in accusative case)				
	a/no	**adjective + ending**		**noun**	
ich habe *I have*	**einen** *a* **keinen** *no*	alt- groß- hässlich- kaputt- klein- neu-	old big ugly broken small new	**-en**	**Bleistift** pencil **Computer** computer **Filzstift** felt tip pen **Füller** fountain pen **Kalender** calendar **Klebstift** glue stick **Kuli** pen **Spitzer** pencil sharpener **Taschenrechner** calculator
du hast *You have* **er/sie/es hat** *he/she/it has*	**eine** *a* **keine** *no*	praktisch- schmutzig- sauber- schön-	practical dirty clean beautiful	**-e**	**Brotdose** a lunch box **Schere** scissors **Schultasche** school bag **Tafel** whiteboard **Wasserflasche** water bottle
wir haben *we have* **ihr habt** *you guys have*	**ein** *a* **kein** *no*	braun- blau- gelb- golden- grau- grün- orang- schwarz-	brown blue yellow golden grey green orange black	**-es**	**Blatt Papier** sheet of paper **Buch** book **Federmäppchen** pencil case **Heft** exercise book **Lineal** ruler **Radiergummi** rubber **Wörterbuch** dictionary
sie/Sie haben *they/you (formal) have*	**viele** *many*	rot- weiß-	red white	**-e**	**Bleistifte** pencils **Kulis** pens **Hefte** exercise books **Scheren** scissors **Stühle** chairs **Taschenrechner** calculators **Tische** tables **Wörterbücher** dictionaries
	keine *no*	hellblau- dunkelblau-	light blue dark blue	**-en**	

Drills

1. Complete the table

Deutsch	English
alt	
	dirty
	green
praktisch	
schön	
	brown
	light blue
kaputt	
	red

2. Translate into English

a. Ich habe einen neuen Füller.

b. Ich habe eine blaue Brotdose.

c. Mein Freund hat ein grünes Heft.

d. Ich habe kein Lineal.

e. Wir haben viele neue Wörterbücher.

f. Ich hätte gern ein neues Federmäppchen.

g. Ich habe keine schöne Wasserflasche.

h. Du hast eine alte Schere.

i. Sie hat ein neues Radiergummi.

j. Es gibt schmutzige Tische.

3. Provide the correct adjective ending

Ich habe …

a. einen schön__ Filzstift.

b. eine neu__ Schere.

c. rot__ Kulis.

d. keinen sauber__ Stuhl.

e. ein grün__ Heft.

f. hellblau__ Bleistifte.

g. keine kaputt__ Stühle.

h. neu__ Tische.

i. einen hässlich__ Füller.

4. Complete with the missing adjective

a. Ich habe eine _____ Schultasche. *I have a red school bag.*

b. Ich habe einen _____ Kuli. *I have a broken pen.*

c. Ich habe einen _____ Füller. *I have a new fountain pen.*

d. Ich habe ein _____ Lineal. *I have a yellow ruler.*

e. Ich habe ein _____ Papier. *I have a white sheet of paper.*

f. Ich habe zwei _____ Scheren. *I have two red scissors.*

g. Ich habe _____ Stifte. *I have blue pens.*

h. Ich habe eine _____ Tasche. *I have a black school bag.*

5. Translate into German

a. I have…

b. a black ruler

c. a green school bag

d. a yellow pencil case

e. two green rulers

f. two blue scissors

g. two white exercise books.

6. Translate into German

a. I have a red pen and a blue fountain pen.

b. Paul has a green school bag.

c. Do you have a white pencil case?

d. Do you guys have any red markers (=*Textmarker*)?

e. I need a pink sheet of paper.

f. We have a yellow exercise book.

g. He has a black and white ruler.

 **THE LANGUAGE GYM**

UNIT 11 (Part 1)
Talking about food:
Likes / Dislikes / Reasons

Grammar Time 9: ESSEN & TRINKEN + gern/lieber/am liebsten

In this unit you will learn how to say:

- What food you like/dislike eating and to what extent
- Why you like/dislike it
- New adjectives
- The present tense of 'essen' *[to eat]* and 'trinken' *[to drink]*
- 'gern', 'lieber', 'am liebsten' to say what you like, prefer, and most like eating

You will revisit the following

- Time markers
- Providing a justification

UNIT 11: Talking about food
Likes / Dislikes / Reasons (Part 1)

Ich esse gern *I like eating*	**Äpfel**	*apples*	**denn es ist ...** *because it is ...*	**ekelhaft**	*disgusting*
	Bananen	*bananas*		**erfrischend**	*refreshing*
Ich esse nicht gern *I don't like eating*	**Brot**	*bread*	**weil es ... ist.** *because it is ...*	**fettig**	*oily, greasy*
	Eier	*eggs*		**geschmackvoll**	*full of taste*
Ich esse lieber *I prefer eating*	**Erdbeeren**	*strawberries*	**Ich finde es ...** *I find it ...*	**langweilig**	*boring*
	Fisch	*fish*		**gesund**	*healthy*
Ich esse am liebsten *I most like eating*	**Fleisch**	*meat*		**lecker**	*tasty*
	Gemüse	*vegetables*		**nahrhaft**	*nutritious*
	Hamburger	*burgers*		**salzig**	*salty*
	Hähnchen	*chicken*		**scharf**	*spicy*
	Honig	*honey*		**süß**	*sweet*
	Käse	*cheese*		**ungesund**	*unhealthy*
	Kartoffeln	*potatoes*		**zäh**	*tough*
	Krabben	*prawns*			
	Nudeln	*pasta*		**reich an ...**	*rich in ...*
	Obst	*fruit*			
	Reis	*rice*		**... Mineralstoffen**	*... minerals*
	Salat	*salad*		**... Proteinen**	*... proteins*
	Schokolade	*chocolate*		**... Vitaminen**	*... vitamins*
	Süßigkeiten	*sweets*			
	Tomaten	*tomatoes*			
Ich trinke gern *I like drinking*	**Cola**	*cola*			
	Kaffee	*coffee*			
Ich trinke nicht gern *I don't like drinking*	**Kakao**	*cocoa*			
	Milch	*milk*			
Ich trinke am liebsten *I most like drinking*	**Saft**	*juice*			
	Tee	*tea*			
Ich trinke lieber *I prefer drinking*	**Wasser**	*water*			

☺ **Es schmeckt mir (gut)!** *It tastes good!* / ☹ **Es schmeckt mir nicht (gut).** *It doesn't taste good.*

Note: "es" here refers to the action of eating/drinking in general. All actions are neuter when expressed as a noun.

 **THE LANGUAGE GYM**

Unit 11. Talking about food (Part 1): VOCABULARY BUILDING (Part 1)

1. Match up

Erdbeeren	eggs
Fleisch	apples
Gemüse	prawns
Hähnchen	milk
Wasser	fruit
Milch	water
Eier	burgers
Krabben	chicken
Hamburger	meat
Obst	strawberries
Äpfel	vegetables

2. Complete

a. Ich esse gern _____.   *I like eating chicken.*

b. Ich esse lieber _____.   *I prefer eating prawns.*

c. Ich esse nicht gern _____.   *I don't like eating apples.*

d. Ich trinke am liebsten _____.   *I like most drinking milk.*

e. Ich trinke lieber _____.   *I prefer drinking coffee.*

f. Ich _____ gern Wasser.   *I like drinking water.*

g. Ich _____ nicht gern Tomaten.   *I don't like eating tomatoes.*

h. Ich hasse _____.   *I hate juice.*

i. Ich mag _____ nicht.   *I don't like fruit.*

j. Ich liebe _____.   *I love eggs.*

3. Translate into English

a. Ich esse gern Obst.

b. Ich esse nicht gern Eier.

c. Ich esse am liebsten Erbsen.

d. Ich mag Hamburger.

e. Ich mag Fleisch nicht.

f. Ich esse lieber Orangen.

g. Ich esse nicht gern Tomaten.

h. Kaffee schmeckt mir nicht.

4. Complete the words

a. Ei_____

b. Bana_____

c. Erb_____

d. Gem_____

e. Hamb_____

f. Kr_____

g. Äp_____

h. Wa_____

5. Broken words

a. I__ e_____ g_____ N_____.   *I like eating pasta.*

b. I__ t_____ g_____ W_____.   *I like drinking water.*

c. I__ e_____ n_____ g_____ F_____.   *I don't like eating meat.*

d. I__ m_____ S_____.   *I like chocolate.*

e. I__ e_____ a___ l_____ G_____.   *I most like eating vegetables.*

f. I__ e_____ g_____ Ä_____.   *I like eating apples.*

g. I__ f_____ M_____ l_____.   *I find milk tasty.*

h. I__ l_____ K_____.   *I love potatoes.*

6. Translate into German

a. I like eating eggs.

b. I prefer eating oranges.

c. I really like eating vegetables.

d. I don't like eating meat.

e. I like fruit.

f. I don't like vegetables.

g. I hate milk.

Unit 11. Talking about food (Part 1): VOCABULARY BUILDING (Part 2)

1. Complete with the missing words. The initial letter of each word is given

a. Ich finde Bananen sehr l_____.
I find bananas very tasty.

b. Ich f_____ Äpfel sehr e_____.
I find apples very refreshing.

c. Ich finde Hähnchen e_____.
I find chicken disgusting.

d. Ich mag F_____ gar nicht.
I don't like meat at all.

e. Ich trinke lieber K_____ als T____.
I prefer drinking coffee to tea.

f. Hamburger sind u_____.
Burgers are unhealthy.

g. Salat ist ziemlich g_____.
Salad is quite healthy.

h. Ich esse keinen R_____.
I eat no rice.

i. Ich esse am liebsten K_____.
I most like eating cake.

j. Ich trinke gern K_____, weil es süß ist.
I like drinking cocoa (hot chocolate), because it is sweet.

2. Complete the table

Deutsch	English
Milch	
	chicken
Gemüse	
Eier	
	tea
	bread
Kartoffeln	
Reis	
	pasta

3. Anagrams

a. pfÄle	g. sseWar
b. iMlhc	h. eTe
c. beerErden	i. ftaS
d. trBo	j. hnHächne
e. meGüse	k. sRie
f. delNun	l. ffartKlneo

4. Broken words

a. I____ e_____ a_ l_____ E_____. *I like most eating eggs.*

b. I____ e_____ l_____ S_____. *I prefer eating salad.*

c. I____ l_____ K_____. *I love potatoes.*

d. R_____ i____ s_____ g_____. *Rice is very healthy.*

e. I____ f_____ K_____ u_____. *I find coffee unhealthy.*

f. F_____ i___ l_____. *fish is tasty.*

g. Indisches Essen i___ s_____. *Indian food is spicy.*

h. S_____ i___ s____. *Chocolate is sweet.*

5. Complete each sentence with a suitable word

a. _____ sind nicht gesund.

b. Kaffee ist sehr _____.

c. Ich mag _____ nicht.

d. Ich liebe _____ und _____.

e. Meine Mutter isst gern _____.

f. Ich esse nicht gern _____, weil es _____ ist.

g. Ich esse lieber _____, denn es ist _____.

h. Findest du Gemüse _____?

Unit 11. Talking about food (Part 1): READING

Hallo! Ich heiße Nils. Was ich gern esse? Ich liebe Meeresfrüchte, also esse ich gern Muscheln und Krabben. Ich finde es superlecker! Ich esse auch gern Fisch, weil es reich an Proteinen ist. Besonders Lachs! Hähnchen finde ich auch sehr lecker. Außerdem esse ich gern Obst, besonders Bananen und Erdbeeren. Sie schmecken so süß! Jedoch esse ich nicht gern Gemüse. Es schmeckt mir nicht. Und du, was isst du gern?

Hallo! Ich heiße Alex. Was ich gern esse? Also, ich liebe Gemüse! Ich esse es jeden Tag. Meine Lieblingsgemüse sind Spinat, Tomaten und Mais. Sie sind reich an Vitaminen und Mineralstoffen. Ich esse auch sehr gern Obst, weil es gesund und lecker ist. Ich hasse Fleisch und Fisch. Es ist reich an Proteinen, aber es schmeckt mir nicht.

Hallo zusammen! Ich heiße Verena. Was ich gern esse? Ich liebe Fleisch, besonders Rindfleisch, denn es ist sehr geschmackvoll. Ich esse auch gern Brathähnchen, es ist schön knusprig und reich an Proteinen. Eier finde ich auch lecker. Sie sind nicht nur gesund, sondern sie sind auch reich an Vitaminen und Proteinen. Obst finde ich ganz gut – ich esse am liebsten Bananen, weil sie lecker und vitaminreich sind. Aber ich hasse Äpfel. Ich finde sie furchtbar!

Guten Tag, ich heiße Jana. Also, ich esse am liebsten Nudeln. Ich finde es sehr lecker und sehr nahrhaft. Aber ich esse kein Fleisch – ich bin Vegetarierin! Jedoch esse ich supergern Obst, weil es süß ist, und ich esse gern Gemüse, weil es gesund ist. Ich hasse Eier. Ich finde sie ekelhaft. Sie sind reich an Proteinen und Vitaminen, aber sie schmecken mir nicht. Ich mag auch Kartoffeln nicht. Ich finde sie langweilig und nicht lecker.

Hi Leute! Ich heiße Freddie. Was ich gern esse? Also, ich liebe Fleisch, zum Beispiel Steak oder Hamburger. Ich finde es lecker und es ist sehr nahrhaft. Aber ich esse nicht gern Fisch – ich finde Fisch ekelhaft! Jedoch esse ich gern Krabben mit Mayonnaise, obwohl es nicht gesund ist. Außerdem esse ich total gern Obst, besonders Bananen, denn sie schmecken einfach fantastisch! Äpfel und Orangen esse ich nicht. Ich hasse sie. Ich esse auch kein Gemüse.

1. Find the German for the following in Nils' text

a. I love seafood

b. I like eating prawns

c. super-delicious

d. rich in proteins

e. salmon

f. moreover, I like eating

g. in particular

h. so sweet

i. however

2. Find the German for the following in Freddie's text

a. What I like to eat?

b. for example

c. very nutritious

d. but I don't like eating

e. however I like eating

f. especially bananas

g. because they taste

h. I hate them

i. although it is not healthy

3. Complete the following sentences based on Alex's text

a. Alex loves_____.

b. He eats them _____.

c. His favourite vegetables are _____,
_____ and _____.

d. He also likes _____ because it is
_____ and _____.

e. He hates _____ and _____.

4. Fill in the table below about Jana

Likes eating most	Likes a lot	Hates	Doesn't like

 **THE LANGUAGE GYM**

Unit 11. Talking about food (Part 1): TRANSLATION

1. Bad translation: spot and correct [IN THE ENGLISH] any translation mistakes you find below

a. Ich liebe Krabben.	*I hate prawns.*
b. Ich hasse Nudeln.	*I hate rice.*
c. Ich esse gern Honig.	*I don't like eating honey.*
d. Ich esse am liebsten Äpfel.	*I like eating apples.*
e. Ich finde Eier nicht lecker.	*I find eggs tasty.*
f. Bananen sind reich an Vitaminen.	*Bananas are very rich in protein.*
g. Ich esse nicht gern Fisch.	*I don't like eating honey.*
h. Ich trinke lieber Mineralwasser.	*I prefer drinking milk.*
i. Ich mag Gemüse nicht.	*I like vegetables.*
j. Ich esse Reis nicht gern.	*I like eating rice.*
k. Obst ist lecker und gesund.	*Vegetables are tasty and healthy.*
l. ich esse am liebsten Kartoffeln.	*I most like eating pasta.*

2. Translate into English

a. Ich mag Meeresfrüchte.	h. Ich trinke lieber Mineralwasser.
b. Ich finde Fisch sehr lecker.	i. Ich esse gern Krabben.
c. Hähnchen ist reich an Proteinen.	j. Ich esse kein Gemüse.
d. Ich esse sehr gern Reis.	k. Ich esse nicht gern Karotten.
e. Fleisch ist ungesund.	l. Der Kaffee ist sehr stark.
f. Ich liebe Kartoffeln.	m. Äpfel schmecken mir nicht.
g. Ich hasse Eier.	n. Ich finde Orangen sehr lecker.

3. Phrase-level translation [En to Ger]

a. I like eating

b. I love

c. I prefer eating

d. I hate

e. rich in proteins

f. because it is

g. I don't like eating

h. I like eating most

i. I find it

j. mineral water

k. orange juice

4. Sentence-level translation [En to Ger]

a. I like spicy chicken a lot.

b. I like oranges because they are healthy.

c. Meat is tasty but unhealthy.

d. This coffee is very sweet.

e. Eggs are disgusting.

f. I love oranges. They are delicious and rich in vitamins.

g. I love fish. It is tasty and rich in proteins.

h. Vegetables are disgusting.

i. I prefer bananas.

j. This tea is sweet.

 **THE LANGUAGE GYM**

Unit 11. Talking about food (Part 1): WRITING

1. Split sentences

Ich esse gern Nudeln, weil	nicht lecker.
Ich mag Kartoffen, denn	sind nicht gesund.
Ich finde Fleisch	sie lecker sind.
Am liebsten esse	ich Reis oder Kartoffeln.
Ich esse jeden Tag	am liebsten?
Hamburger	sie sind reich an Proteinen.
Was isst du	Obst und Gemüse.

2. Rewrite the sentences in the correct order

a. Reis gern Ich esse   Ich esse gern Reis.

b. hasse Ich Gemüse

c. Kaffee gern trinke Ich

d. ich Kartoffeln nicht gern esse

e. Ich lieber trinke Mineralwasser

f. Obst gesund sehr ist

g. mag Ich Erdbeeren, weil lecker sind sie

Note: When "ich" is spelled with a lower-case "i", it does not start the sentence!

3. Spot and correct the grammar and spelling (there may be missing words)

a. Ich gern esse Kartoffeln.

b. Ich nicht gern Erbsen.

c. Am liebsten trinken ich Cola.

d. Ich trink gern Kaffee.

e. Ich esse leiber Nudeln.

f. Ich mag Hänchen.

4. Anagrams

a. heftekal

b. schielF

c. delNun

d. iFhcs

e. desgu

f. ckrlee

g. ilMch

5. Guided writing – write 3 short paragraphs describing the people below using the details in the box [I]

Person	Likes eating most	Likes eating	Doesn't like eating	Hates
Anna	pasta because rich in protein	chicken because tasty	vegetables	eggs because disgusting
Ingo	fish because healthy	straw-berries because sweet	apples	hamburger because unhealthy
Deniz	honey because sweet	fish because tasty	fruit	vegetables because boring

6. Write a paragraph on Toni in German [using the third person singular]

Name:	Toni
Age:	18
Description:	good-looking, tall, sporty, friendly
Occupation:	student
Likes most eating:	chicken
Likes eating:	vegetables
Doesn't like eating:	meat
Food he hates:	fish

Grammar Time 9: ESSEN (to eat) and TRINKEN (to drink)
+ using "gern/lieber/am liebsten" to express preference

Subject-Verb	Adverbs of preference	Food/Drink		Emotive Comment
ich esse *I eat* **du isst** *you eat* **er/sie/es isst** *he/she/it eats* **wir essen** *we eat* **ihr esst** *you guys eat* **sie/Sie essen** *they/you (formal) eat*	**am liebsten** ☺☺☺ **lieber** ☺☺ **gern** ☺	**Äpfel** **Bananen** **Brot** **Eier** **Erdbeeren** **Fisch** **Fleisch** **Gemüse** **Hamburger** **Hähnchen** **Honig** **Käse** **Kartoffeln** **Nudeln** **Obst** **Reis** **Salat** **Schokolade** **Süßigkeiten** **Tomaten**	*apples* *bananas* *bread* *eggs* *strawberries* *fish* *meat* *vegetables* *burgers* *chicken* *honey* *cheese* *potatoes* *pasta* *fruit* *rice* *salad* *chocolate* *sweets* *tomatoes*	**Mmmh!** *Yum!* **Es schmeckt so lecker!** *It tastes so delicious!* **Es schmeckt gut.** *It tastes good.*
ich trinke *I drink* **du trinkst** *you drink* **er/sie/es trinkt** *he/she/it drinks* **wir trinken** *we drink* **ihr trinkt** *you guys drink* **sie/Sie trinken** *they/you (formal) drink*	**nicht gern** ☹ **gar nicht gern** ☹☹	**Apfelsaft** **Bier** **Kaffee** **Kakao** **Limonade** **Milch** **Mineralwasser** **Orangensaft** **Tee** **Wein**	*apple juice* *beer* *coffee* *cocoa* *lemonade* *milk* *mineral water* *orange juice* *tea* *wine*	**Es schmeckt ekelhaft!** *It tastes disgusting!* **Igitt!** *Yuck!*

Author's note:

In English, it is difficult to translate "am liebsten", "lieber", etc. The proper translation into English will always use the verb "to like" or "to prefer", together with "eating" or "drinking". Examples: Ich esse am liebsten Fisch = I most like eating fish; Ich esse lieber Fisch = I prefer eating fish; Ich esse gern Fisch = I like eating fish; Ich esse nicht gern Fisch = I don't like eating fish.

Drills

1. Match

ich esse gern	he really likes eating
wir essen am liebsten	she likes drinking
sie trinkt gern	I like eating
du isst lieber	we most like eating
er isst sehr gern	they don't like drinking
sie trinken nicht gern	you prefer eating

2. Translate into English

a. Ich esse gern Nudeln.

b. Wir essen lieber Obst.

c. Sie isst am liebsten Gemüse.

d. Was trinkt ihr gern?

e. Wir trinken sehr gern Saft.

f. Er isst gern Fleisch.

g. Du isst gern Kartoffeln.

h. Isst du gern Schokolade?

i. Er trinkt gern Milch.

j. Ich trinke nicht gern Tee.

3. Spot and correct the mistakes

a. Mein Vater ist gern Gemüse.

b. Mein Bruder und ich esst gern Obst.

c. Mein Vater esst nicht gern Fleisch.

d. Meine Großeltern trinke lieber Wasser.

e. Was ist du am liebsten?

f. Meine Schwester esst lieber Jogurt.

g. Dein Bruder und du, was isst ihr gern?

h. Was trinke du am liebsten?

4. Complete with the correct form of ESSEN or TRINKEN

a. Mein Vater _____ gern Obst und Gemüse.

b. Meine Brüder _____ nicht gern Reis.

c. _____ du gern Apfelsaft?

d. Meine Mutter und ich _____ gern Salat.

e. Meine Eltern _____ sehr gern Wasser.

f. Meine Schwester _____ total gern heiße Schokolade.

g. Mein Freund _____ nicht gern Wein.

h. Was _____ du zum Frühstück?

5. Translate into German

a. I like eating pasta.

b. We like most drinking orange juice.

c. What do like to you eat?

d. What do you guys like to drink?

e. We really like eating meat.

f. They don't like eating fish.

g. She doesn't like eating vegetables.

h. You like drinking mineral water.

6. Translate into German

a. I like eating meat, because it is tasty.

b. He doesn't like eating potatoes, they are disgusting.

c. I like drinking apple juice. It is delicious and healthy.

d. My parents like eating salad, because it is very tasty.

e. I don't like eating vegetables, they don't taste good to me.

f. I don't like drinking tea or coffee because I find it not tasty.

UNIT 12
Talking about food (Part 2):
What people eat and drink during the day

Grammar Time 10: Word order in main clauses

Question Skills 2: Jobs / School bag / Food

In this unit you will consolidate all that you learnt in the previous unit and learn how to say:
- What meals you eat every day and
- What you eat at each meal
- Word order in main clauses

You will revisit the following:
- The present tense of 'essen' and 'trinken'
- Use of 'gern' and other adverbs of preference to express likes and dislikes

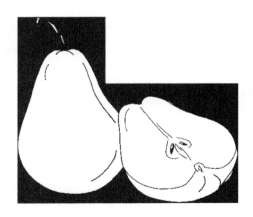

THE LANGUAGE GYM

Unit 12 (Part 2)
Talking about food: Likes / Dislikes / Reasons

Adverbial	Verb-Subject	Adverbial	Object	
Zum Frühstück *For breakfast,*	**esse ich** *I eat*		**Brot mit Käse** **Brötchen mit Nutella**	*bread with cheese* *bread roll with Nutella*
		immer *always*	**Croissant mit Butter** **Eier mit Schinken**	*croissant with butter* *eggs with bacon*
Zum Mittagessen *For lunch,*		**oft** *often*	**Haferbrei mit Honig** **Müsli mit Milch** **Toast mit Marmelade**	*porridge with honey* *muesli with milk* *toast with jam*
Zum Abendessen *For dinner,*		**manchmal** *sometimes*	**Fisch** **Fleisch**	*fish* *meat*
Zwischendurch *In between,*		**selten** *rarely*	**Gemüse** **Hähnchen** **Kartoffeln**	*vegetables* *chicken* *potatoes*
		nie *never*	**Nudeln** **Pfannkuchen** **Reis**	*pasta* *pancakes* *rice*
Zum Nachtisch *For dessert,*			**Salat** **Schnitzel mit Pommes**	*salad* *schnitzel with chips*
		gern ☺	**Eis** **Kekse**	*ice cream* *biscuits*
		lieber ☺☺	**Kuchen** **Obst** **Schokolade**	*cake* *fruit* *chocolate*
		am liebsten ☺☺☺		
Dazu *With that*	**trinke ich** *I drink*	**nicht gern** ☹	**Apfelsaft** **heiße Schokolade** **Kaffee**	*apple juice* *hot chocolate* *coffee*
		gar nicht gern ☹☹	**Limonade** **Milch** **Mineralwasser** **Orangensaft** **Tee**	*lemonade* *milk* *mineral water* *orange juice* *tea*
Ich liebe es, denn *I love it because* **Ich hasse es, denn** *I hate it because*	**es ist so lecker!** *it is so tasty* **es ist so gesund!** *it is so healthy* **es gibt mir Energie!** *it gives me energy* **es macht mich wach!** *it wakes me up* **es schmeckt so gut!** *it tastes so good* **Mmmh!** ☺		**es ist nicht lecker!** *it is not tasty* **es ist so ungesund!** *it is so unhealthy* **es ist viel zu fettig!** *it is much too greasy* **es macht mich krank!** *it makes me ill* **es schmeckt ekelhaft!** *it tastes disgusting* **Igitt!** ☹	

Unit 12. Talking about food – Likes/Dislikes (Part 2): VOCABULARY

1. Match

Wasser	sandwich
Fisch	water
Reis	chicken
Brötchen	fish
Hähnchen	cheese
Fleisch	honey
Nudeln	chips
Pommes	salad
Honig	pancakes
Käse	rice
Pfannkuchen	fruit
Salat	pasta
Gemüse	vegetables
Obst	meat

2. Complete with the missing words

a. Ich esse gern _____. *I like eating fruit.*

b. Ich liebe _____. *I love salad.*

c. Ich mag _____. *I like vegetables.*

d. Ich esse lieber _____. *I prefer eating apples.*

e. Ich finde es sehr _____. *I find it very tasty.*

f. Ich esse gern _____. *I like eating chicken.*

g. Ich mag _____ nicht. *I don't like pancakes.*

h. Ich liebe _____. *I love honey.*

i. Ich hasse _____. *I hate fish.*

j. Es schmeckt einfach _____. *It tastes simply disgusting.*

3. Complete with the missing letters

a. Wa_ _er   *water*

b. Fle_ _ _ _   *meat*

c. Kuc_ _ _   *cake*

d. O_ _ _   *fruit*

e. Äp_ _ _   *apples*

f. Karto_ _ _ln   *potatoes*

g. Hähn_ _ _ _   *chicken*

h. Erdbe_ _ _n   *strawberries*

i. s_ _   *sweet*

j. Apfels_ _ _   *apple juice*

k. Haferb_ _ _   *porridge*

l. R _ _s   *rice*

m. E_ _   *ice cream*

n. K_ _ _ee   *coffee*

o. Br_ _ _hen   *bread roll*

p. le_ _ _r   *tasty*

q. B_ _ _   *bread*

r. K_ _e   *cheese*

4. Match

nahrhaft	unhealthy
fettig	bitter
saftig	juicy
lecker	healthy
gesund	nutritious
ungesund	disgusting
scharf	fatty
vitaminreich	sweet
ekelhaft	rich in vitamins
süß	tasty
bitter	spicy

5. Sort the items below into the appropriate category

a. lecker	e. gut	i. Äpfel	m. bitter	q. Hähnchen	u. Milch
b. süß	f. Nudeln	j. Erdbeeren	n. Fleisch	r. Reis	v. Birnen
c. fettig	g. Schnitzel	k. ekelhaft	o. Jogurt	s. salzig	w. Karotten
d. Fischstäbchen	h. nahrhaft	l. Bananen	p. gesund	t. Spinat	x. Käse

Obst	Gemüse	Adjektive	Fisch & Fleisch	Milchprodukte

Unit 12. Talking about food – Likes/Dislikes (Part 2): READING (Part 1)

Ich heiße Luis. Was ich normalerweise esse? Also, zum Frühstück esse ich meistens Müsli mit Milch und ich trinke einen Becher Kaffee dazu. Das macht mich wach!

Zum Mittagessen esse ich am liebsten Hamburger mit Pommes. Dazu trinke ich meistens ein Glas Orangensaft. Ich weiß, Hamburger sind ungesund, aber ich finde sie total lecker!

Nach der Schule esse ich oft eine Kleinigkeit, wenn ich nach Hause komme. Zum Beispiel esse ich einen Toast mit Marmelade. Dazu trinke ich eine Tasse Tee.

Zum Abendessen esse ich oft etwas Warmes, zum Beispiel Nudeln. Zum Nachtisch esse ich am liebsten ein Eis – mmmh! Ich würde auch gern Käse essen, aber meine Mutter kauft nie Käse. Sie hasst Käse.

Ich heiße Franzi. Was ich normalerweise esse? Zum Frühstück esse ich nicht so viel. Meistens nur ein gekochtes Ei mit Toast. Dazu trinke ich eine Tasse Tee, natürlich mit viel Zucker!

Zum Mittagessen esse ich am liebsten Hähnchen mit Reis und ich trinke ein Glas Mineralwasser. Ich esse auch oft Gemüse, weil es sehr gesund und lecker ist.

Nach der Schule, wenn ich nach Hause komme, esse ich oft ein paar Kekse. Dazu trinke ich einen Orangensaft. Das ist sehr lecker und es gibt mir Energie!

Zum Abendessen esse ich meistens etwas Kaltes, zum Beispiel Brot mit Käse. Dazu esse ich gern Obst, zum Beispiel einen Apfel oder eine Banane. Das ist nicht nur gesund, sondern auch sehr lecker – mmmmh!

1. Find the German for the words below in Franzi's text.

a. a boiled egg   e___ g_____ E_

b. a cup of tea   e____ T_____ T____

c. lots of sugar   v_____ Z_____

d. for lunch   z___ M_____

e. a glass   e___ G_____

f. chicken   H_____

g. healthy   g_____

h. after school   n__ d___ S_____

i. a few biscuits   e__ p_____ K_____

j. energy   E_____

k. vegetables   G_____

l. usually   m_____

m. something cold   e_____ K_____

n. for dinner   z___ A_____

o. for example   z____ B_____

p. not only   n_____ n____

q. but also   s_____ a_____

2. Complete the following sentences based on Luis' text

a. For breakfast, I mostly eat _____ with _____, and I drink a mug of _____ with that.

b. For _____, I most like eating hamburgers with _____.

c. With that, I usually drink a _____ of _____.

d. I know, hamburgers are _____, but I find them really _____!

e. After _____, I often eat something small, when I come _____.

f. For dinner, I usually eat something _____, for example _____.

g. I would also like to eat _____, but my mother never buys cheese, she _____ cheese!

3. Find the German for the following in Luis' text

a. What I normally eat?

b. after school

c. a small thing

d. that makes me awake

e. a cup of tea

f. I would also like to eat

g. for dessert

h. normally

i. for example

j. toast with jam

k. I know

l. my mother never buys

m. she hates cheese

n. a mug of coffee

o. but I find them

Unit 12. Talking about food – Likes/Dislikes (Part 2): READING (Part 2)

4. Who says this, Luis or Franzi? Or both?

a. I would also like to eat cheese.   *Luis*

b. I like most eating chicken for lunch.

c. I usually eat something cold for dinner.

d. I don't eat so much for breakfast.

e. I drink a cup of tee in the afternoon.

f. I like eating fruit.

g. I love the taste of burgers.

h. Burgers are not healthy.

i. For dinner, I eat something warm.

j. I drink orange juice.

k. His mother hates cheese.

l. I eat bread with cheese.

Hallo, ich heiße Jana. Was ich normalerweise esse? Zum Frühstück esse ich meistens sehr viel: eine Schale Müsli mit Jogurt, ein gekochtes Ei mit Toast und auch eine Banane. Dazu trinke ich immer einen großen Becher Kaffee. Das gibt mir Energie für den Tag!

Das Mittagessen esse ich immer in der Schulkantine. Am liebsten esse ich Nudeln mit Tomatensoße und Salat. Dazu trinke ich Apfelsaft. Fleisch oder Fisch esse ich nie, denn ich bin Vegetarierin. Zum Nachtisch esse ich oft Eis oder Obstjogurt.

Nach der Schule esse ich oft ein Stück Kuchen, wenn ich nach Hause komme, und ich trinke ein Glas Milch. Das ist lecker.

Zum Abendessen esse ich nicht so viel. Meistens esse ich nur ein Brot mit Käse. Manchmal esse ich auch eine Suppe, zum Beispiel eine Kartoffelsuppe. Ich liebe Kartoffeln, weil sie so nahrhaft sind!

Vor dem Schlafengehen habe ich immer Hunger und ich würde gern etwas essen, aber meine Mutter erlaubt es nicht, denn es ist nicht gesund!

5. Answer the following questions on Jana's text

a. How much does she eat at breakfast?

b. What does she eat? [3 things]

c. What does this breakfast give her?

d. What juice does she drink at lunch?

e. What does she never eat and why?

f. What does she eat when she comes home?

g. Why does she love potatoes?

h. Why doesn't her mother allow her to eat something before going to bed?

6. Find in Jana's text the following:

a. a word for dessert, starting with O

b. a vegetable starting with S

c. a drink starting with A

d. sweet baked goods starting with K

e. a fruit starting with B

f. a dairy product starting with J

g. an adjective starting with N

h. a container starting with S

i. a verb starting with E

j. a place in school starting with S

k. a type of soup starting with K

l. a noun starting with V

THE LANGUAGE GYM

Unit 12. Talking about food – Likes/Dislikes (Part 2): WRITING

1. Split sentences

Zum Frühstück esse ich	Tee mit viel Zucker!
Manchmal esse	liebsten Orangensaft.
Dazu trinke ich eine Tasse	Warmes, zum Beispiel eine Suppe.
Zum Mittagessen	ich auch Haferbrei.
Fleisch esse ich nie, denn	es reich an Proteinen ist.
Ich trinke am	esse ich oft Nudeln mit Tomatensoße.
Zum Abendessen esse ich oft etwas	meistens Müsli mit Milch.
Ich esse Fisch gern, weil	ich bin Vegetarier.

2. Complete with the correct option

a. Ich esse oft etwas _____, zum Beispiel eine Suppe.

b. Am liebsten _____ ich Hähnchen mit Reis.

c. Normalerweise esse ich Cornflakes zum _____.

d. Ich esse gern Schnitzel mit _____ zum Mittagessen.

e. Zum Abendessen esse ich gern ein _____ mit Käse.

f. Ich esse kein _____, weil ich Vegetarierin bin.

g. Ich liebe _____, weil es sehr süß und lecker ist.

h. Ich trinke gern _____, denn es macht mich wach!

i. Ich trinke gar nicht gern Milch, ich finde das _____!

j. Obst und Gemüse sind sehr gut für die _____.

Gesundheit	Brot	Frühstück	Kaffee	esse
Fleisch	Warmes	Schokolade	ekelhaft	Pommes

3. Spot and correct the grammar and spelling mistakes [note: in several cases a word is missing]

a. Zum Abendessen esse ich gern Hamburger mit Pommes.

b. Ich gern trinke Mineralewasser.

c. Ich gern Fleisch, weil es reich an Proteinen.

d. Ich leibe Orangesaft.

e. Nach der Schule essen ich gern Toast mit Jam.

f. Ich auch eine tasse Tee mit Milch.

g. Ich liebe honig, weil es ist süß.

h. Zum Abendessen ich essen oft Tomatensuppe.

i. Ich esse am leibsten Gemuse, denn es ist gesund.

4. Complete the words

a. z__ M_____   *for lunch*

b. z__ A_____   *for dinner*

c. z____ F_____   *for breakfast*

d. g_____   *healthy*

e. s_____   *sweet*

f. l_____   *tasty*

g. e_____   *disgusting*

6. Sentence level translation [EN - GER]

a. I love fruit juice because it is sweet and refreshing.

b. I don't like salmon because it is disgusting.

c. For dinner, I eat a cheese sandwich.

d. I always drink milk with honey. I like it because it's sweet.

e. I like fish, but chicken is not very tasty.

5. Guided writing – write 2 short paragraphs in the first person [I] using the details below

Person	Breakfast	Lunch	Dinner	Would like to eat
Simon	muesli with milk, orange juice	schnitzel with chips, ice cream	potato soup, mineral water	crabs, but mother hates sea food
Ellen	a boiled egg, toast, coffee	pasta with tomato sauce, cake	fish or chicken with rice, juice	chocolate, but unhealthy

 THE LANGUAGE GYM

Grammar Time 10: Word Order in main clauses

1. Subject – Verb (SV): the 'normal' word order

When the subject starts the sentence, the verb is right next to it (Subject-Verb). Everything else, such as an adverbial or an object, follows after:

Subject–Verb (SV)		Adverbial		Object	
Ich esse	*I eat*	**gern** **immer** **manchmal** **oft**	☺ *always* *sometimes* *often*	**Haferbrei** **Müsli** **Toast**	*porridge* *muesli* *toast*

2. Verb-Subject (Inversion)

When an adverbial starts the sentence …

Adverbial		Verb-Subject (VS)		Object	
Am liebsten **Manchmal** **Meistens** **Dazu**	☺☺☺ *Sometimes* *Usually* *With that*	**esse ich**	*I eat*	**eine Banane** **eine Orange** **einen Apfel**	*a banana* *an orange* *an apple*

… or an object …

Object		Verb-Subject (VS)		Adverbial	
Hamburger **Schwarzbrot** **Spiegeleier**	*Hamburger* *Black bread* *Fried eggs*	**esse ich**	*I eat*	**nicht gern** **selten** **oft** **zum Frühstück**	☹ *rarely* *often* *for breakfast*

… the subject and the verb swap places (Verb-Subject). The normal word order of subject-verb is now the other way around or as linguists like to say: 'inverted', hence the name: 'inversion'.

Inversion also happens in **questions**. In an 'open' question (example 1 below), the inversion follows the question word. In a 'closed' question (example 2) the inversion is located at the beginning:

(1) **Was**	*What*	**isst du**	*do you eat*	**zum Frühstück?**	*for breakfast?*
(2) **Trinkst du**	*Do you drink*	**oft**	*often*	**Tee?**	*tea?*

 **THE LANGUAGE GYM**

Word order in main clauses. Drills (food & drink)

1. Match adverbials

manchmal	usually
dazu	sometimes
am liebsten	for dinner
meistens	with that
nicht gern	☺☺☺
zum Abendessen	☹

2. Underline all SV and circle all VS

a. Ich esse oft Kartoffeln.

b. Manchmal esse ich Nudeln mit Tomatensoße.

c. Meistens trinke ich dazu Orangensaft.

d. Mein Bruder isst gern Hähnchen, ...

e. ..., aber ich esse lieber Fisch.

f. Ich mag am liebsten Lasagne!

g. Was isst du am liebsten zum Abendessen?

3. Sentences with 2 main clauses – underline all SVs and circle all VS

a. Ich esse gern Salat und ich trinke am liebsten Wasser dazu.

b. Du isst gern Gemüse, aber ich esse gern Fleisch.

c. Zu Mittag esse ich oft Salat, aber manchmal esse ich auch Nudeln.

d. Ich esse oft Müsli zum Frühstück und manchmal trinke ich einen Tee dazu.

e. Mein Vater trinkt gern Bier, aber meine Mutter trinkt lieber Wein.

f. Ich finde Lasagne superlecker, aber Fisch finde ich ekelhaft!

g. Ich esse sehr gern Spiegeleier, aber manchmal esse ich auch ein gekochtes Ei.

4. Put the words in the correct order to form sentences [note: start with the underlined word]

a. meine Mutter oft Müsli isst

b. Nudeln ich esse am liebsten

c. trinke ich dazu Apfelsaft

d. isst gern Haferbrei du

e. lieber Hamburger ich esse

f. er gern isst eine Banane

g. trinken wir manchmal Kaffee

h. trinkt Tee deine Oma gern?

i. ich manchmal Toast mit Marmelade esse

j. ich dazu trinke Orangensaft oder Wasser

k. ich finde nicht lecker Schwarzbrot

l. isst mein Freund Hamburger sehr gern

5. Translate into English

a. Ich esse immer Müsli zum Frühstück.

b. Zu Mittag esse ich oft Salat.

c. Manchmal esse ich Hamburger.

d. Mein Bruder isst selten Fleisch.

e. Ich esse nie Schokolade.

f. Du isst meistens Toast mit Marmelade.

6. Translate into German

a. I never eat a banana.

b. Sometimes, I eat an apple.

c. I often drink orange juice, ...

d. ... but I never drink coffee.

e. What do you eat for dinner?

f. My father always eats meat.

THE LANGUAGE GYM

Word order in main clauses. Drills (family, weather, pets)

1. Match adverbials

in meiner Familie	unfortunately
im Sommer	in my family
zu Hause	furthermore
jedoch	in the summer
leider	however
außerdem	at home

2. Underline all SV and circle all VS

a. In meiner Familie gibt es fünf Personen.

b. Ich heiße Martin und ich bin zehn Jahre alt.

c. Zu Hause habe ich einen Hund und einen Fisch.

d. Mein Hund ist laut, aber meine Katze ist leise.

e. Außerdem habe ich ein Pferd.

f. Das Wetter ist im Sommer oft schön.

g. Jedoch ist es im Winter oft kalt.

3. Sentences with 2 main clauses – underline all SVs and circle all VS

a. Ich mag meinen Bruder, denn er ist immer nett zu mir.

b. Meine Schwester mag ich nicht, denn sie ist immer gemein zu mir.

c. Ich habe einen Bruder, aber ich habe keine Schwester.

d. Ich kann nicht Fußball spielen, aber ich kann gut singen.

e. Tanzen kann ich nicht so gut, aber ich kann sehr gut malen.

f. Mein Onkel ist vierzig Jahre alt und meine Tante ist neununddreißig Jahre alt.

g. Ich verstehe mich gut mit meinem Onkel, denn er ist sehr lustig und nett.

4. Put the words in the correct order to form sentences [note: start with the underlined word]

a. meine Mutter <u>ich</u> mag

b. ich kein Haustier <u>zu Hause</u> habe

c. das Wetter <u>manchmal</u> ist schlecht

d. regnet im Winter oft <u>es</u>

e. immer <u>mein Bruder</u> lustig ist

f. kann <u>er</u> gut Fußball spielen

g. ist immer sonnig <u>im Sommer</u> es

h. du aus Deutschland <u>kommst</u>?

i. <u>außerdem</u> ich habe einen Bruder

j. ich habe keine Schwester <u>jedoch</u>

k. ich finde nicht nett <u>meine Schwester</u>

l. meinen Bruder <u>ich</u> finde nervig

5. Translate into English

a. Meinen Bruder finde ich nervig, …

b. …, aber meine Mutter finde ich sehr nett.

c. Leider habe ich kein Haustier.

d. Jedoch habe ich eine Schwester.

e. Meine Schwester isst oft Nudeln.

f. Sie kann gut singen.

6. Translate into German

a. Unfortunately, my brother is not nice.

b. He is often annoying.

c. In the summer, the weather is often bad.

d. But sometimes, the sun shines.

e. Do you have a pet?

f. Sometimes, I would like to have a hamster.

Question Skills 2: Jobs / School bag / Food

1. Translate into English

a. Wo isst du zu Mittag?

b. Was arbeitet deine Mutter?

c. Was hast du in deiner Schultasche?

d. Was ist dein Lieblingsessen?

e. Was ist dein Lieblingsgetränk?

f. Wie oft isst du Fleisch?

g. Magst du Orangensaft?

h. Warum isst du kein Gemüse?

i. Isst du oft Süßigkeiten?

j. Was ist dein Lieblingssport?

k. Wie ist deine Schwester?

l. Mit wem frühstückst du gern?

2. Match the answers below to the questions in activity 1

a. Apfelsaft.

b. Sie ist sehr fleißig und immer hilfsbereit.

c. Fußball.

d. Ja, ich mag das. Ich finde es lecker.

e. Weil ich das nicht mag.

f. Nudeln mit Tomatensoße.

g. Ja, jeden Tag.

h. Ich esse das zweimal pro Woche.

i. Es gibt ein Heft, zwei Bücher, einen blauen Kuli und einen Apfel.

j. Meine Mutter ist Polizistin.

k. In der Schulkantine.

l. Mit meinem Bruder.

3. Provide the questions to the following answers

a. Ich esse kein Fleisch.

b. Ich esse immer Gemüse, denn es ist gesund.

c. Sie arbeitet als Lehrerin.

d. Ich liebe Obst, weil es lecker und nahrhaft ist.

e. Ich spiele Fußball in der Schule.

f. Ich esse oft Krabben.

g. Ich esse fünfmal pro Tag Obst.

h. Ich komme aus München.

i. Nein, ich habe keine Haustiere.

j. Mein Lieblingsgetränk ist Apfelsaft.

k. In meiner Schultasche gibt es einen Taschenrechner, drei Hefte und ein Buch.

4. Complete

a. W___ h_____ d__ i__ d_____ Schultasche?

b. W___ arb_____ du?

c. W__ o___ i___d__ Meeresfrüchte?

d. W___ i___ d_____ Lieblingsgetränk?

e. W___ al_ b_____ du?

f. I____ d__ g___ Fleisch?

g. W_____ k_____st du?

h. W____ i_____ d__ z____ Frühstück?

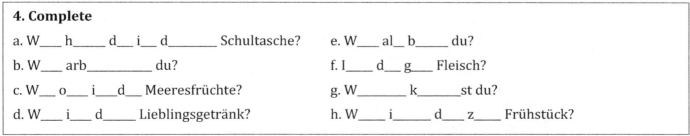

UNIT 13
Talking about clothes and accessories I wear, how often and when

Grammar Time 11: TRAGEN + indefinite article + adjective + noun

Revision Quickie 3: Jobs, food, clothes and numbers 20-100

In this unit you will learn how to:

- Say what clothes you wear in various circumstances and places
- Give a wide range of words for clothing items and accessories
- Use a range of words for places in town
- Make the full present tense conjugation of 'tragen' (to wear)

You will revisit:

- Time markers
- Frequency markers
- Colours
- Self-introduction phrases
- adjective endings in accusative case after "einen/eine/ein"

UNIT 13
Talking about clothes

Wo? / Wann?	VS + Wie oft?	Was?	
Zu Hause *At home,* **In der Disko** *At the nightclub,* **In der Schule** *At school,* **Im Fitnessstudio** *At the gym,* **Am Strand** *At the beach,* **Wenn es draußen heiß ist,** *When it is hot outside,* **Wenn es draußen kalt ist,** *When it is cold outside,* **Wenn ich mit meiner Freundin /mit meinem Freund ausgehe,** *When I go out with my girlfriend /with my boyfriend,* **Wenn ich mit meinen Eltern ausgehe,** *When I go out with my parents,* **Wenn ich Sport mache,** *When I do sport,*	**trage ich immer** *I always wear* **trägt er/sie immer** *he/she always wears*	**einen Anzug** **einen Badeanzug** **einen Gürtel** **einen Hut** **einen Kapuzenpulli** **einen Mantel** **einen Pulli** **einen Rock** **einen Trainingsanzug** **einen Schal** **eine Hose** **eine Halskette** **eine Jacke** **eine Krawatte** **eine kurze Hose** **eine Mütze** **eine Strickjacke** **eine Uhr** **eine Uniform** **ein Kleid** **ein Hemd** **ein T-Shirt** **ein Top** **Jeans** **Ohrringe** **Pantoffeln** **Sandalen** **Schuhe** **Socken** **Stiefel** **Stöckelschuhe**	*a suit* *a swimsuit* *a belt* *a hat* *a hoody* *a coat* *a jumper* *a skirt* *a tracksuit* *a scarf* *trousers* *a necklace* *a jacket* *a tie* *shorts* *a cap* *a cardigan* *a watch* *a uniform* *a dress* *a shirt* *a T-shirt* *a top* *jeans* *earrings* *slippers* *sandals* *shoes* *socks* *boots* *high heel shoes*

Unit 13. Talking about clothes: VOCABULARY BUILDING

1. Match up

ich trage ...	a shirt
ein Hemd	trainers
ein Kleid	trousers
Sportschuhe	a suit
eine Hose	a cap
einen Anzug	I wear ...
eine Mütze	a dress

2. Complete with the missing word

a. Zu Hause _____ ich oft ein T-Shirt.
At home, I often wear a T-shirt.

b. In der Schule trage ich immer eine _____.
At school, I always wear a uniform.

c. Im Fitnessstudio trage ich meistens einen _____.
At the gym, I usually wear a tracksuit.

d. Am Strand trage ich immer einen _____.
At the beach, I always wear a swimsuit.

e. In der Disko trage ich nie _____, sondern ich trage _____.
In the nightclub, I never wear sandals, but I wear high heels shoes.

f. Ich trage meistens _____.
I usually wear earrings.

g. Ich trage eine lange _____.
I wear long trousers.

3. Translate into English

a. Ich trage oft ein T-Shirt.

b. Ich trage manchmal einen Anzug.

c. Ich trage nie einen Pulli.

d. Ich trage sehr oft eine coole Mütze.

e. Ich trage immer eine Uhr.

f. Ich trage meistens Ohrringe.

g. Er trägt oft einen eleganten Anzug.

h. Sie trägt immer braune Sandalen.

i. Ich trage nie ein weißes T-Shirt.

j. Ich trage meistens warme Pantoffeln.

k. Mein Bruder trägt immer Jeans.

4. Anagrams [clothes and accessories]

a. üMtze	e. chSueh	i. oRck
b. hUr	f. demH	j. iekLd
c. zugAn	g. aeJns	k. utH
d. hrOinger	h. lachS	l. eiSftle

5. Associations – match each body part below with the words in the box, as shown in the examples

a. der Kopf   *head*   **Hut**

b. die Füße   *feet*

c. die Beine   *legs*

d. der Hals   *neck*

e. der Oberkörper   *upper body*

f. die Ohren   *ears*

g. das Handgelenk   *wrist*

Schal	Krawatte	Schuhe	Stiefel
Jacke	Hemd	Strümpfe	Hut
Ohrringe	Hose	Rock	Käppi
Halstuch	Uhr	Halskette	T-Shirt

6. Complete

a. Ich trage St_____.
I wear boots.

b. zu H_____
at home

c. Ich habe eine goldene U_____.
I have a golden watch

d. Ich trage ein bequemes H_____.
I wear a comfortable shirt.

e. Ich trage einen blauen A_____.
I wear a blue suit.

f. Mein Bruder trägt eine S_____.
my brother wears a cardigan.

g. Meine Freundin trägt rote S_____.
My girlfriend wears red shoes.

 THE LANGUAGE GYM

Unit 13. Talking about clothes: READING

Ich heiße Lisa. Ich komme aus der Schweiz. Ich bin fünfzehn Jahre alt und ich bin ziemlich sportlich. Ich habe ziemlich viele Klamotten. Ich trage gern Klamotten, die von guter Qualität sind – aber nicht zu teuer! Zu Hause trage ich meistens einen Trainingsanzug. Ich habe vier oder fünf Trainingsanzüge, stell dir vor. Wenn ich mit meinem Freund ausgehe, trage ich Ohrringe, eine Halskette, ein rotes oder schwarzes Kleid und Stöckelschuhe.

Ich heiße Renaud. Ich komme aus Frankreich. Ich bin dreizehn Jahre alt. Ich kaufe gern Klamotten, vor allem Schuhe! Ich habe viele Markenschuhe aus Italien, stell dir vor! Ich liebe italienische Kleidung. Wenn es draußen kalt ist, trage ich meistens einen Mantel und schwarze oder braune Schuhe. Manchmal trage ich eine sportliche Jacke. Wenn es warm ist, trage ich meistens ein T-Shirt, Jeans und Sandalen oder Sportschuhe. Zu Hause habe ich ein Pferd, das Jacques Chirac heißt.

Ich heiße Maria. Ich komme aus Spanien. Ich bin zwölf Jahre alt. Ich kaufe immer Klamotten von Zara. Ich mag Klamotten, die schön sind, aber nicht zu teuer. Markenklamotten mag ich aber nicht! Ich trage immer sportliche Kleidung, zum Beispiel einen Trainingsanzug, T-Shirts und Sportschuhe. Wenn es draußen kalt ist, trage ich eine Jacke und einen Schal aus Wolle. Wenn es draußen heiß ist, trage ich eine Bluse und eine kurze Hose.

Ich heiße Michael und ich komme aus Hamburg. Ich bin vierzehn Jahre alt. In der Schule trage ich immer ein Hemd, Hose und Schuhe. Zu Hause trage ich normalerweise ein T-Shirt und Jeans. Ich habe viele T-Shirts und Jeans zu Hause. Im Fitnessstudio trage ich immer ein Muskelshirt, eine kurze Hose und schwarze Sportschuhe. Wenn ich mit meinen Freunden ausgehe, trage ich eine Jacke, ein Hemd, eine schwarze oder graue Hose und schwarze Schuhe. Und du, was trägst du?

1. Find the German for the following in Lisa's text

a. I am from

b. quite sporty

c. many clothes

d. of good quality

e. not too expensive

f. five tracksuits

g. with my boyfriend

h. earrings

i. a red or black dress

j. high-heel shoes

2. Find the German for the following in Michael's text

a. at school

b. normally

c. many T-shirts

d. at home

e. tank top

f. short trousers

g. a jacket

h. black trousers

i. sports shoes

j. what do you wear?

3. Complete the following statements about Renaud's text

a. He is _____ years old.

b. Above all, he likes buying _____.

c. He has many branded shoes from _____.

d. When it's cold, he usually wears a _____ and _____ or _____ _____.

e. Sometimes he wears a _____ _____.

4. Answer in German the questions below about Maria

Wie heißt sie?

Woher kommt sie?

Wie alt ist sie?

Was mag sie?

Wo kauft sie ihre Klamotten?

Was trägt sie, wenn es draußen kalt ist?

Was trägt sie, wenn es draußen heiß ist?

5. Find someone who ...

a. ... loves branded clothes?
b. ... is from Germany?
c. ... wears a tank top in the gym?
d. ... wears earrings when she goes out with her boyfriend?
e. ... has four or five different tracksuits?
f. ... has a lot of T-shirts and jeans at home?
g. ... is very sporty?
h. ... wears grey or black trousers when going out with friends?

 THE LANGUAGE GYM

Unit 13. Talking about clothes: WRITING

1. Split sentences

Zu	ich ein T-Shirt und eine kurze Hose.
Wenn es draußen	Hause trage ich einen Trainingsanzug.
Im Fitnessstudio trage	schwarze Schuhe.
Wenn es draußen warm ist,	kalt ist, trage ich einen Mantel.
Ich trage nie	blaue Strickjacke.
Wenn ich in die Disko	gehe, trage ich coole Markenschuhe.
Ich trage einen	blauen Pullover.
Ich trage eine	trage ich eine Bluse.

2. Complete with the correct option

a. _____ ich mit meinem _____ ausgehe, trage ich immer elegante Kleidung.

b. In der Schule _____ ich immer eine Uniform.

c. Im Fitnessstudio trage ich weiße _____.

d. Am Strand trage ich ein weißes _____.

e. Wenn es _____ heiß ist, trage ich eine kurze _____ und Sandalen.

f. Zu Hause trägt mein Vater immer _____ Trainingsanzug von Puma oder Nike.

g. Meine Schwester trägt immer braune _____.

h. Ich trage _____ Stöckelschuhe. Ich mag das nicht.

Stiefel	Freund	nie	trage	Wenn
Sportschuhe	einen	draußen	Hose	Muskelshirt

3. Spot and correct the grammar and spelling mistakes [note: in several cases a word is missing]

a. Wenn ich meinen Freunden ausgehe, ich immer coole Schuhe.

b. Zu Hause ich trage am leibsten einen Trainingsanzug.

c. Ich oft trage schwarze Schuhe, wenn ich ausgehe.

d. Mein Bruder tragt immer eine blau Hose.

e. In Schule ich trage immer eine Uniform.

f. Er immer tragt Markenklamotten.

g. Wenn es ist draußen kalt, trage ich einen warme Mantel.

h. Ich tragen gern ein grunes Kleid.

4. Complete the words

a. R_____   *skirt*

b. A_____   *suit*

c. O_____   *earrings*

d. H_____   *trousers*

e. S_____   *shoes*

f. S_____   *scarf*

g. T_____   *tracksuit*

5. Guided writing – write 3 short paragraphs in the first person [I] using the details below

Person	Lives	Wears at home	When going out	Never wears
Anton	Basel	track suit and sports shoes	brown boots	earrings
Vera	München	white T-shirts	jeans, black shoes	a watch
Annette	Linz	jeans and T-shirt	dress and earrings	a scarf

6. Describe this person in German using the 3rd person

Name:	Ron
Lives in:	London
Age :	20
Pet:	A black spider
Hair/eyes:	blond + green eyes
Always wears:	suits
Never wears:	jeans
At the gym wears:	an Adidas tracksuit

Grammar Time 11
TRAGEN + indefinite article + adjective + noun

Subject-Verb	Direct object (Noun phrase in accusative case)				
	a/no	**adjective + ending**		**noun**	
ich trage *I wear* **du trägst** *you wear*	**einen** *a* **keinen** *no*	**alt-** **bequem-** **elegant-** **gestreift-** **kurz-** **lang-** **modisch-**	*old* *comfy* *elegant* *stripy* *short* *long* *trendy*	**-en**	**Anzug** *suit* **Badeanzug** *swimsuit* **Gürtel** *belt* **Hut** *hat* **Kapuzenpulli** *hoody* **Mantel** *coat* **Pulli** *jumper* **Rock** *skirt* **Schal** *scarf* **Trainingsanzug** *tracksuit*
er/sie/es trägt *he/she/it wears* **wir tragen** *we wear* **ihr tragt** *you guys wear*	**eine** **keine**	**neu-** **schick-** **schön-** **warm-** **braun-** **blau-** **gelb-**	*new* *stylish* *beautiful* *warm* *brown* *blue* *yellow*	**-e**	**Bluse** *blouse* **Halskette** *necklace* **Hose** *trousers* **Jacke** *jacket* **Krawatte** *tie* **Mütze** *cap* **Strickjacke** *cardigan* **Uhr** *watch* **Uniform** *uniform*
sie tragen *they wear*	**ein** **kein**	**golden-** **grau-** **grün-** **orang-** **schwarz-**	*golden* *grey* *green* *orange* *black*	**-es**	**Kleid** *dress* **Hemd** *shirt* **T-Shirt** *T-shirt* **Top** *top*
Sie tragen *you (formal) wear*	**ein Paar** *a pair of*	**rot-** **weiß-**	*red* *white*	**-e**	**Jeans** *jeans* **Ohrringe** *earrings* **Pantoffeln** *slippers* **Sandalen** *sandals*
	keine	**hellblau-** **dunkelblau-**	*light blue* *dark blue*	**-en**	**Schuhe** *shoes* **Socken** *socks* **Stiefel** *boots* **Stöckelschuhe** *high heel shoes*

DRILLS

1. Complete the table

Deutsch	English
bequem	
	trendy
	blue
kurz	
warm	
	black
	beautiful
gestreift	
	new

2. Translate into English

a. Ich trage einen bequemen Anzug.

b. Du trägst eine blaue Bluse.

c. Mein Freund trägt ein schickes Hemd.

d. Sie tragen schicke Stöckelschuhe.

e. Tragt ihr eine graue oder eine blaue Uniform?

f. Ich trage ein schönes Top.

g. Er trägt eine gestreifte Krawatte.

h. Meine Schwester trägt einen modischen Rock.

i. Manchmal trage ich ein rotes T-Shirt.

j. Ich trage einen alten Kapuzenpulli.

3. Provide the correct adjective ending

Ich trage ...

a. einen schön__ Mantel.

b. eine neu__ Bluse.

c. rot__ Pantoffeln.

d. keine sauber__ Socken.

e. ein grün__ Kleid.

f. hellblau__ Schuhe.

g. ein gestreift__ Hemd.

h. eine rot__ Strickjacke.

i. einen modisch__ Pulli.

4. Complete with the missing adjective

a. Ich trage eine _____ Uhr.   *I wear a golden watch.*

b. Er trägt eine _____ Hose.   *He is wearing long trousers.*

c. Wir tragen _____ Sandalen.   *We are wearing brown sandals.*

d. Du trägst einen _____ Kapuzenpulli.   *You wear a grey hoody.*

e. Ich trage einen _____ Schal.   *I'm wearing a warm scarf.*

f. Sie trägt ein Paar _____ Schuhe.   *She wears a pair of black shoes.*

g. Mein Opa trägt ein _____ Hemd.   *My grandad wears a white shirt.*

h. Ich trage eine _____ Jacke.   *I wear a stylish jacket.*

5. Translate into German

a. I wear ...

b. a black scarf.

c. a comfy hoody.

d. a yellow blouse.

e. grey trousers.

f. brown shoes.

g. a stripy tie.

6. Translate into German

a. I wear a blue dress and white shoes.

b. Peter wears a brown shirt and a black belt.

c. Do you wear a comfortable uniform?

d. Do you guys wear white sports shoes?

e. I wear clean socks.

f. We wear comfy sandals and short trousers.

g. She wears a white blouse and a blue skirt.

 THE LANGUAGE GYM

Grammar Time 12: Word Order in subordinate clauses

A subordinate clause starts with a subordinate conjunction, which links the subordinate clause to a main clause. The subordinate clause then continues with the subject and potentially some other bits, before finally, the verb stands at the end.

Below, you can find six of the most frequently used subordinate conjunctions in German, and see how they and the other elements in a subordinate clause work together. You could use the extra space in the table to write your own main clauses and some subordinate clauses if you wish. You could also add in more subordinate conjunctions that you will surely come across in your German learning journey!

Main Clause	Subordinate Clause	
	Subord. Conj.	**Subject ... <u>Verb</u>.**
Ich esse oft Spinat, *I often eat spinach*	**weil** *because*	**ich es lecker <u>finde</u>.** *I <u>find</u> it tasty.*
	da *as*	**ich verrückt danach <u>bin</u>.** *I <u>am</u> crazy about it.*
	obwohl *even though*	**mein Bruder das doof <u>findet</u>.** *my brother <u>finds</u> it stupid.*
	wenn *when*	**ich Hunger <u>habe</u>.** *I <u>am</u> hungry.*
	damit *so that*	**ich groß und stark <u>werde</u>.** *I <u>become</u> big and strong.*
Ich denke, *I think*	**dass** *that*	**es supergesund <u>ist</u>.** *it <u>is</u> super-healthy.*

Author's note:

(1) A subordinate clause can stand either before, after, or in the middle of the main clause. If it stands before the main clause, the main clause begins with inversion (VS). Can you spot this in the sentence builder at the beginning of this Unit?

(2) In German, a subordinate clause is always separated from the main clause by a comma.

Drills

1. Match

Deutsch	English
da	that
wenn	so that
obwohl	as
weil	because
damit	when
dass	before
bevor	although

2. Pick the correct option

a. Ich mag meinen Onkel, **damit / weil** er supernett ist.

b. Ich esse gern Fastfood, **obwohl / wenn** es ungesund ist.

c. Ich trage ein T-Shirt, **wenn / dass** es heiß ist.

d. Ich denke, **da / dass** Spinat sehr lecker ist.

e. **Weil / Bevor** ich ins Bett gehe, esse ich oft einen Snack.

f. Ich wohne in Köln, **obwohl / damit** ich aus Berlin komme.

g. **Damit / Weil** ich Hunde liebe, haben wir einen Hund zu Hause.

3. Split sentences

Main clause	Subordinate clause
a. Ich mag meinen Bruder,	weil es gesund ist.
b. Ich esse oft Gemüse,	da sie gut bezahlt ist.
c. Meine Tante findet ihre Arbeit super,	dass Fastfood ungesund ist.
d. Ich liebe Schokolade,	obwohl er oft nervig ist.
e. Mein Vater denkt,	damit er cool aussieht.
f. Ich trage eine Uniform,	weil sie süß und lecker ist.
g. Mein Freund trägt eine dunkle Sonnenbrille,	wenn ich in der Schule bin.

4. Complete with a subordinate conjunction from the box below

a. Ich mag meinen Opa, _____ er sehr großzügig ist.

b. Ich esse oft Schokolade, _____ ich Hunger habe.

c. _____ er oft gemein zu mir ist, liebe ich meinen Bruder.

d. Wir machen viel Sport, _____ es gesund ist.

e. Ich mache Muskeltraining, _____ ich cool aussehe.

obwohl	wenn	weil
damit	da	

5. Connect the clauses, using the subordinate conjunction given in brackets. Take care to put the <u>verb</u> in the resulting subordinate clause into the correct position.

a. Ich trage oft Sandalen. Es ist heiß. (wenn) -

Ich trage oft Sandalen, wenn es heiß <u>ist</u>.

b. Ich trinke oft Orangensaft. Es ist gesund und lecker. (weil) -

c. Ich trage oft Stöckelschuhe. Es ist unbequem. (obwohl) -

d. Ich esse ein Stück Kuchen. Ich komme nach Hause. (wenn) -

e. Ich denke. Es ist sehr ungesund. (dass) -

f. Ich gehe ins Fitnessstudio. Ich werde stark. (damit) -

6. Underline all subordinate clauses in the text below.

Hallo Leute! Ich heiße Arne. Obwohl ich aus Österreich komme, wohne ich in München, im Süden von Deutschland. Wenn ich zu Hause bin, trage ich am liebsten einen Trainings-anzug. Das ist das Allerbeste, weil es total bequem ist. Außerdem trage ich immer Kopfhörer, obwohl das meine Mutter nervig findet. Sie denkt, dass es schlecht für meine Ohren ist. Aber ich trage das, damit ich laut Musik hören kann. Ist doch klar, oder?

THE LANGUAGE GYM

Revision Quickie 3: Jobs, food, clothes and numbers 20-100

1. Complete (numbers)

a. 100   hun_____

b. 90   neun_____

c. 30   dr_____

d. 50   fün_____

e. 80   ach_____

f. 60   sech_____

g. 40   vier_____

2. Translate into English (food and clothes)

a. der Anzug   h. die Socken

b. der Saft   i. der Fisch

c. das Hähnchen   j. der Schal

d. der Rock   k. die Schuhe

e. das Schnitzel   l. das Gemüse

f. das Wasser   m. der Kaffee

g. das Fleisch   n. das Abendessen

3. Write in a word for each letter in the categories below as shown in the example *(there is no obvious word for the greyed out boxes!)*

Buchstabe	Kleidung	essen und trinken	Zahlen	Jobs
S	Schuhe	Saft	sechs	Schauspieler
H				
B				
E				
A				

4. Match up

ich trage	my name is
ich habe	I drink
ich bin	I also have
ich esse gern	I live
ich trinke	I work
ich arbeite	I have
ich wohne	I come from
ich heiße	there is/are
ich komme aus	I wear
es gibt	I am
ich habe auch	I like eating
ich esse oft	I often eat

5. Translate into English

a. Ich trage oft braune Stiefel.

b. Ich esse immer Müsli zum Frühstück.

c. Ich arbeite als Anwalt in der Stadt.

d. Ich trinke gern heiße Schokolade.

e. Ich esse nicht gern Fleisch.

f. Ich esse oft Nudeln mit Tomatensoße.

g. Meine Mutter ist Geschäftsfrau.

h. Ich habe keine Markenklamotten.

i. Ich esse gern Salat zum Mittagessen.

UNIT 14
Saying what I and others do in our free time

Grammar Time 13:
SPIELEN, MACHEN, GEHEN + Use of adverbials to add interest

Grammar Time 14:
3 types of linking words

In this unit you will learn how to:

- Say what activities you do using the verbs 'spielen (play), 'machen' (do) and 'gehen' (go)
- Add information about when, how often, with whom, and for how long you do them
- Use different types of linking words

You will revisit:
- Time and frequency markers
- Weather
- Expressing likes/dislikes
- Adjectives
- Pets

UNIT 14
Saying what I (and others) do in our free time

In meiner Freizeit *In my free time*	**spiele ich oft** *I often play* **spiele ich gern** *I like playing*	**Basketball** **Fußball** **Gitarre** **Handball** **Karten** **Schach** **Tennis** **Trompete**	*basketball* *football* *guitar* *handball* *cards* *chess* *tennis* *trumpet*
Wenn das Wetter gut ist, *When the weather is good,*			
Wenn das Wetter schlecht ist, *When the weather is bad,*	**mache ich oft** *I often do* **mache ich gern** *I like doing*	**Judo** **Karate** **Krafttraining** **Leichtathletik** **Yoga**	*judo* *karate* *weight lifting* *athletics* *yoga*
Wenn ich Zeit habe, *When I have time,* **Wenn ich darf,** *When I am allowed to,* **Wenn ich kann,** *When I can,* **Wenn ich müde bin,** *When I am tired,*	**gehe ich oft** *I often go* **gehe ich gern** *I like going*	**angeln** **joggen** **klettern** **Rad fahren** **reiten** **Ski fahren** **schwimmen** **wandern** **an den Strand** **in den Park** **in die Disko** **ins Schwimmbad** **ins Sportzentrum** **zu meinem Freund** **zu meiner Oma**	*fishing* *jogging* *rock climbing* *cycling* *riding* *skiing* *swimming* *hiking* *to the beach* *to the park* *to the nightclub* *to the pool* *to the sports centre* *to my friend's house* *to my granny's house*
Ich mache das ... *I do that ...*	**jeden Tag** **jedes Wochenende** **zweimal pro Woche** **mit meinem Vater** **mit meiner Schwester** **mit meinen Freunden** **für ein bis zwei Stunden**	*every day* *every weekend* *twice per week* *with my father* *with my sister* *with my friends* *for one to two hours*	

Unit 14. Free time: VOCABULARY BUILDING

1. Match up

ich spiele Schach	I go horse-riding
ich gehe joggen	I play chess
ich gehe reiten	I play basketball
ich spiele Karten	I go hiking
ich mache Karate	I go swimming
ich gehe schwimmen	I do karate
ich gehe wandern	I go jogging
ich spiele Basketball	I play cards

3. Translate into English

a. Ich gehe jeden Tag Rad fahren.

b. Ich gehe oft klettern.

c. Ich gehe zweimal pro Woche klettern.

d. Ich gehe mit meinem Vater reiten.

e. Wenn das Wetter schlecht ist, spiele ich Schach oder Karten.

f. Ich spiele sehr oft Basketball.

g. Ich gehe selten ins Sportzentrum.

h. Ich gehe oft zu meinem Freund.

i. Ich gehe jeden Tag an den Strand.

j. Ich gehe jedes Wochenende angeln.

k. Wenn das Wetter gut ist, spiele ich Golf.

5. ich 'spiele', 'mache' or 'gehe'?

a. Ich _____ Karate.

b. Ich _____ Rad fahren.

c. Ich _____ Schach.

d. Ich _____ Karten.

e. Ich _____ schwimmen.

f. Ich _____ ins Kino.

g. Ich _____ Tennis.

h. Ich _____ Krafttraining.

i. Ich _____ klettern.

2. Complete with the missing word

a. Ich spiele _____.   *I play chess.*

b. Ich gehe _____.   *I go horse riding.*

c. Ich spiele _____.   *I play cards.*

d. Ich gehe _____ fahren.   *I go cycling.*

e. Ich spiele _____.   *I play basketball.*

f. Ich gehe _____.   *I go fishing.*

g. Ich gehe _____.   *I go hiking.*

h. Ich gehe _____.   *I go rock climbing.*

i. Ich gehe _____.   *I go jogging.*

j. Ich mache meine _____.   *I do my homework.*

4. Broken words

a. Ich gehe rei_____.   *I go horse-riding.*

b. Ich gehe schw_____.   *I go swimming.*

c. Ich gehe ang_____.   *I go fishing.*

d. Ich gehe Rad fa_____.   *I go cycling.*

e. Ich spiele Sch_____.   *I play chess.*

f. Ich mache Leichtath_____. *I do athletics.*

g. Ich spiele Kar_____.   *I play cards.*

h. Ich gehe Ski fa_____.   *I go skiing.*

6. Bad translation – spot any translation errors and fix them

a. Ich gehe nie wandern.
I never go swimming.

b. Ich spiele mit meinem Opa Schach.
I play chess with my dad.

c. Ich gehe jeden Tag klettern.
I go rock climbing every weekend.

d. Wenn das Wetter gut ist, gehe ich joggen.
When the weather is good, I go hiking.

e. Ich gehe einmal pro Woche Ski fahren.
I go biking once a week.

f. Ich spiele ziemlich oft Schach.
I quite often play cards.

g. Ich gehe gern klettern.
I like going hiking.

 **THE LANGUAGE GYM**

Unit 14. Free time: READING

Ich heiße Thomas. Ich komme aus Kassel, das ist in der Mitte von Deutschland. In meiner Freizeit mache ich viel Sport. Mein Lieblingssport ist Klettern, stell dir vor! Ich mache das jeden Tag! Wenn das Wetter schlecht ist, bleibe ich zu Hause (*I stay at home*) und ich spiele Karten oder Schach. Ich spiele auch gern PlayStation oder Xbox. Ich mache das sehr oft!

Ich heiße Ronan. Ich gehe gern Rad fahren. Ich mache das jeden Tag mit meinen Freunden. Es ist mein Lieblingssport! Ab und zu gehe ich klettern, joggen oder wandern. Ich spiele nicht gern Tennis oder Fußball, und ich hasse Schwimmen. Ich mache das sehr selten. Zweimal pro Woche gehe ich mit meinem Freund Julian abends in die Disko. Ich liebe Tanzen!

Hallo zusammen! Ich heiße Verónica. Ich komme aus Spanien, aus Barbastro. Ich habe rote Haare und ich bin ziemlich nett und lustig. In meiner Freizeit spiele ich gern Computerspiele und ich höre gern Musik. Ich mache das jeden Tag! Wenn das Wetter schön ist, gehe ich im Park joggen oder ich spiele mit meinem Bruder Tennis. Ich gehe nicht gern ins Fitnessstudio und ich gehe auch nicht gern ins Schwimmbad. Ich finde Schwimmen total doof, weil ich das Wasser nicht mag. Und du, was machst du in deiner Freizeit?

1. Find the German for the following in Thomas' text

a. I do a lot of sport

b. my favourite sport

c. rock climbing

d. every day

e. when the weather's bad

f. I also like playing

g. Imagine!

h. I do that very often

2. Find the German in Ronan's text for

a. I like going biking

b. with my friends

c. now and then

d. I hate swimming

e. into the nightclub

f. I go rock climbing

g. with my friend Julian

h. in the evening (1 word)

3. Complete the following statements about Verónica

a. She is from _____ in _____.

b. She is quite _____ and _____.

c. She likes playing videogames and _____.

d. When the weather is nice she goes _____.

e. She also plays tennis with her_____.

f. She doesn't enjoy the gym nor the _____.

Ich heiße Nicola. Ich komme aus England. In meiner Freizeit lese ich total gern Bücher und Zeitungen. Außerdem spiele ich gern Karten und Schach. Ich bin nicht so sportlich. Jedoch gehe ich manchmal ins Fitnessstudio und ich mache ein bisschen Krafttraining. Ab und zu, wenn das Wetter schön ist, gehe ich mit meinem Hund in den Bergen wandern. Ich liebe meinen Hund! Er heißt Doug und er ist weiß und sehr groß.

4. List 8 details about Nicola

1

2

3

4

5

6

7

8

5. Find someone who...

a. ...enjoys reading newspapers.

b. ...hates swimming.

c. ...does a lot of sport.

d. ... does a little bit of weight lifting.

e. ... goes dancing twice a week.

Unit 14. Free time: TRANSLATION

1. Gapped translation

a. Ich gehe oft in die Disko.
I _____ go to the nightclub.

b. Ich spiele jeden Tag Schach.
I play _____ every day.

c. Ich spiele ziemlich oft Tennis.
I play tennis _____ _____.

d. Ich spiele sehr gern _____.
I really like playing cards.

e. Ich gehe gern _____.
I like going swimming.

f. Manchmal gehe ich klettern. - _____,
I go climbing.

g. Ich mache nie Krafttraining.
I never do _____.

h. Wenn es _____ ist, gehe ich joggen. -
When it is sunny, I go jogging.

2. Translate into English

a. sehr

b. jedes Wochenende

c. wenn das Wetter schlecht ist

d. zu meinem Freund

e. nie

f. jeden Tag

g. ich gehe klettern

h. ich gehe in die Disko

i. ich gehe angeln

4. Translate into German

a. free time: F

b. rock climbing: K

c. swimming: S

d. fishing: A

e. weights: K

f. video games: C

g. chess: S

h. cards: K

i. hiking: W

j. jogging: J

3. Translate into English

a. Ich gehe oft mit meinem Vater angeln.

b. Ich spiele jeden Tag mit meinem Bruder Karten.

c. Ich gehe oft mit meiner Mutter klettern.

d. Ich spiele gern mit meinem besten Freund Schach.

e. Ich spiele jeden Tag mit meinem Bruder PlayStation.

f. Ich gehe jeden Samstag mit meinen Freunden in die Disko.

g. Ich spiele oft mit meiner Freundin Mia Monopoly.

5. Translate into German [note: the initial letters of the words you need are given in brackets]

a. I go jogging. (I g j)

b. I like playing chess. (I s g S)

c. I often go rock climbing. (I g o k)

d. I go swimming with my brother. (I g m m B s)

e. I often do karate. (I m o K)

f. I do yoga with my friends. (I m m m F Y)

g. I go to the nightclub every weekend. (I g j W i d D)

h. I often play video games. (I s o C)

i. I like going cycling. (I g g R f)

j. I play football twice a week. (I s z p W F)

Unit 14. Free time: WRITING

1. Split sentences

Ich gehe nie ins	Tag joggen.
Ich spiele mit meinem	Karate.
Ich gehe oft zu meiner	Bergen klettern.
Ich gehe jeden	Bruder Schach.
Ich spiele sehr	Freundin.
Ich mache oft	ins Fitnessstudio.
Ich gehe sehr gern	Sportzentrum.
Ich gehe in den	gern Karten.

2. Complete the sentences

a. Ich _____ manchmal joggen.

b. Manchmal _____ ich Schach.

c. Ich _____ ab und zu klettern.

d. Ich _____ oft reiten.

e. Ich _____ oft Tennis.

f. Ich _____ zu meinem Freund.

g. In meiner _____ gehe ich oft ins Kino.

h. Ich _____ manchmal ins Sportzentrum.

i. Ich _____ meine Hausaufgaben.

3. Spot and correct mistakes [note: in some cases a word is missing]

a. Ich speile oft Tennis.

b. Ich spiele gern schach.

c. Ich gehe zu mienem Freund.

d. Ich fast nie Fahrrad fahren.

e. Ich mache miene Hausaufgaben.

f. Ich gehen schwimmen.

g. Ich mache krafttraining.

4. Complete the words

a. Scha_____

b. Leichtath_____

c. Kl_____

d. Computer_____

e. Rei_____

f. Ang_____

g. Schw_____

5. Write a paragraph for each of the people below in the first person singular (I):

Name	What I like doing	How often I do that	Who with	What else	Why I (don't) like it
Laura	hiking	every day	with my boyfriend	don't like swimming	hate the water
Dylan	weight-lifting	often	with my friend James	hate football	it's unhealthy
Oskar	skiing	when the weather is nice	alone (=allein)	often go horse-riding	love horses

Grammar Time 13: SPIELEN, MACHEN, GEHEN
+ Use of adverbials to add interest

Subject-Verb		Adverbs/Adverbials		Rest of sentence	
<u>spielen</u>	*to play*				
		gern	☺	**Basketball**	*basketball*
ich spiele	*I play*	lieber	☺☺	**Fußball**	*football*
du spielst	*you play*	am liebsten	☺☺☺	**Karten**	*cards*
er/sie spielt	*he/she plays*	nicht gern	☹	**Korbball**	*netball*
wir spielen	*we play*	gar nicht gern	☹☹	**Schach**	*chess*
ihr spielt	*you guys play*			**Tennis**	*tennis*
sie/Sie spielen	*they / you (formal) play*			**Trompete**	*the trumpet*
		immer	*always*		
		oft	*often*		
<u>machen</u>	*to do*	manchmal	*sometimes*		
		selten	*rarely*	**Hausaufgaben**	*homework*
ich mache	*I do*	nie	*never*	**Kampfsport**	*martial arts*
du machst				**Karate**	*karate*
er/sie macht				**Krafttraining**	*weight lifting*
wir machen		jeden Tag	*every day*	**Leichtathletik**	*athletics*
ihr macht		den ganzen Tag	*the whole day*	**nichts**	*nothing*
sie/Sie machen		nach der Schule	*after school*	**Sport**	*sports*
		am Wochenende	*at the weekend*		
<u>gehen</u>	*to go*				
		allein	*on my own*	**angeln**	*fishing*
ich gehe	*I go*	mit meinem Freund	*with my friend*	**joggen**	*jogging*
du gehst		mit meiner Freundin	*with my friend*	**klettern**	*rock climbing*
er/sie geht		mit meinen Eltern	*with my parents*	**Rad fahren**	*cycling*
wir gehen				reiten	*riding*
ihr geht				**schwimmen**	*swimming*
sie/Sie gehen		für ein bis zwei Stunden	*for 1 to 2 hours*	**wandern**	*hiking*
		den ganzen Tag	*the whole day*		
				an den Strand	*to the beach*
				in den Park	*to the park*
		in den Bergen	*in the mountains*	**in die Disko**	*to the nightclub*
		in der Stadt	*in the city*	**in die Kirche**	*to church*
		am See	*on the lake*	**ins Schwimm-bad**	*to the pool*

Author's note:

*On **the position of adverbs and adverbials**: In German, adverbs and adverbials often stand close to the subject and the verb in the middle of the sentence, as shown in the table. However, if you want to put emphasis on any information that you convey with an adverbial, you can put it also at the beginning or end of the sentence. Feel free to play around with this! Just remember, when you put the adverbial at the beginning of the sentence, do inversion (Verb-Subject) after.*

Drills

1. Match the adverbials

heute	with my friend
nach der Schule	to the park
mit meinem Freund	sometimes
manchmal	with me
in den Park	today
mit mir	after school

2. Complete with the missing <u>adverbials</u>

a. Ich spiele _____ Karten.   *I play cards <u>every day.</u>*

b. Er spielt _____ Basketball.   *He <u>often</u> plays basketball.*

c. Wir spielen _____ Tennis.   *We play tennis <u>the whole day</u>.*

d. Ich gehe _____ an den Strand.   *I go to the beach <u>on my own</u>.*

e. Gehst du _____ angeln?   *Are you going fishing <u>today</u>?*

f. Wir gehen _____ reiten.   *We go horse-riding <u>after school</u>.*

g. _____ mache ich nichts.   <u>*Sometimes*</u>*, I do nothing.*

h. Ich gehe _____ schwimmen.   *I go swimming <u>with my friends</u>.*

i. Sie macht _____ Hausaufgaben.   *She does hwk <u>in the evening</u>.*

3. Complete with the missing <u>verb</u>

a. Ich _____ oft angeln.
I often <u>go</u> fishing.

b. Du _____ selten Sport.
You rarely <u>do</u> sports.

c. Heute _____ ich Schach.
Today, I <u>play</u> chess.

d. Nach der Schule _____ ich nichts.
After school, I <u>do</u> nothing.

e. Wir _____ jedes Wochenende in den Bergen wandern.
We <u>go</u> hiking every weekend in the mountains.

f. Mein Freund _____ am Nachmittag Tennis.
My friend <u>plays</u> tennis in the afternoon.

g. _____ du oft joggen?
Do you <u>go</u> jogging often?

4. Underline SV and circle VS

a. Ich gehe gern an den Strand.

b. Nach der Schule gehe ich Rad fahren.

c. Sie geht nach der Schule reiten.

d. Mit meinen Eltern gehe ich oft klettern.

e. Manchmal spielen wir auch Karten.

f. Mein Bruder spielt immer Trompete.

g. Ich mache jeden Tag Sport.

h. An den Strand gehe ich nicht oft.

i. Wann gehst du ins Schwimmbad?

j. Klettern wir heute?

k. Ich gehe am Wochenende reiten.

5. Complete with the missing subject and verb. Take care to put them in the right order (SV or VS)!

a. _____ jeden Tag mit meiner Mutter Leichtathletik.   <u>*I do*</u> *athletics every day with my mother.*

b. Manchmal _____ Squash im Sportzentrum.   *Sometimes, <u>we play</u> squash in the sports centre.*

c. Sonntags _____ mit meinen Freunden angeln.   *On Sundays, <u>I go</u> fishing with my friends.*

d. _____ am Wochenende ins Kino?   <u>*Are we going*</u> *to the cinema at the weekend?*

e. _____ oft mit meiner Freundin Julia an den Strand.   *I often <u>go</u> to the beach with my friend Julia.*

f. Ab und zu _____ Karate.   *Now and then <u>they do</u> karate.*

g. Wenn es heiß ist, _____ ein Eis.   *When it is hot, <u>I eat</u> an ice cream.*

h. Was _____ in deiner Freizeit?   *What <u>do you do</u> in your free time?*

i. _____ jeden Tag Basketball.   <u>*She plays*</u> *basketball every day.*

6. Complete with *macht*, *spielt* or *geht* as appropriate

a. Meine Mutter _____ nie Sport, sie ist so faul!

b. Mein Vater _____ selten in die Kirche, aber ich gehe oft. Und du?

c. Mein Freund Selim _____ jeden Freitag in die Moschee.

d. Mein Großvater _____ immer Karten mit mir.

e. Mein großer Bruder _____ Karate, stell dir vor, er hat einen schwarzen Gürtel!

f. Mein Freund Dieter _____ immer PlayStation.

g. Mein kleiner Bruder _____ jeden Tag Rad fahren.

h. Meine Oma _____ jeden Tag an den Strand.

8. Translate into English

a. Ich spiele nie Tennis.

b. Sie macht oft ihre Hausaufgaben.

c. Wir gehen jedes Wochenende in die Kirche.

d. Sie gehen nicht oft ins Schwimmbad.

e. Wenn das Wetter gut ist, gehen sie in den Park.

f. Mein Opa spielt gern Schach mit mir.

g. Wenn es regnet, gehe ich ins Fitnessstudio.

7. Complete with *spielen*, *machen* or *gehen* as appropriate

a. Meine Freunde _____ oft Basketball.

b. Meine Brüder _____ jeden Tag Sport.

c. Wir _____ oft Fußball, das ist klasse!

d. Meine Eltern _____ gern schwimmen.

e. Meine Cousins _____ Karate, cool!

f. Mein Freund und ich, wir _____ jedes Wochenende ins Kino. Das ist super!

g. Mein Onkel und meine Tante _____ oft wandern. Ich finde das cool.

h. Meine Freunde _____ oft klettern.

i. _____ Sie gern reiten?

j. Meine Freunde Lisa und Franz _____ sehr gut Schach, stell dir vor!

k. Sie _____ samstags immer ins Schwimmbad. Wie langweilig!

l. Was _____ Sie am Wochenende?

m. Wir _____ an den Strand.

n. Was _____ deine Freunde?

o. Ich denke, sie _____ nichts.

9. Translate into German

a. We never go to the swimming pool.

b. They do sport rarely.

c. She plays basketball every day.

d. When the weather is nice, I go jogging.

e. I rarely do cycling.

f. I often go rock climbing.

g. My father and I often play badminton.

h. My sister plays tennis twice per week.

i. I go to the swimming pool on Saturdays.

j. When the weather is bad, I go to the gym.

k. They rarely do their homework.

l. We never play chess.

Grammar Time 14: 3 types of linking words

Type 1: Co-ordinating Conjunctions:

Co-ordinating conjunctions link two main clauses together. They do not affect the word order.

Main Clause 1	Coord. Conj.	Main Clause 2
Ich habe einen Bruder, *I have a brother*	**und** *and*	ich habe eine Schwester. *I have a sister*
	aber *but*	ich habe keine Schwester. *I have no sister*
Ich mag meinen Bruder, *I like my brother*	**denn** *because*	er ist immer nett. *he is always nice*
*Further co-ordinating conjunctions that you will often see are: **oder** [or] and **sondern** [but]. "sondern" is used to contradict a negative statement, for example: „Ich habe keine Schwester, sondern ich habe einen Bruder" [I don't have a sister, but I have a brother].*		

Type 2: Linking Adverbs:

Linking adverbs form part of a main clause. When they start the clause, they cause <u>inversion</u>:

Main Clause 1	Main Clause 2	
Ich habe einen Bruder, *I have a brother,*	**außerdem** *furthermore,*	<u>habe ich</u> eine Schwester. *I have a sister*
	jedoch *however,*	<u>habe ich</u> keine Schwester. *I have no sister*
*There are many more adverbs such as: **deshalb** [therefore], **trotzdem** [nevertheless], and **auch** [also]. Note that **auch** likes to stand after the verb: „Ich habe **auch** eine Schwester" [I also have a sister].*		

Type 3: Subordinating Conjunctions:

Subordinating conjunctions start a subordinate clause. These are clauses that cannot stand on their own. In a subordinate clause, the <u>verb</u> is at the end.

Main Clause	Subordinate Clause			
Ich mag meinen Bruder, *I like my brother,*	**weil** *because*	er *he*	immer nett *always nice*	<u>ist</u>. *is*
	obwohl *even though*		oft nervig *often annoying*	
*Other frequently used subordinate conjunctions are: **damit** [so that], **dass** [that] as well as **wenn** [when] and **bevor** [before].*				

Drills

1. Match

weil	however
jedoch	because (1)
obwohl	and
denn	even though
und	furthermore
aber	or
außerdem	but
oder	because (2)

2. Pick the correct option

a. Ich heiße Lisa **und / denn** ich bin vierzehn Jahre alt.

b. Ich wohne in Berlin, **oder / aber** ich komme aus Hamburg.

c. Mein Vater kommt aus Köln, **und / jedoch** wohnt er in Wien.

d. Ich kann gut singen, **jedoch / außerdem** kann ich nicht tanzen.

e. Ich mag meine Oma, **weil / obwohl** sie immer nett zu mir ist.

f. Ich mag meine Schwester, **und/ jedoch** ist sie oft launisch.

g. Ich habe eine Katze, **aber / oder** du hast einen Hund.

h. Meine Mutter mag ihre Arbeit nicht, **weil / denn** sie ist nicht gut bezahlt.

3. What type of <u>linking word</u> is it?

a. Ich esse oft Toast mit Marmelade **und** ich trinke Tee dazu.   *type 1*

b. Mein Vater isst oft Pizza, **obwohl** es ungesund ist. - _____

c. Kommst du aus Österreich **oder** kommst du aus der Schweiz?   _____

d. Im Sommer ist das Wetter schön, **aber** im Winter regnet es oft.   _____

e. Ich finde Berlin fantastisch, **denn** die Stadt ist total cool.   _____

f. Mein Hund ist sehr lieb, **jedoch** ist er manchmal ein bisschen gefährlich.

_____

4. Complete with a word from the table below

a. Ich heiße Martin _____ ich bin zwölf Jahre alt.

b. Ich esse oft Fastfood, _____ es superlecker ist.

c. Ich liebe meinen Bruder, _____ er nicht so nett ist.

d. Am Freitag gehe ich ins Kino _____ ich bleibe zu Hause.

e. Ich kann gut Fußball spielen, _____ ich kann nicht singen.

f. Ich habe einen Lieblingsonkel, _____ wohnt er in Afrika.

g. Ich finde Bananen lecker, _____ sie schmecken total gut.

h. Meine Oma ist total lustig, _____ kann sie super kochen.

oder	außerdem	und	weil
aber	jedoch	denn	obwohl

5. Spot the word order error in the <u>second clause of each sentence</u> and re-write it correctly

a. Ich kann gut tanzen, <u>aber kann ich nicht schwimmen</u>.   *I can dance well, but I can't swim well.*

b. Ich esse oft Gemüse, <u>weil es ist lecker</u>.   *I often eat vegetables, because it is tasty.*

c. Meine Mutter ist nett, <u>außerdem sie ist sehr hilfsbereit</u>.   *My mother is kind. Besides, she is very helpful.*

d. Ich mag meinen Opa, <u>jedoch er sehr geizig ist</u>.   *I like my grandad, however, he is very stingy.*

e. Ich esse oft Pommes, <u>obwohl ist es ungesund</u>.   *I often eat chips, even though it is unhealthy.*

f. Ich gehe nicht in den Garten, <u>weil regnet es</u>.   *I don't go into the garden, because it is raining.*

g. Ich mag meinen Bruder nicht, <u>denn ist er doof</u>.   *I don't like my brother, because he is stupid.*

UNIT 15
Talking about weather and free time

Grammar Time 15: SPIELEN, MACHEN, GEHEN (Part 2) + SEIN & HABEN (Part 3)

Revision Quickie 4: Weather / Free time / Clothes

Question skills 3: Clothes / Free time / Weather

In this unit you will learn how to say:
- What free-time activities you do in different types of weather
- Where you do them **and** who with
- Words for places in town

You will also learn how to ask and answer questions about:
- Clothes
- Free time
- Weather

You will revisit:
- Sports and hobbies
- The verbs 'machen', 'gehen' and 'spielen' in the present indicative
- Pets
- Places in town
- Clothes
- Family members
- Numbers from 1 to 100

THE LANGUAGE GYM

UNIT 15
Talking about weather and free time

Adverbial phrase	Verb-Subject	Rest of sentence	
Wenn das Wetter schön ist, *When the weather is nice,* **Wenn das Wetter schlecht ist,** *When the weather is bad,* **Wenn es regnet,** *When it rains,*	**spiele ich** *I play* **spielt meine Freundin Anna** *my friend Anna plays*	Schach Karten Basketball Fußball Tennis mit meinen Freunden mit seinen Freunden mit ihren Freunden	chess cards basketball football tennis with my friends with his friends with her friends
Wenn es schneit, *When it snows,* **Wenn die Sonne scheint,** *When the sun shines,*	**mache ich** *I do* **macht mein Freund Paul** *my friend Paul does*	Judo Karate Leichtathletik meine Hausaufgaben seine Hausaufgaben ihre Hausaufgaben Sport Yoga	judo karate athletics my homework his homework her homework sport yoga
Wenn es bewölkt ist, *When it is cloudy,* **Wenn es heiß ist,** *When it is hot,* **Wenn es kalt ist,** *When it is cold,* **Wenn es neblig ist,** *When it is foggy,* **Wenn es sonnig ist,** *When it is sunny,* **Wenn es stürmisch ist,** *When it is stormy,* **Wenn es windig ist,** *When it is windy,*	**gehe ich** *I go* **geht meine Freundin Mia** *my friend Mia goes*	angeln joggen klettern Rad fahren reiten Ski fahren schwimmen tanzen wandern an den Strand in den Park ins Sportzentrum ins Fitnessstudio ins Schwimmbad zu meinem Freund zu seinem Freund zu ihrem Freund	fishing jogging rock climbing cycling riding skiing swimming dancing hiking to the beach to the park to the sports centre to the gym to the pool to my friend's house to his friend's house to her friend's house
Manchmal *Sometimes* **Unter der Woche** *On weekdays* **Am Wochenende** *At the weekend*	**bleibe ich** *I stay* **bleibt mein Freund Ben** *my friend Ben stays*	zu Hause in meinem Zimmer in seinem Zimmer in ihrem Zimmer	at home in my room in his room in her room

Unit 15. Talking about weather and free time VOCABULARY BUILDING 1

1. Match up

Wenn ...	it is cold
... es kalt ist	it is hot
... es heiß ist	it is cloudy
... das Wetter schön ist	When
... das Wetter schlecht ist	the weather is nice
... es bewölkt ist	It's raining
... es regnet	the weather is bad

2. Complete with the missing word

a. wenn das Wetter _____ ist
when the weather is bad

b. wenn es _____ und _____ ist
when it rains and is cold

c. wenn es _____ und _____ ist
when it is sunny and hot

d. Wenn es stürmisch ist, _____ ich zu Hause.
When it is stormy, I stay at home.

e. Wenn das Wetter _____ ist, gehe ich in den Park.
When the weather is nice, I go to the park.

f. Wenn es _____, gehe ich Ski fahren.
When it snows I go skiing.

g. Wenn das Wetter _____ ist, bleibt mein Freund zu Hause.
When the weather is bad, my friend stays at home.

h. Ich mag es, wenn es _____ ist.
I like it when it's sunny.

3. Translate into English

a. Es ist bewölkt.

b. Wenn es regnet, ...

c. Wenn es kalt ist, ...

d. Wenn es heiß ist, ...

e. Wenn es schneit, ...

f. Wenn das Wetter schön ist, ...

g. Wenn es neblig ist, ...

h. ... spiele ich Tennis.

i. ... gehe ich Ski fahren.

j. ... bleibe ich zu Hause.

4. Associations – match each weather word below with the clothes/activities in the box

1. das Wetter ist schlecht: Sturm, Wind, Regen –

2. das Wetter ist schön: Sonne und Hitze -

3. es schneit und es ist kalt:

Schnee-stiefel	ich bleibe zu Hause	ich gehe Ski fahren	Strand
ich mache nichts	kurze Hose	ich sehe fern	Hut
die Berge	Schal	Schlafanzug	Badeanzug

5. Anagrams [weather]

a. tlak

b. hcöns

c. linebg

d. ergnet

e. wöltkbe

f. chletsch

g. ießh

h. mischtürs

i. digwin

j. nnigso

k. tteWer

l. gtu

6. Complete

a. Das Wetter ist _____. *The weather is nice.*

b. Ich bleibe zu H_____. *I stay at home.*

c. Wenn es r_____. *When it rains.*

d. Ich _____ es, wenn es sonnig ist. *I like it when it's sunny.*

e. Ich _____ an den Strand. *I go to the beach.*

f. wenn es stürmisch _____ *when it is stormy*

g. wenn es _____ ist *when it is hot*

h. wenn es _____ ist *when it is cloudy*

 THE LANGUAGE GYM

Unit 15. Talking about weather and free time: VOCABULARY BUILDING 2

1. Match up

ich spiele Tennis	I go out
ich spiele Karten	in his bedroom
ich gehe reiten	Max goes fishing
ich gehe aus	I play tennis
Max geht angeln	I do horse-riding
in seinem Zimmer	I play cards
ich bleibe zu Hause	swimming
schwimmen	I stay at home

2. Complete with the missing word

a. Ich bleibe _____ meinem Zimmer.
I stay in my bedroom.

b. Mein Freund _____ in den Park.
[My friend goes to the park.

c. Ich gehe zu _____ Freund.
I go to my friend's house.

d. Manchmal gehe ich ins _____.
Sometimes I go to the sports centre.

e. Unter der Woche _____ ich immer meine Hausaufgaben.
I always do my homework on weekdays.

f. Ich mag das _____, weil ich mit meinen Freunden spiele.
I like the weekend because I play with my friends.

g. Meine Freundin Vero _____ immer zu_____ Freund.
My friend Vero always goes to her friend's house.

h. Ich gehe immer _____.
I always go rock climbing.

3. Translate into English

a. Ich gehe zu meinem Freund.

b. Ich gehe reiten.

c. Es ist bewölkt.

d. Ich gehe Rad fahren.

e. Er geht joggen.

f. Er geht ins Sportzentrum.

g. Ich gehe ins Schwimmbad.

h. Er macht Sport.

4. Anagrams [activities]

a. ggenjo	e. ketBallbas	i. daR ahfrne
b. chimmwsen	f. ßblalFu	j. zu ienmem uerFnd
c. dernwan	g. enrtKa	k. gelnan
d. eitenr	h. chSahc	l. zentan

5. Broken words

a. I___ s_____ m____ m_____ F_____ F_____. — *I play football with my friends.*

b. M_____ T_____ M_____ s_____ K_____. — *My aunt Maria plays cards.*

c. I___ g_____ z__ m_____ F_____. — *I go to my friend's house (m).*

d. J_____ g_____ i____ S_____. — *Jens goes to the sports centre.*

e. I___ g_____ r_____, w_____ e__ s_____ i__. — *I go horse riding, when it is sunny.*

f. M_____ F_____ b_____ z__ H_____ ... — *My friend stays at home*

g. ... u_____ m_____ H_____. — *... and does homework.*

6. Complete

a. Ich mache _____. *I do homework.*

b. Er _____ zu Hause. *He stays at home.*

c. Er _____ schwimmen. *He goes swimming.*

d. Ich _____ ins Fitnessstudio. *I go to the gym.*

e. Sie geht ins _____. *She goes to the cinema.*

f. Ich bleibe zu _____. *I stay at home.*

g. Ich gehe _____. *I go rock climbing.*

h. Ich gehe _____ fahren, ... *I go skiing ...*

i. ...wenn es _____. *...when it snows.*

j. in meinem _____ *in my room*

Unit 15. Talking about weather and free time: READING

Ich heiße Pietro. Ich komme aus Italien. Ich bin elf Jahre alt. Ich bin sehr sportlich, deshalb mag ich es, wenn das Wetter gut ist! Wenn die Sonne scheint, gehe ich immer mit meinen Freunden in den Park und wir spielen Fußball. Außerdem, wenn es heiß ist, gehe ich mit meinem Hund an den Strand. Er ist sehr klein und superlustig. Wenn ich an den Strand gehe, trage ich einen Badeanzug, Sandalen und einen Hut.

Ich heiße Isabela. Ich komme aus Rom, in Italien. Ich bin fünfzehn Jahre alt. Ich kaufe gern T-Shirts und Jacken. Ich liebe es, wenn es draußen stürmt! Ich bleibe dann mit meinem kleinen Bruder zu Hause und ich spiele Computerspiele oder Karten mit ihm. Ich finde Unwetter total spannend und interessant. Ich mag es nicht, wenn es kalt ist, denn ich hasse es, einen Mantel oder einen Schal zu tragen. Zu Hause habe ich einen Hund, eine Katze und einen Papagei, der Italienisch spricht!

Ich heiße Ana Laura. Ich komme aus Brasilien. Ich bin zwölf Jahre alt. Mein Hobby ist Singen! Wenn es kalt ist, gehe ich mit meinen Freundinnen ins Einkaufszentrum. Ich trage einen langen Mantel, einen Schal und Stiefel. Ich liebe die Kälte! Mein Lieblingsfilm ist Frozen 2. Wenn es heiß ist, bleibe ich zu Hause. Ich mag die Hitze nicht. Ich gehe auch nie an den Strand. Ich hasse den Strand!

Ich heiße Chloé. Ich komme aus Frankreich. Ich bin vierzehn Jahre alt. Wenn es heiter und sonnig ist, gehe ich immer ins Schwimmbad. Ich gehe auch oft mit meinem Vater mit seinem Boot angeln. Es ist ein bisschen langweilig, aber ich mag es trotzdem. Abends gehe ich mit meinen Freunden aus. Wenn ich in die Disko gehe, trage ich meistens Jeans und ein Hemd. Meine Freundin heißt Sofie. Sie ist nett und intelligent. Wenn das Wetter schlecht ist und es regnet, bleibt sie immer zu Hause und macht ihre Hausaufgaben.

1. Find the German for the following in Pietro's text

a. I come from

b. I am 11 years old

c. therefore, I like it

d. when the sun shines

e. when it is hot

f. into the park

g. with my dog

h. very small

i. to the beach

j. a swimsuit

2. Find the German for the following in Chloe's text

a. when it's clear skies

b. always

c. to the swimming pool

d. I also often go

e. a bit boring

f. I go out with my friends

g. a shirt

h. is called

i. she stays

j. in her house

3. Complete the following statements about Isabela's text

a. She is _____ years old.

b. She likes buying _____ and _____.

c. She loves it when it is _____ outside.

d. When it's stormy, she plays _____ or _____ with her _____ brother.

e. Isabela does not like _____ weather.

f. Her pet can _____ Italian.

4. Answer in German the questions below about Ana Laura

a. Woher kommt sie?

b. Wie alt ist sie?

c. Was macht sie gern in ihrer Freizeit?

d. Was für ein Wetter mag sie?

e. Wohin geht sie, wenn es kalt ist?

f. Was macht sie, wenn es heiß ist?

g. Wie findet sie die Hitze?

h. Was ist ihr Lieblingsfilm?

5. Find someone who

a. Likes to go fishing?
b. Who is from France?
c. Who loves really cold weather?
d. Who has three pets at home?
e. Who thinks that storms are pretty?
f. Who wears jeans to go out?
g. Who goes to the beach with an animal?
h. Who never goes to the beach?
i. Who owns a boat?

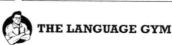 **THE LANGUAGE GYM**

Unit 15. Talking about weather and free time: WRITING

1. Split sentences

Ich mag es, wenn	den Strand.
Ich mag es	ich einen warmen Mantel.
Wenn das Wetter schlecht ist,	es kalt ist.
Wenn es heiß ist, gehe ich an	nicht, wenn es regnet.
Unwetter sind	gehe ich Ski fahren.
Wenn das Wetter schön ist, gehe	bleibe ich zu Hause.
Wenn es sehr kalt ist, trage	sehr schön.
Wenn es schneit,	ich an den Strand.

2. Complete with the correct option

a. _____ es kalt ist, trage ich einen Schal.

b. Unter der _____ mache ich meine Hausaufgaben.

c. Wenn es _____, _____ ich zu Hause.

d. Wenn es neblig _____, gehe ich nicht Ski _____.

e. Wenn es _____ ist, gehe ich surfen.

f. Wenn es _____ ist, gehe ich wandern auf dem Land.

g. Wenn das Wetter _____ ist, bleibt mein Freund Alex in _____ Zimmer.

sonnig	windig	bleibe	fahren	Woche
schlecht	ist	Wenn	regnet	seinem

3. Spot and correct the grammar and spelling mistakes [note: in several cases a word is missing]

a. Wenn es windig ist, ich gehe ins Fitnessstudio.

b. Wenn es neblig, spielt meine Freundin Mia Tennis.

c. Ich liebe Unwetter, denn sie sehr schön.

d. Wenn das Wetter ist schlecht, bleibe ich zu hause.

e. Wenn es neblig ist, speile ich nicht gern Golf.

f. Am Wochende gehe ich mit meinem Hund an die Strand.

g. Wenn es sonnig ist, tragen ich ein weißes hemd.

h. Ich immer trage Sportschuhe, wenn ich Fußball spielen.

i. Du tragst gern warme Klamotten, wenn es ist kalt.

4. Complete the words

a. k_____   *cold*

b. h_____   *hot*

c. b_____   *cloudy*

d. w_____   *when*

e. s_____   *sunny*

f. w_____   *windy*

g. n_____   *foggy*

5. Guided writing – write 3 short paragraphs in the first person [I] using the details below

Person	Lives	Weather	Activity	With
Matthias	Köln	good weather	go to the park	friends
Ingrid	Sylt	sunny and windy	go to the beach	dog
Chris	Wien	cold and rainy	stay home	big sister

6. Describe this person in German using the 3rd person [she]

Name: Hanna

Lives in: Rostock

Age: 13

Pet: a brown dog

Weather: nice and warm weather

Always: goes to the park and plays football with her friends

Never: stays at home and does homework

Grammar Time 15:

SPIELEN, MACHEN, GEHEN (Part 2) & SEIN, HABEN

spielen		*to play*
ich spiele *I play*	**wir spielen** *we play*	Gitarre Karten Volleyball
du spielst *you play*	**ihr spielt** *you guys play*	mit Freunden im Garten
er/sie/es spielt *he/she/it plays*	**sie/Sie spielen** *they/you (formal) play*	im Park in der Sonne

machen		*to do*
ich mache	**wir machen**	einen Ausflug eine Radtour
du machst	**ihr macht**	einfach nichts! Hausaufgaben
er/sie/es macht	**sie/Sie machen**	Karate Yoga

gehen		*to go*
ich gehe	**wir gehen**	in den Park in die Stadt
du gehst	**ihr geht**	ins Schwimmbad Salsa tanzen
er/sie/es geht	**sie/Sie gehen**	zu meinem Freund nach Hause

sein		*to be*
ich bin	**wir sind**	groß klein
du bist	**ihr seid**	glücklich zwölf Jahre alt
er/sie/es ist	**sie/Sie sind**	ein bisschen müde musikalisch

haben		*to have*
ich habe	**wir haben**	kurze Haare braune Augen
du hast	**ihr habt**	einen kleinen Frosch eine süße Katze
er/sie/es hat	**sie/Sie haben**	ein schönes Fahrrad viele Haustiere

Drills

1. Complete with the one of the following verbs: *habe – gehe – bin – spiele – mache*

a. ich _____ Sport

b. ich _____ in den Park

c. ich _____ eine Katze

d. ich _____ Fußball

e. ich _____ Karten

f. ich _____ einen Hund

g. ich _____ fünfzehn Jahre alt

h. ich _____ zwei Haustiere

i. ich _____ ins Kino

j. ich _____ klettern

k. ich _____ Rad fahren

l. ich _____ Schach

m. ich _____ glücklich

n. ich _____ braune Augen

o. ich _____ blonde Haare

2. Rewrite the sentences in the first column in the third person singular

ich	er/sie
Ich spiele Tennis.	Er spielt Tennis.
Ich gehe ins Kino.	
Ich habe eine Katze.	
Ich bin groß.	
Ich mache Yoga.	

3. Translate into English

a. Wir gehen schwimmen.

b. Wir spielen Schach.

c. Sie machen nichts.

d. Sie gehen ins Kino.

e. Wir haben zwei Hunde.

f. Ihr macht Hausaufgaben.

g. Er hat keine Geschwister.

h. Ich komme nicht aus Zürich.

i. Was machst du?

4. Complete

a. Ich g_____ ins Schwimmbad.

b. Meine Mutter g_____ ins Kino.

c. Wir g_____ oft ins Kino.

d. Mein Bruder h_____ eine Katze.

e. Sie s_____ dreizehn Jahre alt, aber ich b_____ elf.

f. Meine Eltern h_____ rote Haare.

g. Mein Bruder und ich m_____ Kampfsport.

5. Complete with the appropriate verb

a. Ich _____ oft mit meinen Eltern ins Kino.

b. Meine Schwester und ich _____ in den Park.

c. Meine Mutter _____ lange blonde Haare.

d. Mein Cousin _____ sehr groß und sportlich.

e. Meine Brüder _____ oft an den Strand.

f. Wenn das Wetter gut ist, _____ er Sport.

g. Sie _____ am liebsten Volleyball.

h. Was _____ du am liebsten in deiner Freizeit?

6. Translate into German

a. I often play tennis in the park.

b. My mother goes into town at the weekend.

c. My brother is tall and slim.

d. He has blond hair and blue eyes.

e. My father is forty years old.

f. My brother goes to the gym.

g. They often go to the swimming pool.

Revision Quickie 4: Clothes/Free time/Weather

1. Activities - Match up

Ich mache Hausaufgaben.	I go to the cinema.
Ich mache Sport.	I go to the swimming pool.
Ich spiele Basketball.	I go to the gym.
Ich spiele Karten.	I go shopping.
Ich gehe ins Kino.	I do the homework.
Ich gehe ins Schwimmbad.	I go swimming.
Ich gehe ins Fitnessstudio.	I do rock climbing.
Ich gehe shoppen.	I do sport.
Ich gehe schwimmen.	I go horse-riding.
Ich gehe reiten.	I go to the beach.
Ich gehe an den Strand.	I play cards.
Ich gehe klettern.	I play basketball.

2. Weather – Complete

a. Es ist k__ __t.

b. Es ist h__ __ß.

c. Es ist son__ __ __.

d. Es ist neb__ __ __.

e. Das Wett__ __ ist sc__ __n.

f. Das We__ __ __ __ __ i__ __ schl__ __ __ __.

g. Es ist stür__ __ __ __ __.

h. Es ist wi__ __ __ __.

i. Es re__ __ __ __.

3. Fill in the gaps in German

a. Wenn es k_____ ist, trage ich einen M_____.   *When it is cold, I wear a coat.*

b. Wenn das W_____ s_____ ist, b_____ ich zu Hause.   *When the weather is bad, I stay at home.*

c. Wenn die S_____ s_____, gehe ich an den S_____.   *When it is sunny, I go to the beach.*

d. Wenn ich Y_____ mache, t_____ ich einen Tr_____.   *When I do yoga, I wear a tracksuit.*

e. Wenn es h_____ ist, gehe ich i____ S_____.   *When it is hot, I go to the swimming pool.*

f. Am Wochenende m_____ ich m_____ H_____.   *At the weekend I do my homework.*

g. Wenn ich Z_____ h_____, g_____ i_____ k_____.   *When I have time, I go rock climbing.*

4. Translate into German

a. when it is hot

b. when it is cold

c. I play basketball.

d. I do my homework.

e. I go rock climbing.

f. when I have time

g. I go to the swimming pool.

h. I go to the gym.

5. Translate into German

a. I wear a coat.

b. We wear a uniform.

c. They play basketball.

d. She goes rock climbing.

e. He has time.

f. They go swimming.

Question Skills 3: Clothes / Free time / Weather

1. Translate into English

a. Was trägst du, wenn es kalt ist?

b. Wie ist das Wetter, wo du wohnst?

c. Was machst du in deiner Freizeit?

d. Machst du Sport?

e. Wie oft spielst du Basketball?

f. Warum magst du Fußball nicht?

g. Wo gehst du klettern?

h. Was ist dein Lieblingssport?

2. Complete with the missing question word

a. _____ wohnst du?

b. _____ Sport machst du?

c. _____ magst du lieber, Tennis oder Schach?

d. _____ gehst du schwimmen?

e. _____ findest du meine Schuhe?

f. _____ machst du gern in deiner Freizeit?

g. Mit _____ spielst du Tennis?

h. _____ oft gehst du reiten?

i. _____ spielst du nicht mit mir? ☹

3. Split questions

Was machst du in	du klettern?
Wie oft gehst	trägst du, wenn es kalt ist?
Gehst du	oft ins Kino?
Mit wem	deiner Freizeit?
Was trägst	du am liebsten?
Was macht	spielst du Schach?
Hast du viele	Klamotten?
Was für Klamotten	dein Bruder nach der Schule?

4. Translate into German

a. What?

b. Where?

c. How?

d. When?

e. With whom?

f. How much?

g. How many?

h. From where?

i. Why?

5. Write the questions to these answers

a. Wenn es kalt ist, trage ich einen Mantel.

b. Am Wochenende mache ich Sport.

c. Ich gehe um fünf Uhr ins Fitnessstudio.

d. Ich habe zwei Trainingsanzüge.

e. Ich spiele mit meinem Bruder Tennis.

f. Ich gehe im Freibad am Stadtrand schwimmen.

g. Ich gehe selten klettern.

6. Translate into German

a. Where do you play tennis?

b. What do you do in your free time?

c. How many shoes do you have?

d. What is your favourite sport?

e. Do you do sport often?

f. When do you do your homework?

UNIT 16
Talking about my
daily routine

Revision Quickie 5:
Clothes / Food / Free Time / Describing people

In this unit you will learn how to say:

- What you do every day
- At what time you do it
- Sequencing events/actions (e.g. using 'then', 'finally')

You will revisit:
- Numbers
- Free time activities
- Nationalities
- Clothes
- Hair and eyes
- Food
- Jobs

UNIT 16
Talking about my daily routine

Meistens *Usually* **Morgens** *In the mornings*	**wache ich ...** *I wake ...* **stehe ich ...** *I get ...*	**um sechs Uhr** **gegen sieben Uhr** **um zehn nach acht** **um Viertel nach acht** **um zwanzig nach acht** **um halb neun** **um zwanzig vor neun** **um Viertel vor neun** **um zehn vor neun**	*at 6 o'clock* *around 7 o'clock* *at 8.10* *at 8.15* *at 8.20* *at 8.30* *at 8.40* *at 8.45* *at 8.50*	**... auf** *... up*

Zuerst *First*	**gehe ich ins Bad** *I go into the bathroom*		**ich packe meine Schultasche** *I pack my school bag*
Dann *Then*	**dusche ich mich** *I have a shower*		**ich putze meine Zähne** *I brush my teeth*
Danach *Afterwards*	**ziehe ich mich an** *I get dressed*		**ich gehe aus dem Haus** *I go out of the house*
Später *Later*	**frühstücke ich** *I breakfast*		**ich fahre mit dem Bus zur Schule** *I go to school by bus*
Mittags *At lunchtime*	**komme ich wieder nach Hause** *I come home again*	**und** *and*	**ich entspanne mich** *I relax*
Nachmittags *In the afternoon*	**esse ich zu Mittag/zu Abend** *I eat lunch/dinner*		**ich mache meine Hausaufgaben** *I do my homework*
Abends *In the evening*	**sehe ich fern** *I watch TV*		**ich spiele am Computer** *I play on the computer*
Zum Schluss *Finally*	**gehe ich <u>um Mitternacht</u> ins Bett** *I go to bed at midnight*		**ich mache das Licht aus** *I switch off the light*

Author's note:

In the column on the very left, you find some very useful adverbs that will allow you to make clear in which <u>sequence</u> or at what <u>time of the day</u> something is happening. Do you remember what happens when you use these kinds of words (adverbs) at the beginning of a sentence? Can you observe this in the table? Discuss your thoughts with a partner or your teacher. You can also check back with the grammar time on word order in main clauses in Unit 12.

 **THE LANGUAGE GYM**

Unit 16. Talking about my daily routine: VOCAB BUILDING (Part 1)

1. Match up

ich stehe auf	I have lunch
ich fahre zur Schule	I have dinner
ich gehe ins Bett	I get up
ich esse zu Mittag	I have breakfast
ich esse zu Abend	I relax
ich frühstücke	I go to school
ich entspanne mich	I come home again
ich komme wieder nach Hause	I go to bed

2. Translate into English

a. Ich stehe um sechs Uhr auf.

b. Ich gehe um elf Uhr ins Bett.

c. Ich esse um zwölf Uhr zu Mittag.

d. Ich frühstücke um sieben Uhr.

e. Ich komme um halb vier wieder nach Hause.

f. Ich esse um sieben Uhr zu Abend.

g. Ich sehe fern.

h. Ich höre Musik.

i. Ich gehe um halb acht aus dem Haus.

3. Complete with the missing words

a. Ich _____ zur Schule.
I go to school.

b. Ich gehe _____ dem Haus.
I leave the house.

c. Ich _____ wieder nach Hause.
I come home again.

d. Ich _____ fern.
I watch TV.

e. Ich _____ Hausaufgaben.
I do homework.

f. Ich _____ Musik.
I listen to music.

g. Ich _____ am Computer.
I play on the computer.

h. Ich esse um zwölf Uhr zu _____.
I have lunch at 12.

i. Dann _____ ich meine Schultasche.
Then, I pack my school bag.

4. Complete with the missing letters

a. Ich __ntspanne __ich.   *I relax.*

b. Ich __omme ...   *I come ...*

c. ... wieder __ach __ause.   *...home again.*

d. Ich h__re Musik.   *I listen to music.*

e. Ich fr__hstüc__e.   *I have breakfast.*

f. Ich e__se zu A__end.   *I eat dinner.*

g. Ich geh__ zur S__hule.   *I go to school.*

h. Ich ste__e au__.   *I get up.*

i. Ich gehe in__ Be__t.   *I go to bed.*

j. Ich esse zu Mi__tag.   *I eat lunch.*

5. Bad translation – spot and correct any translation mistakes. Not all translations are wrong.

a. Ich entspanne mich ein bisschen.   *I shower a bit.*

b. Ich gehe um Mitternacht ins Bett.   *I go to bed at noon.*

c. Ich mache meine Hausaufgaben.   *I do your homework.*

d. Ich frühstücke.   *I have lunch.*

e. Ich fahre zur Schule.   *I come back from school.*

f. Ich komme wieder nach Hause.   *I leave the house.*

g. Ich sehe fern.   *I watch TV.*

h. Ich gehe aus dem Haus.   *I leave school.*

i. Ich putze mir die Zähne.   *I clean my hands.*

6. Translate the following times into German

a. at 6.30 a.m.   *um halb sieben*

b. at 7.30 a.m.

c. at 8.20 p.m.

d. at midday

e. at 9.20 a.m.

f. at 11.00 p.m.

g. at midnight

h. at 5.15 p.m.

i. at 9.45 p.m.

Unit 16. Talking about my daily routine: VOCAB BUILDING (Part 2)

1. Complete the table

ich gehe ins Bett	
	I brush my teeth
ich stehe auf	
	I go back home
ich esse zu Mittag	
ich frühstücke	
	I have dinner
ich höre Musik	
	I leave the house
ich sehe fern	
ich entspanne mich	
	I do my homework
ich ziehe mich an	

2. Complete the sentences using the words in the table below

a. um halb _____   *at seven thirty*

b. _____ fünf Uhr   *at about five o'clock*

c. um acht Uhr _____   *at 8 a.m. in the morning*

d. um zwölf Uhr _____   *at 12 p.m. lunchtime*

e. um Viertel nach _____   *at 11.15*

f. gegen zwanzig _____ drei   *at about 2.40*

g. um _____   *at midnight*

h. gegen vier _____   *at about four o'clock*

i. um _____ nach zehn   *at 10.05*

j. um fünf vor _____ neun   *at 8.25*

gegen	acht	Uhr	morgens	mittags
elf	vor	fünf	halb	Mitternacht

3. Translate into English (numerical)

a. um halb neun   *at 8.30*

b. um Viertel nach neun   _____

c. um fünf vor zwölf   _____

d. um zwölf Uhr mittags   _____

e. um Mitternacht   _____

f. um fünf nach halb acht   _____

g. um Viertel nach zwei   _____

h. abends um halb zehn   _____

4. Complete

a. um h_____ s_____   *at 5.30*

b. g_____ V_____ n____ a_____   *around 8.15*

c. m_____   *at noon*

d. u_ z_____ v_____ n_____   *at 8.40*

e. um M_____   *at midnight*

f. um f_____ n_____ h_____ z_____   *at 11.35*

g. g_____ n_____ U_____   *around 9 o'clock*

h. um z_____ v_____ d_____   *at 2.50*

5. Translate into English

a. Ich stehe um halb sieben auf.

b. Ich komme um vier Uhr wieder nach Hause.

c. Gegen sechs Uhr sehe ich fern.

d. Gegen fünf Uhr mache ich meine Hausaufgaben.

e. Ich frühstücke um Viertel vor sieben.

f. Ich gehe gegen elf Uhr ins Bett.

g. Um ein Uhr esse ich zu Mittag.

6. Translate into German

a. I get up at half past five.

b. I come home again at five o'clock.

c. Around eight o'clock I relax.

d. Then I watch TV.

e. I eat breakfast at quarter past eight.

f. I go to bed around ten o'clock.

g. I switch off the light at midnight.

Unit 16. Talking about my daily routine: READING (Part 1)

Ich heiße Hiroto. Ich komme aus Japan. Mein Tagesablauf ist ziemlich einfach. Meistens stehe ich gegen sechs Uhr auf. Dann dusche ich mich und ich ziehe mich an. Danach frühstücke ich mit meinem Vater und meinem kleinen Bruder. Dann putze ich mir die Zähne. Gegen halb acht gehe ich aus dem Haus und ich fahre mit dem Fahrrad zur Schule. Ich komme gegen vier Uhr wieder nach Hause. Dann entspanne ich mich – meistens sehe ich zuerst ein bisschen fern und dann gehe ich mit meinen Freunden in den Park. Von sechs bis sieben Uhr mache ich meine Hausaufgaben. Um acht Uhr esse ich mit meinen Eltern zu Abend. Ich esse nicht viel, meistens nur einen Hamburger. Danach sehe ich einen Film im Fernsehen und gegen elf Uhr gehe ich ins Bett.

Ich heiße Gregorio. Ich komme aus Mexiko. Mein Tagesablauf ist sehr einfach. Normalerweise stehe ich um Viertel nach sechs auf. Dann dusche ich mich und ich frühstücke mit meinen zwei Brüdern. Dann putze ich mir die Zähne und ich packe meine Schultasche. Gegen sieben gehe ich aus dem Haus und ich gehe zu Fuß zur Schule. Ich komme gegen halb vier wieder nach Hause. Dann entspanne ich mich ein bisschen. Meistens surfe ich im Internet, sehe eine Serie auf Netflix oder chatte mit meinen Freunden auf WhatsApp oder Snapchat. Von fünf bis sechs Uhr mache ich meine Hausaufgaben. Danach, um halb acht, esse ich mit meiner Familie zu Abend. Ich esse Reis oder Salat. Später sehe ich fern und gegen halb zwölf gehe ich ins Bett.

Ich heiße Andreas. Ich komme aus Deutschland. Mein Tagesablauf ist ziemlich einfach. Meistens stehe ich sehr früh auf, gegen fünf Uhr. Ich gehe joggen und dann dusche ich mich und ich ziehe mich an. Danach, gegen halb sieben, frühstücke ich mit meiner Mutter und meiner Schwester. Meistens essen wir Müsli mit Milch und ein bisschen Obst. Dann putze ich mir die Zähne und ich packe meine Schultasche. Gegen Viertel nach sieben gehe ich aus dem Haus und ich gehe zur Schule. Ich komme gegen halb vier wieder nach Hause. Dann entspanne ich mich ein bisschen. Meistens sehe ich fern oder ich chatte mit meinen Freunden im Internet. Von sechs bis acht Uhr mache ich meine Hausaufgaben und um Viertel nach acht esse ich mit meinen Eltern zu Abend. Ich esse nicht viel. Später spiele ich auf der PlayStation bis Mitternacht, dann gehe ich ins Bett.

1. Answer the following questions about Hiroto

a. Where is he from?

b. At what time does he get up?

c. Who does he have breakfast with?

d. At what time does he leave the house?

e. Until what time does he stay at the park?

f. How does he go to school?

2. Find the German for the phrases below in Hiroto's text

a. At around eleven o'clock

b. With my friends

c. I go by bike

d. then I go to the park

e. then I shower

f. I don't eat much

g. from six to seven

h. afterwards I watch a film

3. Find the German for the following phrases/sentences in Gregorio's text

a. I am from Mexico.

b. then I shower

c. with my two brothers

d. then I relax a bit

e. I eat rice or salad.

f. Usually, I surf the internet.

g. Later I watch TV.

4. Complete the statements below about Andreas' text

a. He gets up at _____.

b. He comes back from school at around _____.

c. For breakfast, he eats _____.

d. He has breakfast with _____.

e. After getting up he _____ and then showers.

f. Usually he _____ until midnight.

g. After breakfast, he brushes his teeth and then _____. _____.

Ich heiße Yang. Ich bin zwölf Jahre alt und ich komme aus China. Mein Tagesablauf ist sehr einfach. Meistens stehe ich gegen halb sieben auf. Zuerst dusche ich mich und ich ziehe mich an. Danach frühstücke ich mit meiner Mutter und meinem Bruder Li Wei. Dann putze ich mir die Zähne und ich packe meine Schultasche. Gegen halb acht gehe ich aus dem Haus und ich gehe zur Schule. Gegen vier Uhr komme ich wieder nach Hause. Dann entspanne ich mich ein bisschen. Meistens sehe ich fern, höre Musik oder ich lese meine Lieblingscomics. Von sechs bis halb acht mache ich meine Hausaufgaben. Danach, um acht Uhr, esse ich mit meiner Familie zu Abend. Ich esse nicht viel. Später sehe ich einen Film im Fernsehen und gegen elf Uhr gehe ich ins Bett.

Ich heiße Anna. Ich bin Italienerin. Mein Tagesablauf ist sehr einfach. Normaler-weise stehe ich um Viertel nach sechs auf. Dann wasche ich mich und ich frühstücke mit meiner großen Schwester. Dann putze ich mir die Zähne und ich packe meine Schulsachen. Gegen sieben Uhr fahre ich mit dem Bus zur Schule. Um halb drei komme ich wieder nach Hause. Dann entspanne ich mich ein bisschen. Meistens surfe ich im Internet, sehe fern oder ich lese ein Modemagazin. Von fünf bis sechs Uhr mache ich meine Hausaufgaben. Später, um acht Uhr, esse ich mit meiner Familie zu Abend. Ich esse Obst oder Salat. Dann lese ich ein spannendes Buch und gegen halb zwölf gehe ich ins Bett.

Ich heiße Kim. Ich bin Engländerin und ich bin fünfzehn Jahre alt. Mein Tagesablauf ist sehr einfach. Meistens stehe ich früh auf, gegen halb sechs. Ich mache Sport und dann wasche ich mich und ich ziehe mich an. Danach frühstücke ich gegen sieben Uhr mit meiner Mutter und meiner Stiefschwester. Dann putze ich mir die Zähne und ich packe meine Schulsachen. Gegen halb acht gehe ich aus dem Haus und ich gehe zur Schule. Um drei Uhr komme ich wieder nach Hause. Dann entspanne ich mich ein bisschen. Meistens höre ich Musik oder ich chatte mit meinen Freunden im Internet. Von sechs bis acht mache ich meine Hausaufgaben. Danach, um Viertel nach acht Uhr, esse ich mit meiner Familie zu Abend. Ich esse ziemlich viel. Später sehe ich einen Film im Fernsehen bis Mitternacht, schließlich gehe ich ins Bett.

1. Find the German for the following in Yang's text

a. I am from China

b. my daily routine

c. at first, I shower

d. very simple

e. at around 6.30

f. I don't eat much

g. usually, I watch telly

h. and I go to school

i. I do my homework

j. from 6 to 7.30

k. I watch a movie

2. Translate these items from Kim's text

a. I am English

b. usually

c. at around 5.30

d. with my mum and my stepsister

e. I come back home

f. at three o'clock

g. I have dinner with my family

h. then I relax a bit

i. I brush my teeth

3. Answer the following questions on Anna's text

a. What nationality is Anna?

b. At what time does she get up?

c. What three things does she do after school?

d. How does she go to school?

e. Who does she have breakfast with?

f. At what time does she go to bed?

g. What does she eat for dinner?

h. What does she read before going to bed?

4. Find someone who...

a. ...has breakfast with their big sister.

b. ...does exercise in the morning.

c. ...reads fashion magazines.

d. ...gets up at 5.30 a.m.

e. ...has breakfast with their brother and mother.

f. ...chats with their friends on the internet after school.

g. ...doesn't watch TV at night.

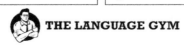

THE LANGUAGE GYM

Unit 16. Talking about my daily routine: WRITING

1. Split sentences

Ich fahre mit	wieder nach Hause.
Ich komme um vier Uhr	Hausaufgaben.
Ich mache meine	dem Bus zur Schule.
Ich sehe	sechs Uhr auf.
Dann spiele ich am	Mitternacht ins Bett.
Ich stehe um	dem Haus.
Ich gehe um	ein bisschen fern.
Ich gehe um elf aus	Computer.

2. Complete with the correct option

a. Ich stehe morgens _____ sieben Uhr auf.

b. Ich mache _____ Hausaufgaben.

c. Ich _____ fern.

d. Ich _____ am Computer.

e. Ich gehe um Mitternacht ins _____.

f. Ich komme um drei Uhr wieder _____ Hause.

g. Ich gehe _____ dem Haus.

h. Ich fahre mit dem _____ zur Schule.

spiele	Bett	um	nach
sehe	meine	aus	Bus

3. Spot and correct the grammar and spelling mistakes [in several cases a word is missing]

a. Ich fahren mit dem fahrrad zur Schule.

b. Ich stehe auf um halb acht.

c. Ich gehen um acht Uhr aus Haus.

d. Ich o komme wieder Hause.

e. Ich fahrt mit Bus zur Schule.

f. Ich gehst um elf Ur ins Bett.

g. Ich essen veirtel vor acht zu Abend.

h. Ich mache um halb sechs miene Hausaufaben.

4. Complete the words

a. Vi_____	*quarter*
b. h_____	*half*
c. um z_____ U_____	*at 10 o'clock*
d. g_____	*at around*
e. u__ a_____ U_____	*at 8 o'clock*
f. zw_____	*twenty*
g. d_____	*then*
h. z_____	*at first*
i. i___ k_____ w_____	*I come back*
j. i___ s_____	*I play*

5. Guided writing – write 3 short paragraphs in the first person [I] using the details below

Person	Gets up	Showers	Goes to school	Comes back home	Watches telly	Has dinner	Goes to bed
Basti	6.30	7.00	8.05	3.30	6.00	8.10	11.10
Luzi	6.40	7.10	7.40	4.00	6.30	8.15	12.00
Mehmet	7.15	7.30	8.00	3.15	6.40	8.20	11.30

Revision Quickie 5: Clothes / Food / Free Time / Describing people

1. Clothes – Match up

ich trage (1)	a woolly hat
einen Anzug	a skirt
eine Wollmütze	a dress
eine Krawatte	a shirt
einen Rock	a T-shirt
ein Kleid	jeans
ein Hemd	a suit
ein T-Shirt	socks
Jeans	trousers
Socken	I wear (1)
eine Hose	a tie

3. Complete the translations below

a. shoes   _Sch_____

b. trousers   _Ho_____

c. hair   _Ha_____

d. curly   _lo_____

e. blue   _bl_____

f. milk   _Mi_____

g. water   _Wa_____

h. pasta   _Nu_____

i. work   _Ar_____

j. clothes   _Klam_____

2. Food – Provide a word for each of the cues below

A fruit starting with **Ä**	Äpfel
A vegetable starting with **T**	
A dairy product starting with **J**	
A meat starting with **Sch**	
A drink starting with **O**	
A drink made using apples starting with **A**	
A sweet dessert starting with **E**	
A fruit starting with **E**	

4. Clothes, Colours, Jobs, Food – Categories

Kleidung	Farben	Berufe	Essen

Hemd	blau	Anwalt	Journalist
Fleisch	rosa	Lehrerin	Hähnchen
Anzug	Koch	Käse	Krawatte
orange	Hut	Reis	rot

5. Match questions and answers

Was ist dein Lieblingsberuf?	Einen Trainings-anzug
Was ist deine Lieblingsfarbe?	Mein Kunstlehrer
Was isst du am liebsten zum Frühstück?	Journalist
Was trägst du im Fitnessstudio?	Schach
Wer ist dein Lieblingslehrer?	Blau
Was ist dein Lieblingsgetränk?	Haferbrei mit Rosinen
Was ist dein Lieblingshobby?	Apfelsaft

6. (Free time) Complete with *mache, gehe* or *spiele* as appropriate

a. Ich _____ jeden Tag Sport.

b. Ich _____ nie Basketball.

c. Ich _____ oft ins Fitnessstudio.

d. Ich _____ immer meine Hausaufgaben.

e. Manchmal _____ ich am Computer.

f. Heute _____ ich nicht ins Schwimmbad.

g. In meiner Freizeit _____ ich gern Judo.

7. Complete with the missing verb, choosing from the list below

a. Ich _____ oft Orangensaft.

b. Ich _____ Erdbeeren!

c. Wenn ich die Hausaufgaben gemacht habe, _____ ich ins Fitnessstudio oder ich _____ am Computer.

d. Ich _____ viel Sport.

e. Morgens _____ ich nicht viel. Nur einen Toast mit Marmelade.

f. Mein Vater _____ als Ingenieur. Ich _____ noch nicht. Ich _____ Student.

g. Ich _____ nicht gern Zeichentrickfilme. Ich _____ Serien auf Netflix besser.

h. Morgens _____ ich gegen sechs Uhr auf.

stehe	spiele	liebe	arbeite
gehe	mache	sehe	bin
arbeitet	trinke	finde	esse

11. Translate into German

a. I play tennis every day.

b. I sometimes wear a jacket.

c. I go to the gym often.

d. I don't like watching cartoons.

e. I get up at around six a.m.

f. I shower twice a day.

8. Adverbs of frequency – Translate

a. nie

b. ab und zu

c. immer

d. jeden Tag

e. selten

f. einmal pro Woche

g. zweimal pro Monat

9. Split sentences (Relationships)

Ich verstehe mich gut mit	Cousine.
Ich verstehe mich nicht	meiner Mutter.
Meine Eltern sind immer	ist supernervig.
Ich	gut mit Max.
Mein Bruder	mich gut mit ihm.
Ich mag meinen	sehr großzügig.
Meine Freundin wohnt	verstehen uns gut.
Ich hasse meine	im Stadtzentrum.
Ich verstehe	Opa sehr!
Mein Bruder und ich	liebe meine Oma.

10. Complete the translation

a. Mein Bruder ist A_____.
My brother is a lawyer.

b. Ich _____ nicht. Ich bin _____.
I don't work. I am a student.

c. Ab und zu _____ ich mit meinem Vater ins Kino.
From time to time I go to the cinema with my father.

d. Ich _____ nie fern.
I never watch TV.

e. Ich _____ meine Lehrer.
I hate my teachers.

f. Meine Eltern sind meistens sehr _____.
My parents are usually very strict.

g. Ich _____ _____ joggen.
I never go jogging.

h. Ich _____ am liebsten _____.
I most like playing chess.

UNIT 17
Describing my house:
- indicating where it is located
- saying what I like/dislike about it

Grammar Time 16: WOHNEN + locations in the dative case
Grammar Time 17: REFLEXIVES (Part 1)
Grammar Time 18: ES GIBT + indefinite article + adjective + noun

In this unit you will learn how to say in German

- Where your house/flat is located
- What your favourite room is
- What you like to do in each room
- The present tense of key reflexive verbs

You will revisit:
- Adjectives to describe places
- Frequency markers
- Countries
- Indefinite article+adjective+noun in the accusative case

UNIT 17 - Describing my house

Ich wohne in einem *I live in a*	**alten**	*old*	**Haus** *house*	**am Stadtrand**	*in the suburbs*
	großen	*big*		**an der Küste**	*on the coast*
	hässlichen	*ugly*		**auf dem Land**	*in the countryside*
Ich wohne in einer *I live in a*	**kleinen**	*small*	**Wohnung** *flat*	**im Stadtzentrum**	*in the city centre*
	neuen	*new*		**in den Bergen**	*in the mountains*
	schönen	*beautiful*			

In meinem Haus/In meiner Wohnung gibt es vier/fünf/sechs Zimmer.
In my house/In my flat there are four/five/six rooms.

Mein Lieblingszimmer ist ... *My favourite room is ...* **Mein Lieblingsort ist ...** *My favourite place is ...*	**das Badezimmer**	*the bathroom*
	der Balkon	*the balcony*
	der Dachboden	*the attic*
	das Esszimmer	*the dining room*
	die Garage	*the garage*
	der Garten	*the garden*
	der Keller	*the cellar*
	das Klo	*the loo*
	die Küche	*the kitchen*
	die Terrasse	*the terrace*
	das Wohnzimmer	*the living room*
	das Zimmer von meinem Bruder	*my brother's room*
	das Zimmer von meinen Eltern	*my parents' room*
	mein Zimmer	*my room*

Hier	*Here*	**kann ich** *I can*	**einfach nichts tun**	*simply do nothing*
Auf dem Balkon	*On the balcony*		**mich gut entspannen**	*relax well*
Auf dem Dachboden	*In the attic*		**mich gut konzentrieren**	*concentrate well*
Auf dem Klo	*On the loo*		**schön in der Sonne sitzen**	*sit nicely in the sun*
Auf der Terrasse	*On the terrace*		**in Ruhe ein Buch lesen**	*read a book in peace*
Im Badezimmer	*In the bathroom*		**in Ruhe fernsehen**	*watch TV in peace*
Im Esszimmer	*In the dining room*		**Hausaufgaben machen**	*do homework*
Im Garten	*In the garden*		**laut Musik hören**	*listen to loud music*
Im Keller	*In the cellar*			
Im Wohnzimmer	*In the living room*			
In der Garage	*In the garage*			
In der Küche	*In the kitchen*			
In meinem Zimmer	*In my room*			

Unit 17. Describing my house: VOCABULARY BUILDING (Part 1)

1. Match up

ich wohne	*in a flat*
in einem Haus	*simply do nothing*
in einer Wohnung	*here I can*
im Wohnzimmer	*in the suburbs*
hier kann ich	*I live*
auf dem Land	*in a house*
am Stadtrand	*in the living room*
einfach nichts tun	*in the countryside*

2. Translate into English

a. Ich wohne in einem alten Haus.

b. Ich wohne in einer neuen Wohnung.

c. Meine Wohnung ist am Stadtrand.

d. Im Wohnzimmer kann ich in Ruhe fernsehen.

e. Mein Lieblingszimmer ist mein Schlafzimmer.

f. Ich bin gern in der Küche, denn sie ist sehr modern.

g. Der Balkon ist mein Lieblingsort in meinem Haus.

h. Ich mag <u>den</u> Balkon, denn hier kann ich mich gut entspannen.

i. Im Garten kann ich in Ruhe ein Buch lesen.

3. Complete with the missing words

a. Ich wohne ___ der Küste.
I live on the coast.

b. Ich _____ mein Haus.
I like my house.

c. Ich _____ in einem alten, aber _____ Haus.
I live in an old but pretty house.

d. Ich entspanne mich _____ im Wohnzimmer.
I like relaxing in the living room.

e. Mein _____ ist am Stadtrand.
My house is in the suburbs.

f. Ich _____ mich nie im Garten!
I never shower in the garden!

g. Ich bin _____ auf dem Klo.
I like being on the loo.

4. Complete the words

a. i__ e_____ H_____
in a house

b. a___ S_____
in the suburbs

c. Das H_____ ist n_____.
The house is new.

d. I____ m_____ den B_____.
I like the balcony.

e. a____ d____ T_____
on the terrace

f. i__ e_____ k_____ W_____
in a small flat

5. Classify the words/phrases below in the table below

a. immer   f. groß   k. in den Bergen

b. spielen   g. manchmal   l. arbeiten

c. nie   h. Esszimmer   m. duschen

d. wohnen   i. schön   n. Zimmer

e. neu   j. klein   o. Küste

Adverbs & Adverbials	Nouns	Verbs	Adjectives
a.			

6. Translate into German

a. I live in an old flat.

b. I live in a new house.

c. in the town centre

d. I like relaxing in the kitchen.

e. I like being in the bathroom.

f. In the garden, I can simply do nothing.

g. My favourite room is the kitchen.

Unit 17. Describing my house: VOCABULARY BUILDING (Part 2)

1. Split phrases

auf der	nichts tun
in der	Terrasse
einfach	einer Wohnung
im	hören
ich wohne in	Balkon
mein Lieblings-	Wohnzimmer
ich mag den	Küche
Musik	ort

4. Broken words

a. Ich entspanne mich g_____. *I like relaxing.*

b. Ich wohne in den B_____. *I live in the mountains.*

c. Ich bin oft im W_____. *I am often in the living room.*

d. Hier kann ich s_____ ... *Here I can ... nicely...*

e. ...in der Sonne s_____. *... sit in the sun.*

f. Mein L_____ ist ... *My favourite room is ...*

g. das K_____ *the loo*

3. Translate into English

a. Ich wohne in einem alten Haus.

b. Es ist am Stadtrand.

c. Es ist groß, aber hässlich.

d. Mein Lieblingsort ist das Klo.

e. Ich bin oft auf der Terrasse.

f. Ich arbeite gern im Esszimmer.

g. Ich entspanne mich gern.

h. Hier kann ich in Ruhe lesen.

i. Ich dusche mich oft im Garten.

2. Complete with the missing word

a. Ich _____ mich gern. *I like relaxing.*

b. Sie ist klein, aber _____. *It (the flat) is small but beautiful.*

c. Es ist im _____. *It (the house) is in the town centre.*

d. Sie ist am _____. *It (the flat) is in the suburbs.*

e. Ich wohne in einem _____ Haus. *I live in a big house.*

f. Das Haus ist in den _____. *The house is in the mountains.*

g. Mein _____-zimmer ist ... *My favourite room is ...*

h. Hier _____ ich einfach nichts tun. *Here I can simply do nothing.*

i. Ich bin gern in meinem _____. *I like being in my room.*

j. Es _____ vier Zimmer. *There are four rooms.*

kann	entspanne	gibt	Stadtzentrum	Stadtrand
großen	Zimmer	schön	Lieblings-	Bergen

5. 'der, 'die' or 'das'?

a. **die** Küche

b. ___ Wohnzimmer

c. ____ Esszimmer

d. ____ Balkon

e. ____ Garten

f. ____ Keller

g. ____ Klo

h. ____ Terrasse

i. ____ Dachboden

j. ____ Arbeitszimmer

6. Bad translation – spot any translation errors and fix them

a. Ich wohne in einem schönen Haus. *I live in a small house.*

b. Mein Lieblingszimmer ist das Wohnzimmer. *My favourite room is the dining room.*

c. Hier kann ich in Ruhe fernsehen. *Here I can relax in peace.*

d. Ich wohne in einer kleinen Wohnung. *I live in a big flat.*

e. Ich mag mein Haus, denn es ist groß und schön. *I don't like my house because it is big and ugly.*

f. Im Esszimmer kann ich gut arbeiten. *In the kitchen I can work well.]*

g. In meinem Zimmer kann ich sehr gut Musik hören. *In my room I can listen to music well.*

 **THE LANGUAGE GYM**

Unit 17. Describing my house: READING

Ich heiße Dante. Ich komme aus Italien. Ich wohne in einem schönen großen Haus an der Küste. In meinem Haus gibt es zehn Zimmer! Mein Lieblingszimmer ist die Küche. Ich bin oft in der Küche, denn ich koche gern, am liebsten Nudeln! Morgens stehe ich immer auf, dann gehe ich ins Bad und ich dusche mich. Dann ziehe ich mich in meinem Zimmer an.

Mein Freund Pablo wohnt in einem kleinen Haus in den Bergen. Er ist sehr lustig und superfleißig. Er mag sein Haus nicht, da es sehr klein ist.

Ich heiße Michael und ich komme aus Basel in der Schweiz. Ich wohne in einem Reihenhaus im Stadtzentrum. Zu Hause sprechen wir Deutsch und Französisch, da mein Vater aus der deutschen und meine Mutter aus der französischen Schweiz kommt. Mein Haus ist klein, aber neu und total schön. Es gibt sechs Zimmer und es gibt auch einen großen Garten. Im Garten wohnt mein Pferd, das Luis heißt. Mein Lieblingszimmer ist das Esszimmer, weil ich supergern esse. In meinem Zimmer kann ich mich sehr gut entspannen. Ich sehe immer Zeichentrickfilme oder Serien auf Netflix. Ich kann hier auch in Ruhe arbeiten, wenn ich Hausaufgaben habe. Das ist super.

Hallo, ich bin Lenny. Ich komme aus Südtirol und ich wohne in einem sehr alten, aber sehr schönen Haus auf dem Land. Ich liebe es! In meinem Haus gibt es fünf Zimmer, aber mein Lieblingszimmer ist das Wohnzimmer – hier kann ich mich jeden Tag nach der Schule entspannen und mit meiner Schwester fernsehen. Jedoch mag ich das Badezimmer nicht, weil es hier manchmal Ratten gibt! Igitt!

1. Answer the following questions about Dante

a. Where is he from?

b. What is his house like?

c. How many rooms are there in his house?

d. Which is his favourite room and why?

e. Where does he get dressed?

f. Where does Pablo live?

g. Does he like his house? (Why?)

2. Find the German for the phrases below in Michaels's text

a. I live in a terraced house

b. at home we speak

c. from French Switzerland

d. there is also a big garden

e. because I really like to eat

f. I always watch cartoons

g. I can work in peace here

h. when I have homework

Ich heiße Ariane. Ich bin aus Österreich. Ich stehe jeden Morgen um fünf Uhr auf, weil ich weit weg von der Schule wohne, am Stadtrand. Ich wohne in einer Wohnung in einem sehr alten Mehrfamilienhaus. Die Wohnung ist sehr alt und ein bisschen hässlich, aber ich mag sie. Im Wohnzimmer kann ich mich sehr gut entspannen, zum Beispiel lese ich Bücher oder ich höre Musik auf Spotify. Aber mein Lieblingszimmer ist mein Zimmer!

3. Find someone who: which person ...

a. ... lives far from school?

b. ... speaks two languages?

c. ... has a really really big house?

d. ... sometimes finds 'unwanted guests' in the bathroom?

e. ... has a big pet that lives outside the house?

f. ... listens to music on a streaming platform?

g. ... is a foodie (loves food)?

h. ... has a friend that doesn't like their house?

4. Find the German for the following phrases/sentences in Ariane's text

a. I am from Austria.

b. I get up at 5 o'clock every morning.

c. far away from school

d. The flat is very old ...

e. ... and a bit ugly ...

f. ... but I like it.

g. for example I read books

 THE LANGUAGE GYM

Unit 17. Describing my house: TRANSLATION

1. Gapped translation

a. Ich wohne in den Bergen.
I live in the _____.

b. Ich wohne in einer kleinen hässlichen Wohnung.
I live in a _____ ugly _____.

c. Sie ist am Stadtrand.
It is in the _____.

d. Ich _____ im _____.
I live in the city centre.

e. In meinem Haus _____ es fünf Zimmer.
In my house there are five rooms.

f. Ich mag die _____ nicht, weil sie sehr _____ ist.
I don't like the kitchen because it's very old.

2. Translate into English

a. an der Küste

b. auf dem Land

c. ich wohne

d. im Stadtzentrum

e. im Esszimmer

f. hier kann ich in Ruhe essen

g. ich entspanne mich gern

h. auf meinem Zimmer

i. auf dem Balkon

3. Translate into English

a. Ich wohne in einem kleinen, aber schönen Haus.

b. Mein Haus ist modern, aber sehr hässlich.

c. Mein Lieblingsort ist der Garten.

d. Hier kann ich mich gut entspannen.

e. Ich mag den Balkon, denn er ist schön groß.

f. Auf meinem Zimmer kann ich in Ruhe Musik hören.

4. Translate into German

a. big   g_____

b. small   k_____

c. in the suburbs   a___ S_____

d. on the coast   a__ d___ K_____

e. the living room   d___ W_____

f. in the dining room i__ E_____

g. ugly   h_____

h. the room   d___ Z_____

i. there are   e___ g_____

j. old   a_____

5. Translate into German

a. I live in a small house.

b. in the city centre

c. in my house there are ...

d. seven rooms

e. my favourite room is ...

f. the living room

g. I like to relax in my bedroom.

h. In the living room I can watch TV in peace.

i. Here I can read a book in peace.

j. I can do my homework in peace.

Grammar Time 16: WOHNEN + locations in the dative case

WOHNEN	Locations in the dative case			
ich wohne *I live* **du wohnst** *you live* **er/sie wohnt** *he/she lives* **wir wohnen** *we live* **ihr wohnt** *you guys live* **sie/Sie wohnen** *they/ you (formal)* *live·*	**in einem** *in a*		**Bungalow** *bungalow* **Wohnblock** *block of flats*	**am* Stadtrand** *in the suburbs* **an der Küste** *on the coast* **auf dem Land** *in the countryside* **im* Stadtzentrum** *in the city centre* **in der Stadt** *in the city* **in den Bergen** *in the mountains*
		alten *old*		
	in einer *in a*	**gemütlichen** *cosy* **großen** *big* **hässlichen** *ugly*	**Doppelhaushälfte** *semi-detached house* **Wohnung** *flat*	
	in einem *in a*	**kleinen** *small* **neuen** *new* **schönen** *beautiful* **ungemütlichen** *uncomfortable*	**Bauernhaus** *farmhouse* **Einfamilienhaus** *detached house* **Hochhaus** *high-rise building* **Mehrfamilienhaus** *multi-family house* **Reihenhaus** *terraced house*	
				*am = an dem on the *im = in dem in the*

Author's note:

When you talk about a place where you live, after prepositions like "in" (in) or "an/auf" (on) the noun phrase is in the **dative case**. *Therefore, in the table above, you can see the dative case versions of the article "a", for masculine (top row), feminine (middle row) and neuter nouns (bottom row). You can also see what the adjective ending looks like in the dative case when it follows an article (always "-en"). In the column on the right, you can see how the prepositions work with the definite article "the" in the dative case, when talking about different locations where your house might be.*

As you do the exercises below, take note of these patterns. Have a chat with your partner/teacher: How do they compare to what you know about the nominative and accusative case patterns?

Drills

1. Match

sie wohnen	I live
wir wohnen	you live
sie wohnt	she lives
ich wohne	we live
ihr wohnt	they live
du wohnst	you guys live

2. Complete with the correct form of 'wohnen'

a. Ich _____ in einem schönen Bauernhaus.
I live in a beautiful farmhouse.

b. Wo _____ du?
Where do you live?

c. Wir _____ in einem Bungalow am Stadtrand.
We live in a bungalow in the suburbs.

d. Sie _____ in einem Haus an der Küste.
She lives in a house on the coast.

e. _____ ihr in einem Haus oder einer Wohnung?
Do you guys live in a house or in a flat?

f. Sie _____ in einer alten Wohnung im Zentrum.
They live in an old flat in the centre.

g. Wir _____ in einem Einfamilienhaus am Stadtrand.
We live in a detached house in the suburbs.

h. Mein Vater _____ in einem Bauernhaus.
My father lives in a farmhouse.

3. Complete with the correct form of 'wohnen'

a. Meine Mutter und ich _____ in Paris. Mein Vater _____ in Madrid.

b. Wo _____ ihr?

c. Ich _____ in London. Mein Bruder _____ in Rom.

d. Meine zwei Onkel _____ in den Vereinigten Staaten, in Los Angeles.

e. Meine Freundin _____ nicht hier.

f. Ich _____ in einem sehr großen Haus am Stadtrand.

g. Du _____ in einem großen Haus.

4. Spot and correct the errors (max 2 per sentence)

a. Ich wohnt in einem Hochhaus im Stadtzentrum.

b. Meine Eltern wohnen in einem Wohnung in Berlin.

c. Meine Freundin wohnen an der Küste.

d. Meine Mutter und ich wohne am Stadtrand.

e. Mein Brüder Max und Leo wohnt in Stuttgart.

f. Meine Opa wohne in einem Reihenhaus in Innsbruck.

5. Complete the translation

a. My siblings live in the countryside.
Meine _____ _____ auf dem _____.

b. I live in a flat
Ich _____ in einer _____.

c. My granny lives in a multi-family house.
Meine Oma _____ in einem _____.

d. We live in the suburbs.
Wir _____ am _____.

e. Where do you live?
Wo _____ du?

f. They live in a small house.
Sie _____ in einem _____ _____.

6. Translate into German

a. My parents and I live in a cosy house.

b. My mother lives in a small house on the coast.

c. My uncle lives in a beautiful house in the mountains.

d. My girlfriend lives in a modern flat in the centre.

e. My sisters live in an old flat in the suburbs.

f. My friend Paco lives in a big flat in the town centre.

 **THE LANGUAGE GYM**

Grammar Time 17: Reflexives (Part 1)

USEFUL VOCABULARY

sich amüsieren	to amuse oneself
sich anziehen	to get dressed
sich baden	to bathe
sich duschen	to have a shower
sich entspannen	to relax
sich fertig machen	to get ready
sich rasieren	to shave
sich schminken	to put make-up on
sich waschen	to wash
sich die Zähne putzen*	to brush one's teeth
sich die Haare kämmen*	to comb one's hair

Present tense of reflexive verbs

	sich duschen	**sich waschen**	**sich die Zähne putzen**
ich	dusche mich	wasche mich	putze *mir* …
du	duschst dich	wäschst dich	putzt *dir* …
er, sie, es	duscht sich	wäscht sich	putzt sich …
wir	duschen uns	waschen uns	putzen uns …
ihr	duscht euch	wascht euch	putzt euch …
sie, Sie	duschen sich	waschen sich	putzen sich …

"mir" and "dir" are indirect object pronouns. You need these here as you are not literally brushing yourself, but your teeth to yourself (dative case)!

1. Complete with <u>mich</u>, <u>sich</u> or <u>uns</u>

a. Sie duschen _____

b. Ich rasiere _____

c. Sie schminkt _____

d. Wir waschen _____

e. Er macht _____ fertig

f. Wir amüsieren _____

g. Sie entspannen _____

h. Ich bade _____

2. Complete with the correct form of the verb

a. _____ _____ _____ sich enstpannen, *she*

b. _____ _____ _____ sich duschen, *we*

c. _____ _____ _____ sich schminken, *I*

d. _____ _____ _____ sich rasieren, *he*

e. _____ _____ _____ sich fertig machen, *they*

f. _____ _____ _____ sich waschen, *you guys*

g. _____ _____ _____ sich amüsieren, *he*

h. _____ _____ _____ die Zähne sich putzen, *you*

3. Translate into English

a. Ich stehe jeden Morgen früh auf, dann dusche ich mich und ich ziehe mich an.

b. Meine Schwester schminkt sich jeden Morgen. Ich finde, sie braucht das nicht.

c. Ich rasiere mich fast jeden Tag. Mein Vater rasiert sich nie!

d. Mein Bruder putzt sich nur einmal am Tag die Zähne. Aber ich putze mir die Zähne dreimal am Tag.

e. Mein Vater hat keine Haare. Also kämmt er sich nie.

f. Meine Mutter hat viele Haare. Sie kämmt sich zwanzig Minuten lang, bevor sie aus dem Haus geht.

g. Wir haben keine Badewanne *[=bath tub]*. Also baden wir uns nie, sondern wir duschen uns immer.

h. Ich wasche mich jeden Abend, bevor ich ins Bett gehe.

 **THE LANGUAGE GYM**

Ich stehe immer um sechs Uhr auf, eine halbe Stunde nach meiner Mutter. Ich wasche mich, ich rasiere mich und ich kämme mir die Haare. Schließlich ziehe ich mich an und gehe in die Küche. Ich frühstücke immer allein, meistens Müsli mit Milch und einen Toast mit Marmelade. Dazu trinke ich einen Becher Kaffee mit Milch. Dann putze ich mir die Zähne und ich mache mich fertig für die Schule. Gegen sieben Uhr gehe ich aus dem Haus. (Nils, 14)

5. Find the German for the English below in Nils's text

a. I always get up

b. I wash

c. I comb my hair

d. then I brush my teeth

e. I get ready

f. I shave

g. mostly muesli with milk

h. with that I drink

6. Complete

a. Ich dusch__ mich.   *I shower.*

b. Er rasier__ sich.   *He shaves.*

c. Wir dusch__ __ uns.   *We shower.*

d. Ihr wasch__ euch.   *You guys wash.*

e. Ich mach__ mich fertig.   *I prepare myself.*

f. Sie kämm__ sich die Haare. *She combs her hair.*

g. Ich putz__ mir die Zähne. *I brush my teeth.*

h. Sie bad__ __ sich.   *They bathe.*

8. Translate

a. Usually, I shower at seven o'clock.

b. He never brushes his teeth.

c. We shave three times a week.

d. They get up early.

e. He never combs his hair.

f. I don't bathe.

g. We prepare ourselves for school.

h. They never relax.

4. Find in Maik's text below the German for:

a. first, she has a shower

b. she puts make-up on

c. he has a shower

d. he combs his hair

e. my mother gets ready for work

f. half an hour later

g. always quite early

h. than my mother

i. a bit

Meine Eltern stehen immer ziemlich früh auf. Meine Mutter steht meistens gegen halb sechs auf. Zuerst duscht sie sich, zieht sich an, schminkt sich und macht sich fertig für die Arbeit. Dann macht sie das Frühstück für meinen Vater und uns, sieht ein bisschen fern und trinkt einen Kaffee. Mein Vater steht eine halbe Stunde später auf. Er duscht sich, rasiert sich, kämmt sich die Haare und zieht sich an. Dann geht er in die Küche und frühstückt mit meiner Mutter. Er geht eine halbe Stunde später als meine Mutter, gegen sieben Uhr, aus dem Haus. (Maik, 12)

7. Complete

a. _____ _____ um sechs Uhr _____.
They get up at six o'clock.

b. _____ _____ _____ um sieben Uhr.
They shave at seven o'clock.

c. _____ _____ _____ jeden Morgen.
I have a shower every morning.

d. ____ _____ _____ nie.
He never shaves.

e. _____ _____ ____ die Zähne.
We brush our teeth.

f. ____ _____ _____ stundenlang.
She puts make-up on for hours.

Grammar Time 18: Was gibt es in deinem Haus?

ES GIBT + indefinite article + adjective + noun

Subject-Verb (+/- adverbial)	Direct object (Noun phrase in accusative case)			
	a/no	adjective + ending	noun	
In meinem Haus gibt es *In my house there is/are* **In meinem Haus haben wir** *In my house we have*	**einen** *a* **keinen** *no*	**dunkl*-** *dark* **elegant-** *elegant*	-en	**Balkon** *balcony* **Dachboden** *attic* **Eingang** *entrance* **Flur** *corridor* **Garten** *garden* **Keller** *cellar*
Unten gibt es *Downstairs there is/are* **Oben gibt es** *Upstairs there is/are* **Im ersten Stock gibt es** *On the 1st floor, there is/are* **Im zweiten Stock gibt es** *On the 2nd floor, there is/are*	**eine** **keine**	**gemütlich-** *cosy* **groß-** *big, large* **hässlich-** *ugly*	-e	**Garage** *garage* **Küche** *kitchen* **Terrasse** *terrace* **Toilette** *toilet* **Treppe** *stairs* **Tür** *door* **Waschküche** *utility room*
Im Keller gibt es *In the cellar there is/are*	**ein** **kein**	**hell-** *bright* **klein-** *small*	-es	**Arbeitszimmer** *study* **Badezimmer** *bathroom* **Esszimmer** *dining room* **Gästezimmer** *guest room* **Klo** *loo* **Schlafzimmer** *bedroom*
Außerdem gibt es *Besides, there is/are* **Leider gibt es** *Unfortunately, there is/are*	**viele**	**modern-** *modern* **schön-** *beautiful*	-e	**Fenster** *windows* **Möbel** *furniture* **Sofas** *sofas*
Ich hätte gern *I'd like to have*	**keine**		-en	**Teppiche** *carpets* **Türen** *doors* **Zimmer** *rooms*

Author's note:
*The adjective "dunkel" (=dark) is normally written with an "e" between the letters "k" and "l". However, whenever it gets an ending, it loses the "e".

THE LANGUAGE GYM

162

Drills

1. Match

es gibt	a large kitchen
wir haben	many sofas
oben	there is
ein kleines Klo	upstairs
eine große Küche	a dark corridor
viele Sofas	we have
außerdem gibt es	a small loo
einen dunklen Flur	besides there is

2. Complete with the missing word

a. Wir haben einen _____ Garten.
We have a big garden.

b. Unten haben wir eine _____ Küche.
Downstairs we have a modern kitchen.

c. In meinem Haus gibt es viele _____ Fenster.
In my house there are many large windows.

d. Unser Haus hat einen _____ Eingang.
Our house has an elegant entrance.

e. In meiner Wohnung gibt es ein _____ Klo.
In my flat, there is a small loo.

3. Circle the adjective with the correct ending.

In meinem Haus gibt es ...

a. einen **große / großes / großen** Garten

b. ein **gemütliche / gemütliches / gemütlichen** Klo

c. ein **helles / helle / hellen** Esszimmer

d. eine **modernen / modernes / moderne** Garage

e. viele **schönes / schönen / schöne** Fenster

f. eine **modern / moderne / modernes** Küche

g. einen **dunklen / dunkle / dunkler** Keller

h. ein **große / großes / großen** Wohnzimmer

i. kein **schönen / schöne / schönes** Schlafzimmer

4. Complete with the adjective ending

In meinem Haus gibt es ...

a. eine groß__ Terrasse

b. einen schön__ Eingang

c. eine klein__ Küche

d. einen hässlich__ Dachboden

e. keinen schön__ Garten

f. eine dunkl__ Treppe

g. ein klein__, aber schön__ Klo

h. viele schön__ Möbel

i. ein hell__ und sehr groß__ Esszimmer

5. Circle the correct article

Ich hätte gern ...

a. **einen / eine / ein** schönen Garten

b. **eine / einen / ein** großes Zimmer

c. **eine / ein / einen** moderne Küche

d. **ein / eine / einen** gemütliches Klo

e. **einen / eine / ein** helles Wohnzimmer

f. **eine / ein / einen** großen Dachboden

g. **ein / einen / eine** schöne Terrasse

h. **eine / einen / ein** neue Tür

i. **ein / einen / eine** großes Zimmer

6. Complete with the endings. Note that leaving the gap blank can be the right option!

a. Wir haben ein__ schön__ groß__ Garten.

b. Im ersten Stock gibt es ein__ klein__ Klo.

c. Außerdem gibt es ein__ gemütlich__ Gästezimmer.

d. Mein Bruder hat ein__ kleiner__ Zimmer als ich.

e. Leider haben wir kein__ schön__ Möbel.

f. Unten gibt es ein__ hässlich__ Keller.

g. Oben gibt es ein__ groß__ praktisch__ Dachboden.

h. Außerdem haben wir ein__ hell__ Badezimmer.

i. Ich hätte gern ein__ größer__ Zimmer.

Ich wohne mit meinen Eltern in einem kleinen Bungalow am Stadtrand. Wir haben ein großes Wohnzimmer und eine schöne neue Küche. Außerdem haben wir ein sehr großes helles Badezimmer. Das finde ich ziemlich cool! Aber: Mein Lieblingszimmer ist mein Zimmer! Ich finde es super, denn es ist groß und gemütlich. Hier kann ich super entspannen und laut Musik hören. Leider haben wir keinen großen Garten, das ist schade. (Lena, 15)

8. Find the German for the English below in Lena's text

a. we have

b. a big living room

c. quite cool

d. a nice new kitchen

e. my favourite room

f. it is big and comfy

g. here I can

h. unfortunately we have

i. that is a shame

9. Answer the following questions about Maik

a. Where is his house located?

b. What is the living room like?

c. Which is his favourite room?

d. What does he have on the wall in his room?

e. What is all the way upstairs?

f. What does he have there?

g. What does he think about his house?

Ich wohne in einem schönen Haus direkt in den Bergen. Das ist so cool! Im Winter kann ich jeden Tag Ski fahren gehen. In unserem Haus haben wir eine moderne Küche, ein gemütliches Wohnzimmer und ein schönes Badezimmer. Mein Lieblingszimmer ist mein Zimmer. Es ist frisch gestrichen und es gibt viele Poster an der Wand. Ganz oben gibt es einen großen Dachboden. Hier gibt es viele alte Skier und auch mein altes Snowboard. (Maik, 14)

7. Find the German for the English below in Ulli's text

a. a small kitchen

b. a little scary

c. not so nice

d. three bedrooms

e. I can't do anything here

f. bigger than mine

g. downstairs

h. there is simply no space

i. at least

Ich wohne mit meinem Bruder und meinen Eltern in einer kleinen Wohnung im Stadtzentrum. Es gibt einen kleinen Flur, eine kleine Küche und ein kleines Klo. Außerdem gibt es drei Schlafzimmer. Leider ist mein Zimmer nicht so schön. Es ist ganz dunkel und auch total klein! Ich finde das nicht gut, denn ich kann hier nichts machen. Es gibt einfach keinen Platz! Immerhin ist das Wohnzimmer ganz gemütlich und es gibt ein schönes Sofa. Hier kann ich mich gut entspannen und mit meinem Bruder fernsehen. Sein Zimmer ist größer als meins. Das finde ich unfair! Unten im Haus haben wir auch einen Keller, aber er ist total dunkel. Das finde ich ein bisschen unheimlich, huaaa! (Ulli, 11)

10. Guided writing – write 2 short paragraphs in the first person [I] using the details below

	Lisa	André
Type of house, location	pretty house in the suburbs	big flat in the town centre
Rooms	modern kitchen, small bathroom, 3 bedrooms	elegant entrance, old kitchen
Favourite room (reason), activity	own room (cosy), can read a book in peace	living room (bright and cosy), watch TV
Would like to have	a bigger garden	a brighter room

UNIT 18
Saying what I do at home, how often, when and where

Grammar Time 19: Destinations vs Locations

Grammar Time 20: SPIELEN, MACHEN, GEHEN (Part 3)

In this unit you will learn how to provide a more detailed account of your daily activities building on the vocabulary learnt in the previous unit.

You will revisit:
- Time markers
- Reflexive verbs
- Parts of the house
- Description of people and places
- Telling the time
- The verbs 'machen, 'spielen' and 'gehen'

Unit 18
Saying what I do at home, how often when and where

Wann? [When?]	VS	Wohin? [Whereto?]	+	Was machst du? [What do you do?]
Morgens *In the morning* **Nach dem Frühstück** *After breakfast* **Nachmittags** *In the afternoon* **Abends** *In the evening*	**gehe ich** *I go*	**auf den Balkon** *onto the balcony* **auf den Dachboden** *onto the attic* **in den Garten** *into the garden* **in den Keller** *into the cellar*	**und** *and*	**ich entspanne mich** *I relax* **ich esse etwas** *I eat something* **ich gehe ins Internet** *I go online* **ich höre Musik** *I listen to music* **ich lese ein Buch** *I read a book* **ich lese ein Magazin** *I read a magazine* **ich mache Hausaufgaben** *I do homework* **ich mache einfach nichts** *I simply do nothing* **ich mähe den Rasen** *I mow the lawn* **ich poste etwas im Internet** *I post something online* **ich putze mir die Zähne** *I brush my teeth* **ich quatsche mit meiner Oma** *I chat with my nan* **ich schlafe ein bisschen** *I sleep a bit* **ich sehe einen Film** *I watch a film* **ich sehe fern** *I watch TV* **ich sehe Serien auf Netflix** *I watch series on Netflix* **ich spiele PlayStation** *I play PlayStation* **ich skype mit meinem Opa** *I skype with my grandad* **ich übe Klavier** *I practise the piano* **ich ziehe mich an** *I get dressed*
	gehe ich oft *I often go*	**auf die Terrasse** *onto the terrace* **in die Küche** *into the kitchen* **in die Garage** *in the garage*		
Wenn ich Zeit habe, *When I have time,* **Wenn ich Hunger habe,** *When I am hungry,* **Wenn ich müde bin,** *When I am tired,* **Wenn ich Ruhe brauche,** *When I need quiet,* **Bevor ich schlafen gehe,** *Before I go to sleep,*	**gehe ich gern** *I like going*	**in mein Zimmer** *into my room* **ins Arbeitszimmer** *into the study* **ins Badezimmer** *into the bathroom* **ins Esszimmer** *into the dining room* **ins Wohnzimmer** *into the living room*		

Unit 18. Saying what I do at home: VOCABULARY BUILDING [PART 1]

1. Match up

ich lese Comics	I chat with
ich sehe einen Film	I mow the lawn
ich esse etwas	I watch a film
ich lese ein Magazin	I eat something
ich ziehe mich an	I read a magazine
ich quatsche mit	I shower
ich mähe den Rasen	I get dressed
ich dusche mich	I read comics

2. Translate into English

a. Meistens dusche ich mich gegen sieben Uhr.

b. Ich gehe oft ins Wohnzimmer und sehe fern.

c. Bevor ich schlafen gehe, lese ich ein spannendes Buch.

d. Wenn ich Ruhe brauche, gehe ich in mein Zimmer.

e. Abends quatsche ich oft mit meinem Vater.

f. Wenn ich Hunger habe, gehe ich in die Küche und esse etwas.

g. Manchmal gehe ich ins Wohnzimmer und spiele PlayStation mit meinem Bruder.

h. Wenn ich Zeit habe, gehe ich in den Garten und ich spiele Fußball.

3. Complete with the missing words

a. Ich _____ mich an.   *I get dressed.*

b. Ich _____ einen Film.   *I watch a film.*

c. Ich _____ ein Buch.   *I read a book.*

d. Ich _____ mir die Zähne.   *I clean my teeth.*

e. Ich dusche _____.   *I have a shower.*

f. Ich _____ etwas.   *I eat something.*

g. Ich _____ ins Internet.   *I go online.*

h. Ich höre _____.   *I listen to music.*

i. Ich _____ fern.   *I watch TV*

j. Ich _____ ein bisschen.   *I sleep a bit.*

4. Complete the words

a. ich q_____	*I chat*	g. ich g_____	*I go*
b. ich s_____	*I watch*	h. ich s_____	*I play*
c. ich h_____	*I hear*	i. ich ü_____	*I practise*
d. ich m_____	*I make*	j. ich p_____	*I post*
e. ich p_____	*I clean*	k. ich m_____	*I mow*
f. ich s_____	*I sleep*	l. ich l_____	*I read*

5. Classify the words/phrases below in the table below

a. gegen sechs Uhr
b. immer
c. nie
d. in meinem Zimmer
e. ich sehe fern
f. ich spiele PlayStation
g. ich wasche mich
h. auf dem Balkon
i. ich putze mir die Zähne
j. manchmal
k. jeden Tag
l. ich höre Musik
m. ich lese Comics
n. ich spiele Fußball
o. im Badezimmer
p. ich übe Gitarre

Time phrases	Locations in the house	Things you do in the bathroom	Free-time activities
a.			

6. Fill in the table with what activities you do in which room

ich spiele am Computer	in meinem Zimmer
ich sehe fern	
ich dusche mich	
ich mache meine Hausaufgaben	
ich übe Trompete	
ich entspanne mich	
ich lese ein spannendes Buch	

Unit 18. Saying what I do at home: VOCABULARY BUILDING [PART 2]

7. Complete the table

English	Deutsch
	ich ziehe mich an
I shower (myself)	
	ich mache Hausaufgaben
I sleep a little	
	ich esse etwas
	ich quatsche mit meinem Bruder
I relax	

8. Multiple choice quiz

	Option a	Option b	Option c
nie	always	never	sometimes
manchmal	sometimes	always	never
Zimmer	room	lounge	garden
ich sehe	I shave	I watch	I go out
ich esse	I drink	I go out	I eat
ich lese	I read	I watch	I relax
ich gehe aus	I mow	I go out	I sleep
Küche	bedroom	lounge	kitchen
ich spiele	I rest	I play	I prepare
ich höre	I listen to	I read	I play
ich schlafe	I sleep	I relax	I read
immer	always	never	every day

9. Anagrams

mi tenGar   *im Garten*   *in the garden*

uaf med konBal

chmalman

ni der üKech

afu mde olK

chi esel

hic hese refn

10. Gap-fill from memory

a. Ich _____ ein spannendes Buch.

b. Ich _____ mir die Zähne im Bad.

c. Ich _____ Serien auf Netflix.

d. Ich _____ nie Popmusik.

e. Ich _____ meine Hausaufgaben.

f. Ich _____ oft Fotos auf Instagram.

g. Am Wochenende _____ ich Fahrrad.

h. Ich _____ gegen ein Uhr aus dem Haus.

i. Ich _____ das Abendessen.

j. Ich _____ Karten im Wohnzimmer.

11. Complete based on the translation in brackets

a. G_____ halb a_____ p_____ ich m_____ die Z_____.
Around seven thirty, I brush my teeth.

b. G_____ V_____ nach s_____ f_____ ich.
Around a quarter past seven I have breakfast.

c. W_____ i___ H_____ h____, g____ i___ in die K_____.
When I'm hungry, I go to the kitchen.

d. I___ s_____ i_____ f____, bevor i____ s_____ g____.
I always watch telly before I to sleep.

e. I___ l____ o___ e___ B_____ i____ W_____.
I often read a book in the living room.

f. I__ h____ am liebsten M_____ i__ m_____ Z_____.
I most like listening to music in my room.

g. G____ f_____ m_____ i___ m_____ H_____.
At around five I do my homework.

12. Broken words

a. die K_____   *the kitchen*

b. auf die Ter_____   *onto the terrace*

c. manch_____   *sometimes*

d. im_____   *always*

e. auf dem B_____   *on the balcony*

f. ich lese ein B_____   *I read a book*

g. in meinem Z_____   *in my room*

h. ich esse e_____   *I eat something*

i. Ch_____   *I chat*

Unit 18. Saying what I do at home: READING

Ich heiße Fabian. Ich komme aus Frankfurt. Zuhause habe ich einen Hund. Ich stehe früh auf, um Viertel nach fünf. Dann gehe ich ins Fitnessstudio und ich mache Krafttraining. Wenn ich wieder nach Hause komme, dusche ich mich. Mein Bruder Max ist sehr faul – er macht nie Sport. Deshalb ist er ein bisschen pummelig. Nachmittags bin ich meistens in meinem Zimmer und ich lese Comics oder ich höre Musik. Unter der Woche, wenn ich wieder nach Hause komme, mache ich meine Hausaufgaben mit meiner Mutter im Wohnzimmer. Ich finde das super, denn meine Mutter ist sehr schlau und sie kann mir super helfen. Schließlich gehe ich um neun Uhr ins Bett. Wo? In meinem Zimmer – ist doch klar! ☺

Ich heiße Eddie und ich wohne in Dänemark. Jeden Tag stehe ich morgens um fünf Uhr auf, stell dir vor! Zuerst dusche ich mich, dann frühstücke ich im Garten. Ich gehe um sieben Uhr aus dem Haus und ich reite auf meinem Pferd zur Schule. Das macht Spaß! Wenn ich wieder nach Hause komme, gehe ich in mein Zimmer und ich skype mit meiner Oma in England. Danach fahre ich Fahrrad im Garten und ich spiele mit meinen zwei Hunden. Manchmal bin ich im Zimmer von meinem Bruder und ich sehe Zeichentrickfilme oder ich poste Fotos auf Instagram. Mein Bruder Samuel postet Videos auf TikTok. Ich mag meinen Bruder, weil er sehr lustig und immer aktiv ist. Er kann super tanzen! Ich quatsche total oft mit ihm und wir spielen sehr oft Karten. Samuel und ich – wir sind wie beste Freunde!

Ich heiße Valentina und ich komme aus Italien. Ich wache immer früh auf, gegen halb sieben. Dann gehe ich ins Bad und ich dusche mich. Ich frühstücke nie morgens, aber meine Schwester Valeria isst immer Müsli mit Milch mit meinem Vater im Esszimmer. Ich gehe immer zu Fuß zur Schule. Ich komme meistens gegen halb vier wieder nach Hause. Dann gehe ich ins Wohnzimmer und ich sehe ein bisschen fern. Manchmal gehe ich auch in mein Zimmer und ich poste etwas im Internet oder ich sehe Serien auf Netflix. Später, gegen acht Uhr, gehe ich in die Küche und ich mache mit meinem Vater das Abendessen in der Küche. Am liebsten mache ich einen grünen Salat, das finde ich total lecker! Ich gehe oft spät ins Bett, um zehn Uhr.

1. Answer the following questions about Fabian

a. Where is he from?

b. What animal does he have?

c. What does he do after he wakes up?

d. Why is Max a bit chubby?

e. Where does he do his homework on weekdays?

f. Who helps him with his homework?

g. Where does he go to bed?

2. Find the German for the phrases below in Eddie's text

a. imagine

b. first I shower

c. out of the house

d. on my horse

e. I go to my room

f. I skype with my granny

g. in my brother's room

h. I chat really often

i. we are like best friends

3. Find the German for the following phrases/sentences in Valentina's text

a. I come from Italy.

b. I always wake up early.

c. I never have breakfast.

d. Valeria always eats with my dad.

e. in the dining room

f. into the living room

g. I most like making

4. Find someone who: which person ...

a. ... wakes up earliest?

b. ... has a family member that likes to dance?

c. ... likes to watch videos of people dancing?

d. ... has nothing for breakfast?

e. ... has a really lazy brother?

f. ... likes to prepare healthy food?

g. ... has a family member that is their best friend?

h. ... goes to school in the most exciting way?

Unit 18. Saying what I do at home: WRITING

1. Split sentences

Ich quatsche	das Essen.
Ich entspanne	meinem Bruder.
Ich mache	mit meiner Mutter.
Ich poste Fotos	mich im Garten.
Ich mache meine	ein spannendes Buch.
Ich gehe in	auf Instagram.
Ich spiele mit	die Küche.
Ich lese	Hausaufgaben.

2. Complete with the correct option

a. Ich stehe um sechs Uhr morgens _____.

b. Ich spiele Fußball im _____ .

c. Ich sehe einen Film in _____.

d. Ich höre Musik in der _____.

e. Ich mache das _____ mit meinem Vater.

f. Ich _____ mir die Zähne.

g. Ich _____ gern Science-Fiction-Filme.

h. Ich _____ auf meinem Pferd zur Schule.

Küche	auf	sehe	meinem Zimmer
reite	Essen	putze	Garten

3. Spot and correct the grammar and spelling mistakes [note: in several cases a word is missing]

a. ich dusche mich Badezimmer

b. ich frühstücke in Kuche

c. ich lese in mienem Zimmer

d. ich speile computer

e. ich gehe in der Garten

f. ich mache meine hausaufgaben

g. ich siehe Serien auf Netflix

h. ich riete auf meine Pferd

i. im Zimmer meinem Bruder

4. Complete the words

a. ich früh_____	*I have breakfast*
b. in der K_____	*in the kitchen*
c. in meinem Z_____	*in my room*
d. die G_____	*the garage*
e. Ich g____ a___ d___ H_____.	*I leave the house.*
f. im W_____	*in the living room*
g. im E_____	*in the dining room*
h. im B_____	*in the bathroom*
i. Ich s_____ F_____ ...	*I watch films ...*
j. ... i___ W_____	*... in the living room*

5. Guided writing – write 3 short paragraphs in the first person [I] using the details below

Person	Gets up	Showers	Has breakfast	Goes to school	Afternoon activity	After dinner activity
Marcel	6.15	in bathroom	kitchen	with brother	make the food in the kitchen	watch TV in living room
Tim	7.30	in shower	dining room	with mother	do homework on the balcony	read a book
Marianne	6.45	in bathroom	living room	with uncle	listen to music in garden	post photos to Instagram

Grammar Time 19:
Destinations vs Locations

Wohin gehst du? *Where are you going?*		Wo bist du? *Where are you?*	
Ich gehe *I go*	**auf den** Balkon — *onto the balcony* **in den Garten** — *into the garden* **in den Keller** — *into the cellar* **an den Strand** — *to the beach* **in den Park** — *to the park*	**Ich bin** *I am*	**auf dem** Balkon — *on the balcony* **im Garten** — *in the garden* **im Keller** — *in the cellar* **am Strand** — *on the beach* **im Park** — *in the park*
	auf die Terrasse — *onto the terrace* **in die Garage** — *into the garage* **in die Küche** — *into the kitchen* **in die Schule** — *to school* **in die Stadt** — *into town*		**auf der** Terrasse — *on the terrace* **in der Garage** — *in the garage* **in der Küche** — *in the kitchen* **in der Schule** — *in school* **in der Stadt** — *in town*
	auf das Dach — *onto the roof* **ins Wohnzimmer** — *into the living room* **in mein Zimmer** — *into my room* **ins Kino** — *to the cinema* **ins Stadion** — *to the stadion*		**auf dem** Dach — *on the roof* **im Wohnzimmer** — *in the living room* **in meinem Zimmer** — *in my room* **im Kino** — *in the cinema* **im Stadion** — *in the stadium*
	in die Berge — *into the mountains*		**in den** Bergen — *in the mountains*

Author's note:

*When prepositions like "in", "an" and "auf" are used to express movement towards a place, then the noun phrase that follows the preposition is in the **accusative case** (left column). When they are used to refer to a place where something is happening or where you are located, then the **dative case** is used (right column).*

*Some combinations of prepositions and definite articles are often shortened: in + dem = **im** / an + dem = **am** / in + das = **ins** / an + das = **ans**.*

Destinations vs Locations. Drills

1. Match

im Badezimmer	into the garden
in die Küche	in the bathroom
im Garten	in the living room
ins Badezimmer	into the living room
im Wohnzimmer	in the kitchen
in der Küche	into the bathroom
ins Wohnzimmer	into the kitchen
in den Garten	in the garden

2. Complete with the preposition and article

a. Ich gehe __ins__ Badezimmer.
I go into the bathroom.

b. Ich bin _____ Wohnzimmer.
I am in the living room.

c. Mein Vater arbeitet _____ Arbeitszimmer.
My father is working in the study.

d. Wir gehen _____ Garten und spielen Fußball.
We go into the garden and play football.

e. Mein Opa geht _____ Keller und spielt Saxophon.
My grandad goes into the cellar and plays the saxophone.

f. Wir fahren am Wochenende _____ Berge!
We're going into the mountains at the weekend!

g. Ich frühstücke immer _____ Küche.
I always have breakfast in the kitchen.

3. Underline the correct option

a. Ich lese ein Buch **im Badezimmer / ins Badezimmer**.

b. Nach dem Essen gehe ich **im Garten / in den Garten**.

c. Ich entspanne mich **auf der Terrasse / auf die Terrasse**.

d. Ich putze mir **im Badezimmer / ins Badezimmer** die Zähne.

e. Mein Onkel geht oft **an den Strand / am Strand**.

f. Meine Mutter ist **auf dem Dach / auf das Dach**.

g. Ich bin oft **in der Garage / in die Garage**.

h. Meine Schwester geht **in der Küche / in die Küche**.

4. Complete the <u>location</u> with the missing word

a. Ich bin auf ____ Balkon.

b. Ich lese ein Buch auf ____ Terrasse.

c. Ich esse etwas in ____ Küche.

d. Mein Fahrrad ist in ____ Garage.

e. Die Katze ist auf _____ Dach.

f. Ich sehe ____ Wohnzimmer fern.

g. Ich mähe den Rasen ____ Garten.

5. Complete the <u>destination</u> with the missing word

a. Ich gehe auf ____ Balkon.

b. Ich gehe auf ____ Terrasse.

c. Ich gehe in ____ Küche.

d. Ich gehe in ____ Garten.

e. Ich gehe oft ____ Stadion ...

f. ... und dann an ____ Strand.

g. Ich fahre in ____ Stadt, ...

h. ... dann ____ Fitnessstudio.

i. Um zehn gehe ich ____ Bett.

6. Complete the <u>destination or location</u> with a word from the box below

a. Wenn ich Hunger habe, gehe ich in die _____.

b. Wenn ich müde bin, lege ich mich ins _____.

c. Wenn es sonnig ist, chille ich im _____.

d. Morgens gehe ich ins _____ und ich dusche mich.

e. Das Auto ist in der _____.

f. Die Katze entspannt sich oben auf dem _____.

g. Am Wochenende fahren wir an den _____.

h. Ich mache Krafttraining im _____.

Küche	Dach	Garten	Strand
Fitnessstudio	Garage	Bett	Badezimmer

 **THE LANGUAGE GYM**

172

Grammar Time 20:

SPIELEN, MACHEN, GEHEN (Part 3) + Reflexives (Part 2)

1. Complete with 'mache', 'spiele' or 'gehe'

a. ich _____ meine Hausaufgaben

b. ich _____ Schach

c. ich _____ klettern

d. ich _____ ins Schwimmbad

e. ich _____ am Computer

f. ich _____ das Essen

g. ich _____ Karten

h. ich _____ einfach nichts

3. Complete with the appropriate verb

a. Meine Mutter _____ jeden Samstag in die Kirche.

b. Meine Schwester _____ nie ihre Hausaufgaben.

c. Wir _____ jeden Tag Basketball.

d. Meine Eltern _____ nicht viel Sport.

e. Meine Brüder _____ oft Schach.

f. Meine Freundin und ich _____ zu Fuß zur Schule.

g. Was _____ du?

h. Wohin _____ ihr?

i. Was _____ du beruflich?

j. Meine Onkel _____ Fußball mit uns.

k. Meine Freunde _____ oft ins Stadion.

l. Mein Vater _____ oft Tennis.

m. Im Sommer _____ meine Eltern und ich manchmal klettern.

n. Am Wochenende _____ meine Eltern und ich einfach nichts.

2. Complete with the missing forms of the present tense of the verbs below

	machen	gehen	spielen
ich *I*		gehe	spiele
du *you*	machst		
er, sie, es *he/she/it*			
wir *we*			
ihr *you guys*	macht		spielt
sie, Sie *they, you (formal)*		gehen	

4. Complete with the correct form of spielen

a. ich _____ Tennis

b. du _____ Karten

c. Sie _____ Gitarre

d. ich _____ im Garten

e. wir _____ manchmal

f. Was _____ du?

g. er _____ Cricket

h. ihr _____ Rugby

i. du _____ Klavier

j. es _____ im Garten

k. du_____ gern

l. sie_____ Schach

5. Complete with the correct form of gehen

a. ich _____ ins Kino

b. du _____ nach Hause

c. sie _____ auf den Balkon

d. er _____ in die Küche

e. ich _____ surfen

f. wir _____ an den Strand

g. du _____ ins Bad

h. ich _____ zur Schule

i. wir _____ aufs Klo

j. ihr _____ segeln

k. du _____ in den Park

l. Sie _____ wandern

THE LANGUAGE GYM

Drills

Present tense of reflexive verbs

	sich waschen	sich duschen	sich anziehen
ich	wasche mich	dusche mich	ziehe mich ...an
du	wäschst dich	duschst dich	ziehst dich ...an
er, sie, es	wäscht sich	duscht sich	zieht sich ...an
wir	waschen uns	duschen uns	ziehen uns ...an
ihr	wascht euch	duscht euch	zieht euch ...an
sie, Sie	waschen sich	duschen sich	ziehen sich ...an

USEFUL VOCABULARY

ich amüsiere mich	I amuse myself
ich bade mich	I bathe
ich dusche mich	I have a shower
ich entspanne mich	I relax
ich kämme mir die Haare	I comb my hair
ich mache mich fertig	I get ready
ich putze mir die Zähe	I brush my teeth
ich rasiere mich	I shave
ich wasche mich	I wash
ich ziehe mich an	I get dressed

6. Translate into English

a. Wir spielen oft am Computer.

b. Mein Bruder macht nie Krafttraining.

c. Meine Schwester spielt jeden Tag Korbball.

d. Mein Vater spielt am liebsten Tennis.

e. Was arbeitet ihr?

f. Wohin geht ihr nach der Schule?

g. Mein Bruder und ich spielen oft Schach.

h. Meine Eltern und ich gehen oft klettern.

i. Mein Bruder geht nie ins Kino.

j. Mein bester Freund geht jeden Samstag ins Stadion.

7. Complete with the correct verb ending and reflexive pronoun

a. Meine Mutter putz__ _____ die Zähne.

b. Mein Bruder wäsch__ _____ nie.

c. Ich dusch__ _____ oft.

d. Mein Vater rasier__ _____ jeden Tag.

e. Du mach__ _____ fertig.

f. Wir bad____ _____ gegen sieben Uhr.

g. Wann zieh__ du _____ an?

h. Rasier__ ihr _____ nie?

i. Amüsier__ du _____?

8. Translate into German

a. We have a shower at six.

b. He showers, then he shaves.

c. I shower at around seven.

d. My father never shaves.

e. My brothers never wash.

f. He gets dressed.

g. They have a bath.

h. She gets ready.

i. He brushes his teeth.

j. When do you guys relax?

 THE LANGUAGE GYM

UNIT 19
My holiday plans

Revision Quickie 6: Daily Routine/ House/ Home life/ Holidays

Question Skills 4: Daily routine / House / Home life / Holidays

In this unit you will learn how to talk about:

- What you intend to do on future holidays
- Where you are going to go
- Where you are going to stay
- Who you are going to travel with
- How it will be
- Means of transport

You will revisit:
- The verb 'gehen'
- Free-time activities
- Previously seen adjectives

UNIT 19
My holiday plans

Diesen Sommer werde ich *This Summer, I will*	**mit meiner Familie** *with my family* **mit dem Auto** *by car* **mit dem Flugzeug** *by plane* **mit dem Schiff** *by ship* **mit dem Zug** *by train*	**nach Deutschland** *to Germany* **nach Österreich** *to Austria* **in die Schweiz** *to Switzerland* **dorthin** *there*	**fahren** *go/drive* **fliegen** *fly* **reisen** *travel*	**Das wird super!** *That will be great!* **Das wird Spaß machen!** *That will be fun!*
Wir werden *We will*	**eine Woche** *one week* **zwei Wochen** *two weeks*	**dort** *there* **auf einem Campingplatz** *on a campsite* **in einem günstigen Hotel** *in a reasonable hotel* **in einem Luxushotel** *a luxury hotel*	**bleiben** *stay* **wohnen** *stay/live*	**Ich freue mich schon darauf!** *I am looking forward to it already!*
Ich werde *I will* **Wir werden** *We will* **Ich würde gern** *I would like to* **Wir würden gern** *We would like to*	**an den Strand gehen** **die Sehenswürdigkeiten besichtigen** **eine Stadtrundfahrt machen** **Fahrrad fahren** **in der Sonne liegen** **lecker essen** **neue Leute treffen** **nichts tun** **nur essen und schlafen** **Party machen** **Souvenirs kaufen** **Salsa tanzen** **Sport machen** **tauchen gehen** **Ukulele spielen**		*go to the beach* *visit the sights* *do a city tour* *go biking* *lie in the sun* *eat tasty food* *meet new people* *do nothing* *only eat and sleep* *party* *buy souvenirs* *dance Salsa* *do sport* *go diving* *play the ukulele*	**Das wird der Hammer!** *That will be awesome!* **Das wird total langweilig!** *That will be really boring!*

Unit 19. My holiday plans: VOCABULARY BUILDING

1. Match up

Diesen Sommer ...	in the holidays
... werde ich	to lie in the sun
nach Deutschland	This summer
in den Ferien	to travel
in der Sonne liegen	to stay
ich würde gern	to Germany
bleiben	I would like to
reisen	I will

2. Complete with the missing word

a. Ich werde mich _____ und ...
I will relax and ...

b. ... nur essen und _____.
... only eat and sleep.

c. Ich werde _____ gehen.
I will go diving.

d. Wir werden mit dem _____ nach Italien reisen.
We will travel by car to Italy.

e. Ich werde auf einem _____ bleiben.
I will to stay on a campsite.

f. Das wird _____ machen.
That will be fun.

g. Wir werden lecker _____.
We'll eat tasty food.

h. Ich werde mit dem _____ reisen.
I'm going to travel by train.

3. Translate into English

a. Diesen Sommer werde ich nach Italien fliegen.

b. Wir werden drei Wochen dort bleiben.

c. Ich werde nach Kuba fliegen.

d. Wir werden jeden Tag Souvenirs kaufen.

e. Ich würde gern jeden Tag Party machen.

f. Ich werde mit meinen Freunden spielen.

g. Ich würde gern nur essen und trinken.

h. Ich werde mich entspannen.

i. Ich werde mit meinem Bruder Sport machen

4. Broken words

a. Ich werde es_____ und tri_____.   *I will eat and drink.*

b. Wir werden nichts ma_____.   *We will do nothing.*

c. Ich werde 2 Wochen bl_____.   *I will stay for 2 weeks.*

d. Ich w_____ gern ...   *I would like to ...*

e. eine Stadtrundf_____ machen.   *to do a city tour*

f. Fahrrad fa_____   *to go biking*

g. in der Sonne li_____   *to lie in the sun*

h. Ich werde Souvenirs ka_____.   *I'll buy souvenirs.*

5. 'gehen, 'spielen' oder 'machen'?

a. Karten _____

b. klettern _____

c. ins Kino _____

d. eine Stadtrundfahrt _____

e. tauchen _____

f. Party _____

g. mit Freunden _____

h. Sport _____

i. Schach _____

j. an den Strand _____

6. Bad translation: spot any translation errors and fix them

a. Diesen Sommer werden wir ...
Last summer I will ...

b. Ich werde in den Ferien nach Argentinien reisen.
We will travel to Argentina in the holidays.

c. Wir werden eine Woche in einem Hotel bleiben.
We will stay in a flat for two weeks.

d. Ich würde gern jeden Tag tauchen gehen.
I would like to go skiing at the weekend.

e. Wir werden viel Sport machen und jeden Tag an den Strand gehen. -
We will do no sports and go to town every day.

f. Ich werde mit dem Zug dorthin reisen.
I will travel there by plane.

g. Ich werde jeden Tag neue Leute treffen.
I will see new animals every day.

 THE LANGUAGE GYM

Unit 19. My holiday plans: READING (Part 1)

Ich heiße Hugo. Ich komme aus Köln, aber ich wohne in Berlin. Diesen Sommer werde ich mit meinem Freund Alex nach Cádiz fahren. Das ist im Süden von Spanien! Wir werden mit dem Auto reisen und vier Wochen dort bleiben. Wir werden jeden Tag an den Strand gehen! Wir werden auch lecker essen. Ich werde nicht die Sehenswürdigkeiten besichtigen, weil das total langweilig ist. Ich liege lieber in der Sonne!

Ich heiße Deryk und ich komme aus Kanada. In meiner Familie gibt es vier Personen. Am liebsten mag ich meine Frau Anna. Diesen Sommer werden wir zuerst nach England und dann nach Québec in Kanada reisen. In England werde ich Bücher lesen und mich entspannen und dann werde ich in Kanada Ski fahren und mit meinen Freunden Party machen. Anna wird Fahrrad fahren und lecker essen, zum Beispiel „Poutine" – das sind Pommes mit Käse, stell dir vor! Mmmh, lecker!

Hallo! Ich bin Dino und ich bin aus Venedig in Italien. Diesen Sommer werde ich in den Ferien nach Mexiko fliegen. Ich werde zwei Wochen dort bleiben, allein, und ich werde in einem Zelt am Strand übernachten. Ich werde jeden Tag Sehenswürdigkeiten, Museen und Kunstgalerien besichtigen. Sport werde ich nicht machen, aber Kultur, ja, das liebe ich! - Und du, was wirst du in den Ferien machen?

Ich heiße Diana. Ich komme aus Polen, aber ich wohne in China. Diesen Sommer werde ich mit meiner Freundin Olivia nach Chile reisen. Wir werden mit dem Schiff fahren, denn wir haben viel Zeit! Ich werde fünf Wochen dort bleiben und in einem Luxushotel wohnen. Ich tanze total gern, also werden wir jeden Tag tanzen gehen. Ich werde auch viel essen und trinken. Ich werde nicht ins Museum gehen, weil ich das nicht so spannend finde.

1. Find the German for the following in Hugo's text

a. I am from

b. but I live in

c. this summer I will

d. with my friend

e. we will travel there

f. every day

g. I am not going to

h. I prefer lying in the sun

2. Find the German for the following in Diana's text

a. by boat

b. we have a lot of time

c. I will stay there 5 weeks

d. I really like dancing

e. so/therefore we will

f. I will also

g. eat lots

h. not so exciting

3. Complete the following statements about Deryk

a. He is from _____.

b. The person he likes most in his family is _____.

c. They will travel to _____ and _____.

d. Deryk is going to _____ and _____.

e. Anna is going to _____ and _____.

f. 'Poutine' is made up of _____ and _____.

4. List any 7 details about Dino (in 3rd person) in English

1.

2.

3.

4.

5.

6.

7.

5. Find someone who ...

a. ... likes being out at sea for long periods.

b. ... loves learning about culture.

c. ... prefers the beach to visiting the sights.

d. ... has opposite interests to Dino.

e. ... is going to travel by car.

 THE LANGUAGE GYM

Unit 19. My holiday plans: READING (Part 2)

Hallo! Ich heiße Marlene. Ich komme aus Hamburg. Zu Hause habe ich eine Schildkröte, stell dir vor! Sie ist sehr langsam und sehr faul, aber ich liebe sie. Sie ist meine beste Freundin! Diesen Sommer werde ich mit meiner Familie an den Chiemsee fahren. Das ist im Süden von Deutschland. Wir werden für drei Wochen dort bleiben und in einem superschicken Luxushotel wohnen. Das wird der Hammer! Wir werden jeden Tag schwimmen gehen und viel in der Sonne liegen. Hoffentlich wird das Wetter gut! Wir werden auch mit dem Auto nach München fahren und die Sehenswürdigkeiten besichtigen, zum Beispiel die Frauenkirche und den Olympiapark. Ich freue mich schon darauf!

Ich heiße Franziska und ich komme aus Innsbruck, in Österreich. Diesen Sommer werde ich für eine Woche mit meinem Bruder Stefan nach Wien fahren. Wir werden mit dem Zug dorthin reisen, denn das ist günstig und bequem. In Wien werden wir natürlich in den Prater gehen, das ist ein Freizeitpark mit vielen Attraktionen! Außerdem werden wir viele Souvenirs kaufen und lecker essen. Ich möchte auch mindestens einen Tag einfach nichts tun und mich im Hotel entspannen. Mein Bruder und ich werden auch viel Musik hören. Magst du Musik? Unsere Lieblingsband heißt Queen und meine Lieblingsmusik ist Rockmusik!

Ich heiße Nikolas und ich wohne in Basel, im Norden der Schweiz. Diesen Sommer werde ich nach Hamburg reisen. Das ist im Norden von Deutschland. Ich werde mit dem Auto dorthin reisen und zwei Wochen in einem günstigen Hotel in der Stadtmitte wohnen. In Hamburg würde ich gern den Hafen besichtigen. Er ist sehr groß und berühmt und man kann super Fischbrötchen essen! Ich werde auch das Miniatur-Wunderland besichtigen. Das ist eine riesengroße Modelleisenbahn. Ich freue mich schon darauf, denn ich habe selbst eine Modelleisenbahn zu Hause! Ich habe auch einen Freund in Hamburg, der Julius heißt. Wir werden zusammen in die Kneipe gehen und ein Bier trinken. Das wird supercool sein!

1. Answer the following questions about Marlene

a. Where is she from?

b. What animal does she have?

c. Who will she go on holiday with?

d. Where will they stay?

e. What will they do every day?

f. What does she hope for?

g. How will they get to Munich?

h. What will they do there?

2. Find the German in Nikolas' text

a. this summer

b. by car

c. in a reasonable hotel

d. the harbour

e. big and famous

f. a model railway

g. who is called Julius

h. I'm looking forward to it already

3. Find the German for the following phrases/sentences in Franziska's text

a. with my brother Stefan

b. a leisure theme park

c. with lots of attractions

d. furthermore we will

e. I would also like to (3 words)

f. simply do nothing

g. our favourite group

h. cheap and comfortable

4. Find someone who: which person ...

a. ... is going to travel south?

b. ... is going to the pub with a friend?

c. ... has a slow moving pet?

d. ... is going to relax for a day and do nothing?

e. ... is going to see some big ships?

f. ... is going to travel by train?

g. ... is going to stay in an expensive accommodation?

h. ... is going to stay away the longest?

Unit 19. My holiday plans: TRANSLATION/WRITING

1. Gapped translation

a. *I will travel to Germany.*
Ich _____ nach Deutschland reisen.

b. *I will go by car.*
Ich werde mit dem _____ fahren.

c. *We will stay there for one week.*
Wir werden eine Woche dort _____.

d. *I will stay/live in a reasonable hotel.*
Ich _____ in einem günstigen Hotel _____.

e. *We will go to the beach every day.*
Wir _____ jeden Tag an den _____ gehen.

f. *When the weather is nice, I will lie in the sun.*
Wenn das Wetter _____ ist, werde ich in der Sonne _____.

g. *I will take lots of photos.*
Ich werde viele Fotos _____.

2. Translate into English

a. ein Eis essen

b. Souvenirs kaufen

c. sich entspannen

d. Fotos machen

e. an den Strand gehen

f. jeden Tag

g. mit dem Flugzeug

h. tauchen gehen

i. Party machen

3. Spot and correct the grammar and spelling mistakes [note: in several cases a word is missing]

a. Ich werden viel Sport machen.

b. Ich werde ein Woche dort blieben.

c. Ich werde in eine Luxushotel wohnen.

d. Ich werde auf einem Campingplatz.

e. Ich jeden Tag Fußball spiele.

f. Wir werde in der stadt party machen.

g. Ich werde an Strand gehen.

h. Ich werde spielen mit meine Freunden.

4. Categories: Positive or Negative?   *Write P or N*

a. Das wird Spaß machen: **P**

b. Das wird langweilig:

c. Das wird fantastisch:

d. Das wird total doof:

e. Das wird interessant:

f. Das wird schrecklich:

g. Das wird spannend:

h. Das wird ekelhaft:

i. Das wird schlecht:

j. Das wird schön:

5. Translate into German

a. I will relax.

b. I will go diving.

c. We will go to the beach every day.

d. I would like to lie in the sun.

e. I would like to visit the sights.

f. I will stay in a hotel.

g. We will stay on a campsite.

h. We will travel by plane.

i. I will go/drive by car.

j. It will be fun!

THE LANGUAGE GYM

Revision Quickie 6: Daily Routine/House/Home life/Holidays

1. Match-up locations

am Stadtrand	in the garden
im Badezimmer	in the living room
in der Küche	in my room
in meinem Haus	in my house
im Garten	in the shower
in meinem Zimmer	in the dining room
im Esszimmer	in the bathroom
in der Dusche	in the kitchen
im Wohnzimmer	in the suburbs

2. Complete with the missing letters

a. ich du_____ mich   *I shower*

b. ich st_____ auf   *I get up*

c. ich se_____ fern   *I watch TV*

d. ich le_____ Comics   *I read comics*

e. ich ge_____ aus dem Haus   *I leave home*

f. ich ko_____ in der Schule an   *I arrive at school*

g. ich fa_____ mit dem Bus   *I go by bus*

h. ich zi_____ mich an   *I get dressed*

i. ich frühstü_____   *I eat breakfast*

3. Spot and correct any of the sentences below which do not make sense

a. Ich dusche mich im Wohnzimmer.

b. Ich esse in der Garage.

c. Ich mache das Essen im Badezimmer.

d. Ich wasche mir die Haare in der Küche.

e. Ich fahre mit dem Bett in die Schule.

f. Ich spiele Tischtennis mit meinem Hund.

g. Das Sofa ist auf dem Klo.

h. Ich sehe im Ofen fern.

i. Ich schlafe im Keller.

j. Ich parke das Auto in meinem Zimmer.

4. Split sentences

Ich sehe	mit dem Bus.
Ich höre	Müsli mit Milch.
Ich lese	fern.
Ich fahre	einen Kaffee.
Ich frühstücke	Musik.
Ich fliege	ein spannendes Buch.
Ich trinke	Hausaufgaben.
Ich poste Fotos	in die Karibik.
Ich mache	auf Instagram.
Ich liege	Karten.
Ich arbeite	in der Sonne.
Ich spiele	im Büro.

5. Match the opposites

gut	ungesund
nett	schlecht
leicht	schön
spannend	gemein
gesund	schwierig
hässlich	langweilig
teuer	schnell
langsam	groß
oft	billig
nie	selten
klein	immer

6. Complete with the missing words

a. Ich reise _____ dem Flugzeug nach Japan.

b. Ich fahre mit meinen Eltern _____ Italien.

c. Ich wohne _____ einem Hotel.

d. Ich gehe oft _____ den Strand.

e. Wir bleiben _____ einem Campingplatz.

f. Ich werde einmal ____ Woche in den Park gehen.

g. Ich gehe _____ Internet.

h. Ich poste Fotos _____ Instagram.

7. Draw a line in between each word

a. ichspielegernTennis

b. ichsehefernundichhöreMusik

c. inmeinerFreizeitgeheichoftinsKino

d. ichwerdemitdemAutonachItalienfahren

e. wirwerdeneineWochedortbleiben

f. ichwerdejedenMorgenandenStrandgehen

g. amSamstagwerdeichPartymachen

h. ichmachenieHausaufgaben

8. Spot the translation mistakes and correct them

a. Ich stehe früh auf.
I go to bed early.

b. Ich hasse Basketball.
I hate volleyball.

c. Ich werde ins Kino gehen.
I am going to go to the beach.

d. Heute werden wir nichts tun.
Today, I will do nothing.

e. Ich werde klettern gehen.
I will go horse-riding

f. Ich werde mit dem Auto reisen.
I will travel by plane

g. Ich werde in einem Luxushotel wohnen.
I am going to stay in a cheap hotel.

h. Ich werde einen Film sehen.
I am going to watch a series.

9. Translate into English

a. ich reise mit dem Bus

b. ich werde zu Hause bleiben

c. ich werde Tennis spielen

d. ich wasche mich

e. ich sehe einen Film

f. ich räume mein Zimmer auf

g. ich esse Gemüse

h. ich esse Eier zum Frühstück

i. ich mache nichts

j. ich arbeite am Computer

10. Translate into English

a. Zuerst dusche ich mich und dann frühstücke ich.

b. Morgen werde ich nach Japan reisen.

c. Ich entspanne mich in meinem Zimmer.

d. Ich spiele nie Basketball, aber oft Fußball.

e. Ich stehe jeden Tag früh auf, und du?

f. Ich esse normalerweise nichts zum Frühstück.

g. Ich werde mit dem Auto nach Italien fahren.

h. In meiner Freizeit spiele ich oft Schach.

i. Ich bin nicht oft im Internet. Ich finde das langweilig.

11. Complete with the missing letters

a. I eat breakfast   ich frühs_ _ _ _ _

b. I watch   ich s_ _ _

c. I do   ich m_ _ _ _

d. I clean   ich p_ _ _ _

e. I read   ich l_ _ _

f. I work   ich ar_ _ _ _ _

g. I fly   ich fl_ _ _ _

h. I sleep   ich sc_ _ _ _ _

i. I go   ich g_ _ _

Question Skills 4: Daily routine/House/Home life/Holidays

1. Complete the questions with the correct option

Wohin	Wann	Wie viele	Was
Warum	Welche	Wie oft	Seit wann

a. _____ stehst du auf?

b. _____ machst du in deiner Freizeit?

c. _____ gehst du nach der Schule?

d. _____ Musik hörst du am liebsten?

e. _____ Haustiere hast du?

f. _____ bist du Vegetarier?

g. _____ putzt du dir die Zähne am Tag?

h. _____ spielst du Gitarre?

3. Match each statement below to one of the questions included in activity 1 above

a. Zwei, einen Hamster und ein Pferd.

b. Am liebsten Popmusik.

c. Weil ich Tiere liebe.

d. Gegen sieben Uhr.

e. Ich spiele oft Fußball.

f. Zweimal, einmal morgens und einmal abends.

g. Seit drei Jahren.

h. Ich gehe mit meinen Freunden in die Stadt.

5. Translate

a. Where is your house?

b. Where do you go after school?

c. What do you do in your free time?

d. Since when do you play chess?

e. What is your favourite food?

f. How many siblings do you have?

g. Who is your best friend?

2. Split questions

Wie viel	spielst du nicht Fußball im Park?
Was isst du	gehst du ins Fitnessstudio pro Woche?
Was machst	Taschengeld bekommst du?
Kannst du	dein Lieblingszimmer?
Warum	zum Frühstück?
Wie oft	Hockey spielen?
Was ist	du in deiner Freizeit?
Wohin wirst du	deine beste Freundin?
Wer ist	im Sommer fahren?

4. Translate into German

a. Who?

b. When?

c. Who with?

d. Why?

e. How many?

f. How much?

g. Which music?

h. Where to?

i. Do you do ...?

j. Can you ...?

k. Where is ...?

l. How many pets?

m. What?

n. Will you ...?

VOCABULARY TESTS

On the following pages you will find one vocabulary test for every unit in the book. You could set them as class assessments or as homework at the end of a unit. Students could also use them to practise independently.

1a. Translate the following sentences (worth one point each) into German

What is your name?	
I am called Alex.	
How old are you?	
I am five years old.	
I am seven years old.	
I am nine years old.	
I am ten years old.	
I am eleven years old.	
I am twelve years old.	
I am thirteen years old.	
Score	**/10**

1b. Translate the following sentences (worth two points each) into German

What is your brother called?	
What is your sister called?	
My brother is called Markus.	
My sister is fourteen years old.	
My brother is fifteen years old.	
I am called Lena and I live in Berlin.	
I have a brother, he is called Linus.	
I have no siblings.	
That is the capital of Switzerland.	
That is the capital of Austria.	
Score	**/20**

1a. Translate the following sentences (worth one point each) into German

My name is Julia.		
I am eleven years old.		
I am fifteen years old.		
I am eighteen years old.		
My birthday is ...		
... on 4th of May.		
... on 5th of June.		
... on the 6th of September.		
... on the 10th of October.		
... on the 11th of July.		
Score	**/10**	

1b. Translate the following sentences (worth two points each) into German

I am 17 years old. My birthday is on the 21st of June.		
My brother is called Simon. He is 19.		
My sister is called Kathrin. She is 22.		
My brother's birthday is on March 23rd.		
My name is Sinan. I am 15. My birthday is on the 27th of July.		
My name is Angela. I am 18. My birthday is on 30th June.		
When is your birthday?		
Is your birthday in October or in November?		
My brother is called Peter. His birthday is on January 31st.		
Is your birthday in May or June?		
Score	**/20**	

1a. Translate the following sentences (worth one point each) into German

black hair	
dark brown eyes	
blonde hair	
blue eyes	
My name is Benjamin.	
I am 12 years old.	
I have long hair.	
I have short hair.	
I have green eyes.	
I have brown eyes.	
Score	**/10**

1b. Translate the following sentences (worth two points each) into German

I have grey hair and blue eyes.	
I have straight red hair.	
I have curly white hair.	
I have brown hair and brown eyes.	
I wear glasses and I have wavy hair.	
I wear no glasses, but I have a beard.	
My brother has blond hair and freckles.	
My brother is 22 years old, and he has medium-length black hair.	
Do you wear glasses?	
My sister has green eyes and curly black hair.	
Score	**/20**

1a. Translate the following sentences (worth one point each) into German

My name is		
I come from		
I live ...		
in a house		
in a flat		
in a modern building		
in the suburbs		
in the town centre		
in the country		
in Berlin		
Score	**/10**	

1b. Translate the following sentences (worth two points each) into German

My brother is called Maik.		
My sister is called Jenny.		
I live in an old building.		
I live in a small house.		
I live in a beautiful house in the mountains.		
I live in an ugly house in the town centre.		
I am 15 and I live in Cologne, in the west of Germany.		
I come from Basel but live in the centre of Lucerne.		
I come from Austria and I live in a nice house in Vienna.		
I live in a small flat in the countryside.		
Score	**/20**	

1a. Translate the following sentences (worth one point each) into German

The weather is ...	
nice	
bad	
it is	
cold	
warm	
sunny	
overcast	
clear skies	
it rains	
Score	**/10**

1b. Translate the following sentences (worth two points each) into German

The weather is nice in Berlin.	
It is often sunny.	
It is sometimes too cold.	
It rarely snows.	
It often rains, where I live.	
In the summer, it is always hot.	
There are often thunderstorms.	
The weather is bad in the autumn.	
I love it when it is hot.	
I find the weather here o.k.	
Score	**/20**

1a. Translate the following sentences (worth one point each) into German

There is ...		
my big sister		
my little brother		
my little sister		
my father		
my mother		
my uncle		
my auntie		
my male cousin		
my female cousin		
Score	/10	

1b. Translate the following sentences (worth two points each) into German

In my family there are four people.		
There is my father, my mother and my two brothers.		
I get along well with my brother.		
My sister is 22 years old.		
My brother is 16 years old.		
My grandad is 78.		
My grandma is 67.		
My uncle is called Josef and he is 54.		
My auntie is called Annika and she is 44.		
My female cousin Lisa is 17 years old.		
Score	/20	

THE LANGUAGE GYM

1a. Translate the following sentences (worth one point each) into German	
He is	
She is	
tall	
pretty	
a bit chubby	
funny	
always nice to me	
very muscular	
quite annoying	
usually friendly	
Score	**/10**

1b. Translate the following sentences (worth two points each) into German	
My mother is quite strict.	
My father is very stubborn but nice.	
My big sister is always hard-working	
My little brother is a bit lazy.	
In my family there are five people.	
I get along with my sister because she is nice to me.	
I don't get along with my brother because he is super-annoying.	
I love my grandparents because they are funny and generous.	
What are your parents like?	
I like my uncle because he is always friendly and ready to help.	
Score	**/20**

1a. Translate the following sentences (worth one point each) into German

I can		
swim		
cook		
dance		
play the guitar		
you can		
we can		
juggle		
ride the unicycle		
sing		
Score	**/10**	

1b. Translate the following sentences (worth two points each) into German

I can sing well.		
I cannot dance.		
We can work in a team.		
My uncle can play the guitar very well.		
I can sing and cook well.		
My granny can do Yoga. Imagine!		
My favourite aunt is super-funny, and she can play football well.		
I like my uncle because he can cook.		
What can you do?		
My big brother can draw very well.		
Score	**/20**	

THE LANGUAGE GYM

1a. Translate the following sentences (worth one point each) into German

I have…	
a dog	
a cat	
a horse	
a budgie	
a parrot	
a snake	
a frog	
two dogs	
two rabbits	
Score	**/10**

1b. Translate the following sentences (worth three points each) into German

I have a parrot. He is called Rico.	
I have a turtle who is called Speedy.	
At home, we have two fish.	
My sister has a spider.	
I don't have pets.	
My uncle Dieter has a snake.	
It (the snake) is called Gonzalo.	
I would like to have a horse.	
I have a cat. She is very cute.	
How many pets do you have at home?	
Score	**/30**

1a. Translate the following sentences (worth one point each) into German

He is a cook.		
She is a journalist.		
She is a lawyer.		
He is a nurse.		
He is a house-husband.		
She is a doctor.		
He is a teacher.		
She is a businesswoman.		
He is a hairdresser.		
She is a farmer.		
Score	**/10**	

1b. Translate the following sentences (worth three points each) into German

My uncle is a cook.		
My mother is a nurse.		
My grandparents don't work.		
My sister works as a teacher.		
My auntie is an actress.		
My (male) cousin is a student.		
My cousins are lawyers.		
He likes his work because it is exciting.		
She likes her work because it is rewarding.		
He hates his work because it is stressful.		
Score	**/30**	

THE LANGUAGE GYM

1a. Translate the following sentences (worth two points each) into German

I am taller than my brother.	
I am shorter than my sister.	
I am sportier than him (he).	
He is chubbier than her (she).	
She is funnier than him (he).	
My grandad is stricter than my gran.	
We are lazier than you guys.	
My dog is noisier than my cat.	
My rabbit is cuter than my horse.	
My uncle is slimmer than my father.	
Score	**/20**

1b. Translate the following sentences (worth 3 points each) into German

My brother is more generous than my cousin.	
My mother is a bit smarter than my father.	
My uncle is not as good-looking as my father.	
My older sister is a lot more talkative than my younger sister.	
My sister and I are not as tall as my cousins.	
My grandfather is not as strict as my grandmother.	
My friend Max is a lot friendlier than my friend Alex.	
My rabbit is a lot cheekier than my guinea pig.	
My cat is a lot faster than my dog.	
My parrot not as dangerous as my turtle.	
Score	**/30**

 **THE LANGUAGE GYM**

1a. Translate the following sentences (worth one point each) into German

I have a pen.	
I have a ruler.	
I have a rubber.	
In my bag I have…	
in my pencil case	
my friend Julian	
Anna has …	
I have no exercise book.	
it is green (the exercise book)	
The pencil sharpener is yellow.	
Score	**/10**

1b. Translate the following sentences (worth three points each) into German

In my bag I have four books.	
I have a yellow pencil case.	
I have a red water bottle.	
I have no black markers.	
There are two blue pens.	
My friend Miriam has a purple lunch box.	
Do you guys have a rubber?	
Do you have a red pen?	
Is there a ruler in your pencil case?	
What is there in your school bag?	
Score	**/30**

1a. Translate the following sentences (worth three points each) into German

I like drinking milk	
I like eating chocolate.	
I don't like eating meat.	
I prefer eating fish.	
Fruit is very healthy.	
Honey is too sweet.	
I most like drinking tea.	
I hate milk.	
I love water.	
I like cheese.	
Score	**/30**

1b. Translate the following sentences (worth five points each) into German

I like eating chocolate because it is tasty.	
I like eating apples because they are healthy.	
I most like eating fruit because it is rich in vitamins.	
I don't like eating steak, because it is too greasy.	
However, I like eating fish because it is rich in proteins.	
I love potatoes, they are my favourite food!	
Furthermore, I like eating fruit because it is tasty and rich in vitamins.	
What do you like to eat and drink?	
I like drinking coffee even though it is unhealthy.	
I prefer drinking tea because it is healthier than coffee.	
Score	**/50**

1a. Translate the following sentences (worth one point each) into German

for breakfast		
for lunch		
for dinner		
I often eat		
with that, I drink		
it is tasty		
it is disgusting		
too fatty		
I love it.		
Yum!		
Score	**/10**	

1b. Translate the following sentences (worth three points each) into German

I eat muesli with milk for breakfast.		
I sometimes eat bread with cheese.		
I never eat something warm (=*etwas Warmes*) for dinner.		
I prefer eating something cold.		
My sister often eats toast with jam .		
I hate it, because it is too sweet!		
I most like eating pasta with tomato sauce for lunch.		
With that I usually drink orange juice.		
My brother prefers drinking water, because it is healthy.		
I love coffee for breakfast, because it wakes me up!		
Score	**/30**	

1a. Translate the following sentences (worth two points each) into German	
I wear / I am wearing	
At home I wear ...	
I often wear ...	
a comfy hoody	
a white shirt	
a cool hat	
a warm jacket	
black trainers	
an elegant uniform	
brown boots	
Score	**/20**

1b. Translate the following sentences (worth three points each) into German	
I often wear a green jumper.	
At home, I wear a track suit.	
At school, we wear a blue uniform.	
At the beach I wear a red bathing suit.	
My sister always wears jeans.	
My brother never wears a watch.	
My mother wears branded clothes.	
I very rarely wear a suit.	
My girlfriend wears a trendy dress.	
My brothers always wear trainers.	
Score	**/30**

1a. Translate the following sentences (worth two points each) into German

I do homework		
I play football		
I go rock climbing		
I go cycling		
I play the trumpet		
I go to the swimming pool		
I do sport		
I go horse riding		
I play tennis		
I go to the beach		
Score	**/20**	

1b. Translate the following sentences (worth five points each) into German

In my free time, I often play chess with my brother.		
I play PlayStation every day.		
I sometimes go swimming with my friends.		
My brother and I often go to the gym.		
I do weights and go jogging every day.		
When the weather is nice, we go hiking.		
When the weather is bad, I play chess.		
My father goes swimming at the weekend.		
My younger brothers go to the park after school.		
In my free time, I go rock climbing or to my friend's house.		
Score	**/50**	

1a. Translate the following sentences (worth two points each) into German

when the weather is nice	
when the weather is bad	
when it is sunny	
when it is cold	
when it is hot	
I go skiing	
I play with my friends	
I play chess	
I go to the gym	
I go cycling	
Score	**/20**

1b. Translate the following sentences (worth four points each) into German

When the weather is nice, I go jogging.	
When it rains, we go to the sports centre and do weights.	
At the weekend, I do my homework and I go to the gym.	
When it is hot, she goes to the beach or she goes cycling.	
When the sun shines, I go jogging with my father.	
When it is stormy, we stay at home and play cards.	
When it is sunny, they go to the park and play football.	
At the weekend, I go to the beach with my girlfriend.	
We never do sport. We play on the computer or we watch TV.	
When it snows, we go to the mountains and ski.	
Score	**/40**

1a. Translate the following sentences (worth one point each) into German

I get up		
I have breakfast		
I eat		
I drink		
I go to bed		
around six o'clock		
I relax		
at lunchtime		
at midnight		
I do my homework		
Score	**/10**	

1b. Translate the following sentences (worth three points each) into German

Around 7.00 in the morning I have breakfast.		
I shower then I get dressed.		
I eat then I brush my teeth.		
Around 8 o'clock in the evenings I have dinner.		
I go to school by bus.		
In the afternoons I watch TV.		
I come home again at 4.30		
From 6 to 7 I play on the computer		
Afterwards, around 11.30, I go to bed.		
My daily routine is simple.		
Score	**/30**	

1a. Translate the following sentences (worth one point each) into German

I live ...	
in a new house	
in an old house	
in a small house	
in a big house	
in the countryside	
in the mountains	
in an ugly flat	
in the suburbs	
in the centre of town	
Score	**/10**

1b. Translate the following sentences (worth three points each) into German

In my house there are four rooms.	
My favourite room is the kitchen.	
I like relaxing in the living room.	
In my flat there are seven rooms.	
My parents live in a big house.	
My uncle lives in a small house.	
We live in a detached house.	
My friend Max lives in a farmhouse.	
My uncle lives in Hamburg.	
My parents and I live in a nice house.	
Score	**/30**

1a. Translate the following sentences (worth one point each) into German

I chat with my mother.		
I play PlayStation.		
I read magazines.		
I read a book.		
I watch a film.		
I listen to music.		
I relax.		
I do my homework.		
I watch TV.		
I leave the house.		
Score	**/10**	

1b. Translate the following sentences (worth three points each) into German

In the mornings, I go onto the balcony and relax.		
I often go to the living room and watch TV.		
When I am hungry, I go to the kitchen and I eat something.		
I never go into the cellar, because it is too dark.		
In the evenings, I watch series on Netflix.		
I have breakfast normally at around 7.30		
After school I go into the garden and relax.		
When I have time, I play with my brother		
My favourite room is my room, because it is big and bright.		
I sometimes watch a film in my room.		
Score	**/30**	

1a. Translate the following sentences (worth two points each) into German

I will	
with my family	
... to Germany	
to travel	
we will	
in a hotel	
to stay	
I will go to the beach.	
I will do sport.	
That will be fun!	
Score	**/20**

1b. Translate the following sentences (worth five points each) into German

We will buy souvenirs and clothes.	
I will stay for a week in a cheap hotel.	
We will stay there for three weeks and eat tasty food every day.	
We will go to the beach every day and lie in the sun.	
This summer, I will go to Italy with my family.	
We will go to Spain for two weeks, and we will travel by plane.	
I would like to do sport, go to the beach and dance.	
We will spend three weeks in Austria, we will stay on a campsite.	
We will stay in a luxury hotel and meet new people.	
That will be fun! I am already looking forward to it!	
Score	**/50**

THE LANGUAGE GYM

The End

We hope you have enjoyed using this workbook and found it useful.

As many of you will appreciate, the penguin is a fantastic animal. At Language Gym, we hold it as a symbol of resilience, bravery and good humour; able to thrive in the harshest possible environments and with, arguably, the best gait in the animal kingdom (black panther or penguin, you choose).

There are several hidden penguins (pictures) in this book, did you spot them all?